T0182544

Taking the State out of the Body

A Guide to Embodied Resistance to Zionism

Eliana Rubin

Taking the State out of the Body: A Guide to Embodied Resistance to Zionism
© 2024 Eliana Rubin
This edition © 2024 PM Press

ISBN: 979-8-88744-062-0 (paperback)
ISBN: 979-8-88744-071-2 (ebook)
Library of Congress Control Number: 2024930557

Front cover design by Roan Boucher
Interior design by briandesign
Illustrations by Saba Taj

10 9 8 7 6 5 4 3 2 1

PM Press
PO Box 23912
Oakland, CA 94623
www.pmpress.org

Printed in the USA.

Contents

Acknowledgments

The lineages that taught me:
This book reflects a collective body of knowledge developed through lived experiences of trauma, oppression, healing, and liberation. It was developed, edited, and molded by a variety of people. Where they are known, they are cited. Where they are unknown, they are honored in a commitment to a continued decolonial praxis. My own learning and transformation have been shaped by generations of diasporic Jews, Black feminists, queer and trans revolutionaries, sex workers, Indigenous leaders, and cultural movements of resistance in the United States, Palestine, and around the world.

The people who held me:
Zoë, Zora, Jay, Yashna, Kym, Sijal, Springer, Becca, Lewis, Ociele, Carleigh, Bridget, Sophia, Savannah, Sara, Jonah, Alli, Toby, Robert, Rachel, and Sadie.

The editors who guided me:
Jade Brooks and Sandra Korn contributed extensive developmental edits to add nuance to the political analysis and bring relevance to somatics for anti-Zionist organizing. Yashna Maya Padamsee collaborated on several of the somatic practice instructions through direct editing as well as live co-teaching practice.

The lands that shaped me:
Coast Miwok, Ramaytush, Lisjan, and Chochenyo Ohlone land: the bay, the Pacific Ocean and the redwoods.
Shakori, Eno, Sissipahaw, Saponi, and Occaneechi land: the river and the red clay.

The marine mammals that taught me:
This book was written to a soundtrack of whale sounds. Their brilliance, echolocation, and magic are woven between the words.

Author's Note: A Guide to Embodied Practices and Lineage

You are invited to engage with practices when the time is right for you and at your own pace. With everything, practice consent, self-responsiveness, accessibility, and mutual care. The practices are intended as applied learning and transformation—before entering, read through the guide below as well as the content of the preceding chapter to better land the social, political, and/or ecological relevance of the practices.

Key
Number of People
♟ = 1 person   ♟ ♟ =2 people   ♟ ♟ ♟ = 3 or more people
Time
🕑 = 5–10 minutes   🕑 🕑 = 15–20 minutes   🕑 🕑 🕑 = 30+ minutes
Level of Intensity (on scale of 1–10)
☆ = 1–3   ☆ ☆ = 2–5   ☆ ☆ ☆ = 5–7

Guidance
- Honor depth of practice: The purpose of including somatic practices is to deepen your integration of the reading material and to invite an embodied presence and curiosity. Following along through the practices in this book is not a substitute for being in a room with a practitioner and/or group. For the integrity of your own practice as well as the safety of others, I do not recommend attempting to lead these practices. I do encourage you to try on the practices for yourself: with friends, comrades, a book club, or other learning community. If you are interested in deepening, I encourage you to find a practitioner, teacher, and/or organization in which you can learn.

- Go slowly: Read through the whole practice before beginning. Make sure you are in the right place and have what you need to engage fully in the practice. Depending on your level of comfort and experience in somatic practice, there may be some that are better to just read and come back to when you have more direct support and guidance. Especially if these are new practices, you may find yourself stuck in the intellectual experience rather than the embodied practice. Remember that practice takes time and is all about supported repetition.

- Accessibility: With every practice, we will center our different body's needs. It's the principle of the practice that matters, not the mechanics. All practices can be done seated, standing, or lying down. At times, I will specify different options, and I invite you to innovate. You can always practice the principle energetically without physically moving at all. In addition, if a practice indicates multiple people, and you are practicing alone, I invite you to practice with a tree, plant, art, or anything else you can connect to—it could even just be the wall!

- Partner practices: Always practice consent. Check in before making any physical contact and make sure you are both on the same page about the scope of the practice and what you might be getting into together.

- Reflection questions: In some of the practices, you'll be asked to notice what happens in your body. For many of us, this is a tall order, remember that even just noticing you can't feel, or noticing places of numbness can be a powerful practice. Some questions that may help that reflection:
  - How is your breath?
  - Does your temperature shift?
  - Do certain muscles tighten or contract?
  - Are there places in your body that feel soft and open?
  - In what parts of your body do you notice more or less sensation?
  - What other senses are heightened or dampened as you practice?

- Level of intensity: You will notice the key only goes to a 7 on a scale of 1–10. This is to guide you towards choosing content for practices that your body is able to metabolize. To avoid overwhelming your system, start with an example for practice that is closer to a 3 or 4 in intensity (e.g. in the boundary practice, practice saying "no" to being asked to facilitate a meeting before you practice saying "no" to an intimate violation). Don't go straight for the big pressures, especially if you're practicing without support.

- Support and aftercare: This book is not a substitute for therapy, and some of the practices may surprisingly evoke strong emotions. Don't worry—you are not alone in that experience. I recommend being intentional about the physical and emotional space you are in before engaging in the more intense somatic practices. Make sure you have time afterward to process, integrate, and re-contain. You always have your breath to guide you. If you find yourself unsettled or activated and can't self-regulate, please reach out to a therapist, practitioner, or trusted friend for support.

- Lineage: The embodied practices included in this book draw from a range of traditions, methodologies, and peoples across time and place. The somatic practices in particular are largely shaped by the teachings of generative somatics, an organization co-founded by Spenta Kandawalla and Staci K. Haines. These lineages draw from many Black, Jewish, Asian, and Indigenous healing traditions that the organization is in an ongoing process of naming and honoring. In the somatic lineages I draw on, some of the teachers I have learned from over the years include: Spenta Kandawalla, Cassielle Bull, Dona Hirschfeld White, Phillippe Citrine, Gesine Wenzel, Staci K. Haines, Elizabeth Ross, Prentis Hemphill, Jennifer Ianello, MawuLisa Thomas-Adeyemo, Yashna Maya Padamsee, Nathan Shara, Kai Cheng Thom, and adrienne maree brown. In addition to somatics, you will find practices from Theater of the Oppressed that I learned through teacher training with the Mandala Center for Change. The rest of the practices have come to me from my Jewish and queer lineages as well as my own healing process: through movement practices, dreams, relationships, and other experiences with the lands and communities to which I belong. For more on honoring the different roots of practices, please read the "Embodiment Lineage" section in chapter 5.

Introduction

This is a book about bodies: bodies that transgress borders, bodies that heal, bodies that form movements together. It is a book that invites you deeper into relationship with your own body along with the communities and ecosystems you live in. This book embraces an internationalist and somatic approach to healing and liberation, in an effort to disentangle the state from the body.

Politicized somatics is a theory and methodology of embodied practice, healing, and change that grows our capacity to feel a wider range of sensations and align our actions with our values. The root of "somatics," "soma," means "the living organism or body in its wholeness." Somatic practices are designed to support more choiceful, impactful, and resilient bodies and movements. Being brought into politicized somatics was the integration of worlds I had been searching for my entire life. Through years of engaging in healing practices, ritual facilitation, birth work, farming, and domestic and international political organizing, I experienced the immense fissures between these. I sensed these fissures of amnesia in the moments we forgot the interdependent nature of our survival. These relationships of interdependence have been fractured by colonization, enclosed by borders, and violated by heteropatriarchy.

For the purposes of this book, "the state" is meant to represent these different systems of violence, extraction, and repression. It does not refer to visionary politics of a socialist state or liberatory forms of nationalism (such as Black nationalism) that aim to push back against dominant and oppressive systems. In this book, "the state" refers to a collection of government bodies that purport themselves to represent people's interests but in actuality represent the interests of the elite, namely profit.

This definition of the state also includes the politics of ethnonationalism that require a dominant and homogenized social, cultural, and historical identity. The state—as is grappled with on the left, from anarchists to socialists—has solidified the impacts of histories of fascism, nationalism, imperialism, capitalism, militarism, colonialism, and Zionism, including but not limited to racism, sexism, ableism, homophobia, transphobia, classism, and xenophobia. So when we address the state, we intervene in all of these systems of oppression and their intersections. This book is meant to reweave what the state tries to take from us: our connections with each other, our bodies, our movements, and ecologies.

I am engaging with this process of reweaving and re-membering through my own social location as a queer Ashkenazi Jewish femme living on unceded Indigenous land on Turtle Island. I recognize the many contradictions in my reality: I am part of a diasporic people, yet I am a settler; I am part of multiple communities targeted by white nationalists, yet I benefit from white supremacy. It is not in spite of these contradictions but because of them that this book has become a generative practice of being with complexity and discomfort as a way of wrestling with what love and justice look like in the body. In fact, in Jewish texts before being co-opted by the state, the word "Israel" referred to "wrestling."

Taking the State out of the Body grapples with my experiences as a Jewish anti-Zionist organizer and queer somatic practitioner over the past decade. Writing it has been a collective process nurtured by many friends, comrades, leaders, and movements. I began writing in 2018 amid sociopolitical conditions vastly different from those that exist for me today. I was living in my hometown in the San Francisco Bay Area and organizing with the International Jewish Anti-Zionist Network (IJAN). I would often write at Hasta Muerta, an anarchist cafe and bookshop, or Reem's, a Palestinian-Syrian owned Arab bakery, both in Oakland. I was embedded in the fringes of queer anti-Zionist Jewish community—I helped lead two-hundred-person liberation seders for Passover, put on raunchy drag shows for Purim, and hold crusty witchy rituals for the High Holidays. In my organizing with IJAN we would support our Palestinian partner organizations, defend against Zionist backlash, run campaigns to expose Zionist institutions, and facilitate workshops on unlearning Zionism. It was also in this time that I went more deeply into my training with Generative Somatics (gs) as a tool for interrupting the weaponization of Jewish trauma as a justification for colonization and genocide in Palestine. My life was full, and my love for the movements, community, and land that grew me was infinite. After moving every year of my adult life as my people were displaced and priced out, while simultaneously watching homes burn and developing chronic health conditions from wildfire smoke, I made the difficult decision to uproot and find a more stable home. On a walk among the redwoods in the Oakland hills I felt my ancestors whispering at my back "Go, you know how to move. And it's time, it's now. Go." I had spent years courting the idea of moving to Durham, North Carolina—heavily influenced by the people I had come to know, the queer Jewish community, the magic of the Eno River, and the town's deep political history, including recent anti-Zionist organizing wins to stop police exchanges with Israel. Then, in the midst of this life transition, in 2020, we faced what would become an ongoing global pandemic that changed the fabric of society and how we relate to each other and our bodies. I was finishing the first draft of my manuscript at this time and scrambled to incorporate learnings from the pandemic: from the impact on our relationships to our bodies, to mutual aid networks, to the failures of the state. I ended up pausing the writing, as the day-to-day needs of my body, my communities, and my move to Durham required every bit of energy.

Soon after landing in my new home, I was hosting Shabbat dinner with a few friends. We went around the table and took turns sharing about big projects we were trying to birth into the world: from challenging the International Holocaust Remembrance Alliance definition of antisemitism, which included any criticism of Israel, to new creative endeavors. As each person shared, we offered support and insight and cheered each other on. It came to be my turn, and I felt my heart race. The devastation of living through a Trump presidency, climate crisis, personal loss, and the pandemic had weakened my resolve to finish this project. But as I sat around the Shabbat table, belly full of challah, eyes glimmering in the candlelight, and listening to new and old friends share so vulnerably, I decided to declare right then and there that I would bring this book to completion. For any other writers or creatives out there, you may relate to the gut-wrenching twists and turns that followed as I moved toward publishing. My manuscript finally landed in the hands of my publisher on October 4, 2023. Just a few days later, on October 7, we witnessed an armed uprising in Gaza and the ensuing intensification of ethnic cleansing and genocide. Now, here I am writing this on day 144 of Israel's unrelenting military attack against Palestinians. It has been excruciating to write

3

through these times of loss, isolation, rage, and agony. Yet it is with every word I write, with every cell of my body, that I resist the oppressors' trappings of complacency and despair. So, while in many ways the terrain has shifted over the course of writing these past five years, and it is impossible to do justice to all that has transpired, it also remains fundamentally the same struggle against ethnonationalist state.

For this book, I have chosen a particular focus on Jewish communities that, like many, have used politicized healing to resist fascism for generations. As a member of this community, I know how important it is to reclaim Jewish histories and connections to land outside of and beyond the state of Israel, alongside a broader decolonial practice of honoring Indigenous peoples and lands on which we currently live. The Nazi genocide and earlier pogroms—targeted killings and removal of Jews throughout the nineteenth and twentieth century—not only killed millions of my people but also fractured or entirely erased many parts of our traditions and history. What remained has been deeply impacted by Jewish assimilation, as well as the impacts of intergenerational trauma. Further, the somatic, emotional impacts of this violent upheaval from place have been weaponized to justify the colonization of Palestine. When we look back at times of heightened antisemitism and fascism in Europe, we find Jewish rabbis, philosophers, psychologists, and healers offering embodied practice for resilience and resistance. Wilhelm Reich (1896–1957) wrote *The Mass Psychology of Fascism* and developed much of the language and mapping of the body that contemporary somatics draws on. He took the political analysis formed by Marxism and the psychoanalysis formed by Freud to show the ways fascism and other dominant ideologies get engrained in the body. We also have other Jewish ancestors of embodied practice like Elsa Gindler—a founding practitioner in the field of somatic bodywork and sensory awareness, and Laura and Fritz Perls, the early originators of Gestalt, a form of psychotherapy that centers the whole-body integration of sensory experience. Looking back even further, we find embodied practices inscribed into the foundations of Judaism from ritual bathing, mikvahs; to wrapping prayer boxes around the arms, tefillin; to the morning blessings for our sacred and mundane bodies, Shacharit; to the weekly commitment to rest and the world to come, Shabbat. For all these reasons and more, I find the practice of politicized healing and resilience in Jewish communities to be a compelling case study for embodied resistance to fascism and other forms of state repression. I hope that

4

readers who are Jewish will be encouraged to engage in politicized healing as our people have used for generations, and I hope readers who are not Jewish will be inspired to explore their own rich lineages and build on their practices of embodied resistance.

As a queer Jew, I have witnessed time after time how the embodiment of ancestral trauma in the Jewish community and the embodiment of homonationalism in the queer community can lead to support for the settler-colonial nation-state of Israel.[1] This book will explore how collective trauma impacts the entire community within structural oppression and state violence. Then it will go deeper into interrogating nationalism as a depoliticized response, where traumatized people seeking state recognition end up supporting new regimes of state violence, like military occupation. I see these as case studies for the ways nationalism and state violence use identities as leverage to engrain oppression into our bodies. The embodiment of nationalism obscures our historical roles in political struggles and inhibits contemporary participation in social movements, particularly the movement to decolonize Palestine. My hope is that this book will bring people together across a wide spectrum of political tendencies and spiritual or religious traditions, to build a shared analysis and practice of embodied resistance. I argue that the tension in Jewish communities around Zionism, Israel, and Palestine often stems from a trauma response that puts people into a state of reactivity—unable to listen, empathize, or find a way forward together toward justice. I invite you to read and engage with this material knowing that for some people it may feel incomplete or challenging; you may require additional support. This book is shaped as a somatic intervention: there is space for building our muscles over time, and there is also a strong yet malleable skeleton that holds certain political lines as a practice of integrity and accountability to bodies on the front lines of systemic trauma, violence, and oppression. I welcome you to practice this with me: we can hold each other and make our way over the inevitable gaps and places this book fails to maintain these embodied politics.

In this book I use "I", "we," and "you" as an invitation to bring these concepts home to our own bodies and experiences. The times I use "we" may not speak to you specifically, but I choose this language as a way of naming collective bodies impacted by the issues this book addresses. I also find that this language can invite us into deeper interdependence and solidarity as we feel for the bigger "we" to which we all belong.

Reading this book is meant to be an intimate experience, moving from a more intellectual political framework, slowly spiraling in, moving closer to the bone.

Through this book we will develop an understanding of the Nazi genocide as an experience of collective trauma, unclouded by Zionist and Jewish exceptionalist rhetoric, to see that it was not only Jews targeted by the Nazis but also others, "deviant" bodies who didn't fit within "Aryan" standards. Using this lens, the focus shifts from a Jewish victim narrative to a narrative of collective struggle against fascism, acknowledging the immense loss in all of these communities while also lifting up both Jews and non-Jews who were part of building resistance to white nationalism.

We will also build an understanding of fascism through the theory and practice of somatics. Fascism—as defined by activist writers like Ejeris Dixon and Shane Burley—is an ultranationalist, antidemocratic, far right movement rooted in rigid, identity supremacy political practices. Within fascism, this majority sees themselves as victims needing to fight marginalized communities for their survival and purity of the "master race."[2] When bodies are targeted in this way and deemed "other," it causes an embodied experience of shame and trauma, leaving a hole in individual and collective bodies. This gap in peoples' sense of safety, security, and selfhood is what the Zionist project took advantage of by persuading Jewish refugees to settle in Palestine. It is also the gap within which capitalism, militarism, and patriotism disguise themselves as meeting our needs for safety and belonging. This book emphasizes the parallels in resisting imperialism and colonialism in language, land, culture, and bodies found across many movements for indigenous self-determination.

One of the insidious impacts of colonization and imperialism that we will address is the hyper-valuing of individualism, with a simultaneous collapsing of codependence and interdependence. White Christian supremacist heteropatriarchal cultures of individualism sell us the idea that our own success, wealth, and fame are more important than our connections with each other and the land. Because interdependence is necessary for survival, these systems of trauma and oppression end up putting us in perpetual states of alarm and create engrained neural pathways that leave us feeling unsafe in our environment. Ultimately, this divides us from each other and further perpetuates a kind of individualism that capitalism requires. In this book we will examine how practices of politicized embodied transformation can heal internalized oppression and restore symbiotic and interdependent relationships with land and all the bodies, creatures, and cultures inhabiting it.

In addition to the overt expressions of individualism within a colonial framework, individualism also shows up inside our systems of care and healing modalities. Most embodiment practices can be traced through ancient indigenous traditions from all around the world. Many of these traditions have been stolen, co-opted, erased, and exterminated through processes of colonization. Despite facing such immense repression, many of these indigenous traditions and peoples are still thriving and resisting. I have made every attempt to name these lineages where I know them and to honor and grieve all the unknown. The criminalization and targeting of indigenous healing practices is a tool to repress community resilience and ensure complacency under colonial regimes. From the burning of political and spiritual books and the burning of witches to the evangelical missions to spread Christian hegemony, the tools we need to heal and dismantle the state have been targeted and attacked. This book argues that to be in right relationship with our ancestral lands and traditions, as well as the land that we live on or occupy (which, due to settler colonialism, are often different from our ancestral lands), we must re-attune to the sensations in our bodies as an internal act of decolonization. We will explore the use of embodied practices and rituals from Jewish, somatic, and land-based traditions to support the integration of these concepts.

Each chapter begins with an allegory that is grounded in human, animal, fungal, or plant bodies. These are intended not just to be symbolic but also to be living demonstrations of the principles we are exploring. Through these allegories we can expand what we think of as a body to include more of our inseparability from other living beings. The allegorical bodies that will guide us through the book include Calendula, Redwoods, Fascia, the Vagus Nerve, Oak, and Mycelium. If at any point you feel lost in your head, try to spend time with these bodies of knowledge. Sit at the base of a redwood or oak tree and notice what stories emerge. Drink calendula tea and allow each sip to be an invitation into your ancestral legacies of resistance. Receive, or give yourself bodywork that focuses on your fascia as a permeable membrane to down-regulate your nervous system defense response. Sink your hands into the soil and see what networks of mycelia you have access to at your fingertips. All of these ways of building embodied knowing are just as important as reading the words in this book—if not more so. Whatever you have access to, even just with your imagination, I invite you to build this embodied wisdom with me.

Each chapter ends with a section on embodied practice. These are invitations to explore the concepts presented in your body—to engage different parts of yourself in your learning, development, and transformation. We can know something in our heads without embodying it in our lives; embodied practices are critical for moving from theory into action, from awareness toward healing. Just remember to follow your own body's needs—it's the principle of the practice that matters, not the mechanics. You will find an appendix in the back of the book that orients you to the practices and what you might need to engage in them as you go. Practice is foundational not only to embodiment but also to Jewishness. In second book of the Torah, the Book of Deuteronomy, Jews practice retelling. We acknowledge in this that repetition is core to our spiritual practice and that there are always multiple ways of telling a story. So I invite you to practice again, to return again, as we do through the wheel of Jewish time and space and the arc of somatic transformation.

In the first chapter, "Calendula: Resisting Ethnonationalism," we probe into the roots of Zionism, fascism, US imperialism, and antisemitism to deconstruct the narrative that a sense of safety is something that can be "obtained" through the state. We will explore the principle of *doykeit* (Yiddish for "hereness") as well as other varied traditions of statelessness.

In chapter 2, "Redwoods: Collective Trauma," we will explore the ways trauma and oppression get internalized in our bodies. We will illuminate both the distinctions and similarities across bodies. We will look at the histories and current expressions of collective trauma in indigenous, immigrant, Black, and Jewish communities. This chapter is intended to ground us in the context of the wide expanse of bodies across time and place before taking a deeper dive into Jewish anti-Zionist histories.

Chapter 3, "Fascia: Borders and Walls," goes on to illuminate how our bodies get enclosed by militarized borders, policing, colonization, and heteronormativity. Chapter 4, "Vagus Nerve: Membranes and Boundaries," is more of a somatic intervention that explores how to hold more permeable and vulnerable boundaries that create space for deeper relationship with ourselves, each other, and the land, rather than the fracturing caused by rigid borders and ethnonationalism. It is also in this chapter that I introduce polyvagal theory and its contributions to transformative healing justice. Polyvagal theory, first introduced in 1994 by Stephen Porges, is a theory of how our nervous system has evolved and functions to regulate emotions, respond to fear, and make connections with others. This chapter provides a scientific foundation for somatic approaches to healing trauma and reaffirms the prioritization of building embodied intimate connections.

Chapter 5, "Oak: Individualistic Embodiment," exposes how individualism shows up in our approaches to care, (dis)ability, and healing. We will deconstruct contemporary orientations to self-care and myths around self-reliance. In the last chapter, "Mycelium: Collective Care," we will root into interdependence and transformative justice, grounding them in Jewish ancestral teachings. This chapter invites us into embodied experiences of sustained connection in community and across movements for justice.

As you open this book, I invite you to skip around, read it in circles, without a beginning or an end. If you are already primed to dive into the content around Zionism, you may want to skip ahead; if not, start from the beginning to root into a broader decolonial, antiracist context. Each chapter spirals around the core ideas that bring the book together: collective trauma, collective accountability, and collective care. Some of the chapters have fewer words and more room for embodied practices. I encourage you to pause and notice sensations in your body frequently as you read. There is a principle in trauma healing called titration, based on chemistry experiments in which you slowly alternate in adding one solution to the other rather than flooding the system all at once. We can also think about this in the way plants absorb water, slowly allowing each drop of water to percolate through the soil. Also, you can expect repetition throughout the chapters as part of this practice of embodiment. As we revisit ideas, they will become more familiar, more intimate, and sink deeper into our bones. While training to be a somatics practitioner, I learned that it takes three hundred times to learn something in your head and three thousand times to learn it in your body.[3] So let this book be a practice of embodiment in and of itself.

In order to build international movements of solidarity, we must deconstruct notions of borders and nationalism as well as build a trauma-informed embodiment practice to generate a sense of safety in our individual and collective bodies. With this deeply political commitment to healing and transformation, we can strengthen our resolve toward decolonizing relationships with our bodies, each other, and the land. When we unlearn the ways the state confines our bodies and heal the ways we have internalized these systems of oppression, we open up possibilities for collective transformation. Along with the internalized experiences of oppression and trauma, our collective bodies have the capacity to experience immense joy and pleasure together. The theory and practices in this book are intended to liberate this energy in our bodies that is otherwise suppressed by the state.

A book represents just one of many forms of creative resistance in movements for justice, from protests in the street, to political research and education, to long-haul community organizing. While I am holding critiques of certain organizing cultures, I do not intend to overstate the importance of healing. We need a strategic analysis. Yes, the individual matters. Healing matters. Metabolizing our grief and trauma particularly as it is being weaponized matters. But that alone will not win us freedom. And, yes, building social movements matters. Yet without the skills to sustain connection with ourselves, each other, and the land, these movements alone cannot win us freedom. We need to be precise with our analysis of power and motive —and we need to make room for the messiness and complexities inside of our relationships to power. For example, all the Jews in the world could withdraw their support for the state of Israel, and that would not be enough. The United States would find another way. Because contrary to the narratives they spin about Israel being for the safety of Jews, the root motive is imperialism. They want us to think it's about Jewish safety, and at times our Jewish identity–based resistance plays right back into it. So in this book, when we address the importance of individual and collective healing, we remember to situate it in a broader commitment to joint struggle with anti-imperialist movements for freedom internationally.

Taking the State out of the Body guides us in building embodied and interdependent relationships to safety and belonging rather than relying on militarized borders, policing, and nationalism. This book is an invitation to cultural workers, organizers, healers, feelers, and anyone else who seeks to understand how we can shift our relationships to safety and belonging from being mediated by the state to being experienced in our bodies and communities.

CHAPTER 1

Calendula: Resisting Ethnonationalism

When Nazi Germany was occupying the Netherlands, the Dutch Resistance wore calendula flowers to show solidarity with Jews in both a material and rhetorical fashion. The Dutch authorities collaborated with the Nazis more than any other country in the region, killing one hundred thousand Jews, which was about 75 percent of the total Jewish population of the Netherlands at the time. Calendula flowers were used to mark safe people and places for Jews to hide. Throughout history, in the face of extreme conditions, wherever there has been fascism, there has been resistance to fascism. Calendula flowers symbolize opposition to nationalism and solidarity with all oppressed peoples.

Calendula's vibrant orange and yellow flowers bloom in the peak of summer in the Northern Hemisphere. These bold, sticky flowers dry into clusters of crescent moon-shaped seed pods that look otherworldly. We can always turn to calendula to remember the incredible resilience and protection that seeds provide, each generation building on the last.

"One nation under God." Recited daily by children at schools across the United States, the Pledge of Allegiance inspires nationalism—a form of devotion to the nation-state—founded on the idea that the United States is a single nation with divine support. In the United States, nationalism is used to drum up support for imperialism, war, and globalization, all under the guise of securing a land of "liberty and justice for all." This settler narrative is shaped by racialized capitalism and colonization. "For all" is rooted in a false homogeny given that this country is occupied by settlers from different European nations as well as immigrant populations from nations around the world. Beyond that, this land consists of numerous different Indigenous nations, making it international in and of itself. Anticolonial movements led by Indigenous activists and scholars in the United States challenge us to understand that the colonization of this land is not complete. Instead, struggles for Indigenous nationhood give space to a future of Indigenous autonomy, sovereignty, and self-determination.

While this book is focused on nationalism in the United States and Zionism in Palestine, we know that nationalism shows up internationally in a variety of ways that support authoritarian regimes—from Venezuela to Russia to the Philippines. It also must be noted that there are forms of nationalism rooted in resistance to colonization and liberatory politics, such as Black nationalism and indigenous struggles to be recognized as sovereign nations, including in Palestine. Scholar Mark Rifkin distinguishes between these anticolonial modes of resistance and statist nationalism: "Not all nationalisms are equivalent; not all movements that might be termed nationalist seek to achieve statist modes of governance; and not all efforts to achieve relative political autonomy through the adoption of state-like governance can be understood as oppressive purely on that basis."[1] One such movement is the Idle No More movement in Canada that calls for Indigenous sovereignty and the protection of land, water, and sky. Anishinaabe and Nehayo writer Tara Williamson writes, "Idle No More is about nationhood. Not nation-state-hood, but nationhood—the ability to take care of the land, our children, and our families in the way we best know how. While the Canadian government currently plays heavily into our ability to function as self-determining nations, we know that true self-governance has to come from ourselves.... The best way to demand self-determination is to be self-determining."[2]

The Idle No More movement has explicitly asserted its solidarity with other indigenous peoples resisting settler colonialism, including Palestinians. "We know what it is to be denied our right to life by colonizers who could not see our humanity; those who only viewed our bodies as obstacles to possessing the land and its resources. In solidarity, Native Americans work to prevent the loss of Palestinian homelands, because we recognize that what is occurring is not just a loss of land, but an erasure of our knowledge, our history and our ancestors."[3]

Zionism is a form of Jewish nationalism that serves a strategic alliance with US imperialism while propelling the ongoing occupation of Palestine.

Zionism serves many functions in Palestine just as nationalism does in the United States. Despite common narrative, safety and security is not the primary motive in either of these cases. Theodore Herzl, a founder of Zionism, spoke in 1956: "I achieved a freer attitude toward antisemitism, which I now began to understand historically and to pardon. Above all, I recognized the emptiness and futility of trying to 'combat' antisemitism."[4] Political Zionism has at its foundation a commitment to forming the nation-state of Israel in the historic land of Palestine, leveraging religion as a justification for ethnonationalism. Originally a British imperial project, Israel is now heavily funded and backed by the United States, which then profits from the occupation of Palestine. The United States uses Israel as an ally for resource extraction and militarism and as a beacon of imperialism in the Middle East. Israel plays a role in repression internationally through the export of military goods, training of police, and collaboration with fascist regimes. From cooperation with the Nazi regime in Germany to Israeli prime minister Benjamin Netanyahu's alliances with US president Donald Trump and Russian president Vladimir Putin, Zionism has consistently aligned itself with populist nationalism. Right-wing populism guises itself through anti-elitist sentiments claiming to speak for the common people, while in practice it is the cause of increased violence and repression.

With the centering of Zionism in Jewishness, there is an implicit erasure of Jewish identity outside of the nation-state of Israel. This conflation is one of many ways that Zionism not only misuses but also perpetuates antisemitism by confusing the varied historical and contemporary roles of Jews in the Zionist project, including their resistance to it. At the same time, the state of Israel has continued to consolidate the relationship between Israeli nationality and Jewishness, through its 2018 Nation-State Law. In writing about the connections between Kashmiri and Palestinian resistance to colonial occupation, scholar activist Zanaib Ramahi writes, "Ethno-nationalism is rooted in colonial narratives that dictate a racial hierarchy of belonging in which the subordination of some members of the population, the out-group, is structurally entrenched and often backed up with physical violence. As per its Nation State Law, Israel is not a state of its citizens, but rather belongs to Jewish people that have membership and belonging in the state. The full privileges of membership in Israel are extended exclusively to its Jewish population."[5]

Within progressive movements, the issue of Palestine is often left out from broader conversations around imperialism. Palestinians are not invited to the table (especially outside the framework of friendly Arab-Israeli/Muslim-Jewish "peace talks"). Time after time, I have seen the Palestinian struggle sidelined because of false claims of antisemitism. I believe that people's confusion around the histories and current expressions of antisemitism in relationship to Zionism has allowed this gap to exist in our movements and led to inability to address the real harm of both antisemitism and Zionism.

Still today we hear echoes of the fascism and white nationalism of 1930s Europe in countries all around the world. Authoritarian regimes are gaining power, including Bolsonaro in Brazil, Modi in India, and Duterte in the Philippines. We have also seen incredible and successful uprisings against repressive governments from Hong Kong to India, Iraq, and Lebanon. White nationalists in the United States were emboldened by the election of Donald Trump to the presidency. The Trump administration and its many outspoken antisemitic, racist, Zionist, and homophobic politicians included the egregious former White House chief strategist, Steve Bannon. During the Trump's presidency, the United States backed the establishment of Jerusalem as the capital of Israel, supported the expansion of settlements, and declared Israel the exclusive homeland for the Jewish people in alignment with the Knesset's passage of the Nation-State Basic Law in 2018. Israel is now backed by the Biden administration, the US military industrial complex, and billions of US tax dollars, and we are witnessing Israel's attempt to "complete" the colonization of Palestine by way of committing a genocide in Gaza. The days, weeks, and months that have followed the armed uprising of Palestinians on October 7, 2023, have seen the most brutal exertion of Israel's dominance over Palestinian land and people since the Nakba and founding of the state of Israel in 1948. As of this writing, tens of thousands of Palestinians have been killed, millions have been displaced from their homes in Gaza, and those who have resisted on either side of the apartheid wall have been brutally repressed.

In the meantime, while the expansion of the Zionist project has supposedly been to keep Jewish people safe, attacks on Jewish communities have actually increased internationally, most notably in the United States. In addition to antisemitic attacks fueled by white nationalism, Zionism and US imperialism have positioned Jews as middlemen in the so called "conflict" in the Middle East. This scapegoating has caused a rise in anti-Jewish hatred as Jews are more and more visible in taking on a settler colonial role in the State of Israel. Scapegoating is one of the hallmarks of antisemitism which we will get into more in the next chapter, for now we can see clearly the shared interests of Zionism, antisemitism, and all forms of racism.

In this chapter, we will disentangle Zionism from Jewishness to reveal histories of joint struggle and possibilities for dismantling nationalism and colonialism.[6] From Audre Lorde and other second-wave, intersectional, and Black feminists we learn that the personal is political, and the political is personal. Always. There came a time in my politicization where that meant disentangling my own understandings of Jewishness, antisemitism, and Zionism. I grew up in a deeply rooted, culturally Jewish community in the Bay Area that shaped me in so many ways, particularly around interdependence, collective care, generative conflict, and holding contradictions. Our family went to services at Beth Shalom in San Francisco, where Rabbi Alan Lew's sermons caused me to doze off as a young child. (I became very familiar with the texture of the red velvet benches in our synagogue.) When I rediscovered Rabbi Lew's teachings as an adult, I was deeply moved by the legacies he carried and communicated through his mindfulness-based Jewish practices. I remember our community pouring out onto the streets on Purim singing and dancing; reflecting on our commitments to love and justice on Rosh Hashanah at the lake in the Presidio; sitting shiva when a community member died; and the many social events where I would be pulling on my mom's clothes trying to get her to stop schmoozing and take me home. In all of these different experiences, the biggest contradiction I found in our community was the steadfast commitment to justice that seemed to stop when it came to the movement for a free Palestine. After countless attempted interventions and difficult conversations, I decided it was time to deepen my own understanding of the ways Zionism had co-opted my own people's histories in service of the oppression of Palestinian people and colonization of their ancestral homelands. I wish I could say I come from a lineage of communist Jews who rallied against the state, but I have not found family stories of Jewish resistance, at least in the tattered records and stories I have been able to access. Instead, I have found stories of my family surviving by moving year after year to avoid the pogroms and other predecessors to the Nazi genocide in eastern Europe. I learned stories of how my grandparents and great grandparents faced antisemitism and assimilated into whiteness. I began searching for deeper meaning and connection to a purpose and politics outside the confines of US-centered movements.

It was 2012, and Palestinian resistance (and thus repression) was increasing in both the West Bank and Gaza. I decided it was time to make a leap and travel to Palestine to ground my emerging analysis in lived experience. My way of getting there was through a program called Birthright, which takes young American Jews on free trips to Israel as a way of seeding Zionist propaganda in young people and encouraging them to join and support the colonization of Palestine. Using the free ticket, and with anarchist zines and directories of infoshops in my luggage, I began the trip planning to leave their curated Zionist tour to participate in Palestine solidarity activism during the olive harvest in the West Bank. What I did not know was that my life's work would be transformed by the experience. While I was there, I was filled with shame and disgust for how symbols of Judaism were being used to support the nation-state of Israel. I watched Israeli soldiers give alcohol to these young Americans, particularly young women and femmes, as the soldiers' roles were romanticized, masculinized, and misrepresented as critical to our safety. Actually, these young men were steeped in a violent rape culture that, in addition to the impacts of war and militarism, made me and all of us more vulnerable to gendered violence. I witnessed Israeli tanks (from the US-based Caterpillar company) with Jewish stars bulldoze Palestinian villages, saw roads leading through the West Bank designated exclusively for Jewish settlers, and saw towering walls with Israeli flags flying in the wind. I knew deep in my bones that this was not the safety I wanted and not the liberation our revolutionary ancestors fought and died for.

As part of transforming the pain I felt, and in alignment with my commitments to justice, I was drawn to take action against the present conditions of suffering while also learning more about the historical context. I joined weekly protests at the wall that prevents Palestinians in the West Bank from accessing Jerusalem, hospitals, and workplaces in Israel—and that often cuts right through their families' land. I participated in direct action at Israeli settlements, defended Palestinian farmland in the West Bank, and gained a more experiential understanding of the violence within the walls of occupied Palestine.

One of the direct actions I participated in was at a Rami Levy grocery store in a "Jewish only" settlement, Ramla, outside of the Palestinian city of Ramallah. It was an action against a grocery chain in a major settlement in the West Bank, taken as part of the boycott, divestment, and sanctions movement that seeks to defund those who profit from

Israeli apartheid.[7] After a nonviolent protest inside the store, the Israeli army arrived and escalated the action, resulting in two Palestinians being beaten and arrested. One of those two was Bassem Tamimi, the head of the popular committee of Nabi Saleh, who had just recently been released from Israeli prison for organizing in his Palestinian village. I watched while his wife tried to follow and de-arrest him, and the army shoved her back. I stepped in front of her to offer a shield, and then a sound bomb went off. The next thing I knew, I had been hit over the head and was face down on the pavement, with four soldiers kicking and grabbing at me. I was carried away and aggressively restrained, as is standard practice for the Israeli police and military.

I spent the following eight days lost in different army tanks, hospitals, and jail cells. Shortly after being detained, the Palestinians were sent to a separate facility, as Israelis and internationals experience an entirely different system (a telltale sign of an apartheid state). The Israeli soldiers mocked me for being a self-hating Jew as I sat on the floor in the corner waiting for a lawyer. When we were taken to a hospital for our injuries, one of the Israelis looked at me with disdain and spit on me. The only moments I felt remotely okay were the moments of collective care—when I had been wearing the same clothes for a week and my cell mate put me in the shower and gave me her fresh T-shirt, and when, across language barriers, we found moments of laughter and dance, and when I missed a meal and friends hid food for me. Once I finally received a court case, I was told my options were either to make *aliyah* (Jewish immigration to Israel) or to be deported. Join the Zionist project or never come back. I chose the latter and boarded a ferry to Greece to meet up with activists I had met in Palestine.

Three days after I was released, the Jewish matriarch of our family, my grandmother, died. We had a fraught relationship, largely because I didn't conform to her standards around gender. In the years before her death, we tried to bridge the gaps between us. I remember her sending me a newspaper clipping about the healing benefits of turmeric when I was in herb school. We loved each other deeply but just never saw eye to eye—especially around Zionism. The last time I saw her before she died, she had told me two things: to break up with my partner at the time (she wasn't wrong about that) and to have a wonderful time in our people's holy land. Reckoning with her death was a practice of holding multiple truths. While I was devastated to lose this precious ancestor, I also felt so unresolved about how she saw me and the world we lived in. Just a few days after her death, the local Jewish Federation sent out a memorial for her, soliciting donations for the Israel Terror Relief Fund. I still remember opening this email and feeling the rage pulsing through my body. I was enraged by the cynical manipulation of my family's grief to instill allegiance to the state of Israel at all costs. After spending this time in the belly of the beast, there was no turning back. I had slept beside countless migrant workers from around the world stuck in the Israeli deportation center and seen Palestinian activists incarcerated in the cruelest of conditions. Witnessing and experiencing this level of suffering connected me to my own ancestral legacy of resistance and fortified my commitment to fight all forms of racism and fascism, including both Zionism and anti-semitism. It also reminded me of the ways trauma and oppression get inscribed in our bodies and set me on a path toward bringing together the healing work I had been practicing with the political work I was engaged in. The personal is political.

As my US citizenship allowed me to return to my home in the San Francisco Bay Area, Bassem Tamimi remained in Israeli military prison until the following year. At this point, it was the end of 2012, and awareness around the siege on Gaza was increasing in the United States. I attended a meeting for new members of the International Jewish Anti-Zionist Network and began organizing alongside recently mobilized activists as well as seasoned movement leaders. The International Jewish Anti-Zionist Network (IJAN) officially formed in 2008 as an anti-imperialist and decolonial organization rooted in decades of relationship with Arabs and Palestinians on the ground and in diaspora. IJAN has always been uncompromising in its commitment to Palestinian freedom and self-determination. At a time where a Jewish anti-Zionist movement in the US was yet to form, IJAN played a critical role in pushing other Jewish organizations to move from liberal anti-occupation frameworks to becoming explicitly anti-Zionist. To this day, IJAN continues to be a force of political clarity and principled struggle in the landscape of Jewish anti-Zionism. Contrary to the Zionist narrative that those who criticize Israel are self-hating Jews, my involvement in IJAN brought me closer to my Jewishness. At the same time, it transformed my relationship with decolonial movements to defend life and land. Nurturing this political home and my commitments to healing and transformation has allowed me to stay centered in the midst of increased polarization and pressure. This has meant more successfully moving people in my community toward liberatory politics by meeting them with understanding rather than rhetoric and leading with power rather than fear. By connecting with our Jewish ancestral lineages in ways are accountable to collective histories and in sync with current expressions of resistance to fascism, we can break through cycles of violence to create more liberatory futures for all. For me, this has become possible through deepening my understanding and practice of joint struggle. "A core tenet of the way IJAN organizes is joint struggle—recognizing the particular stakes of different communities and sectors in the general struggle against Zionist repression, militarism, and imperialism. The stake of each movement is specific, but we share a commitment to principles of universal liberation, justice, equity, never sacrificing any aspect of one community or movement's struggle for freedom for the sake of advancing another's. We recognize that our struggles are bound together, and that we must find ways of organizing together that strengthen all of our movements."[8]

Zionism: The Construction of Jewish Nationalism

Zionism is an ideology of Jewish nationalism that led to the founding of the state of Israel in Palestine and continues to inform the expansion of the settler-colonial state. While Israel is only seventy-six years old, and political Zionism is around 150 years old, our Jewish ancestors built stateless communities for centuries—some might even say thousands of years—in places around the world. During extreme anti-Jewish violence in Europe, many poor and working-class Jews were part of an international opposition to capitalism and racism joining across ethnicity and religion to resist oppression and find safety through solidarity. Many became communists and anarchists and were instrumental in social movements around the globe, including the Russian Revolution, the radical workers' movement in the United States, and the Jewish Labor Bund in eastern Europe. During the same time period, many middle- and upper-class central and western European Jews sought democratic and economic rights in European countries. It wasn't until the end of the nineteenth century that a group of elitist white men struggling for power formed Zionism as a political project and response to antisemitism. In the 1870s, European Zionists began establishing what they called "population centers" for Jewish immigration in Palestine with British imperial support. In 1896 founding Zionist Theodor Herzl wrote *The Jewish State*, prompting British Christian missionaries like Reverend William Hechler to garner their political and material resources to support this nationalist project. In 1917 Britain issued the Balfour Declaration, in which they officially declared support for Palestine as the national home for Jewish people, to keep Jewish pogrom refugees out of Britain. This move was also part of a broader strategy of British imperialism to secure power in the region, including access to the Suez Canal, which was critical in expediting the extraction of natural resources from the region. Between 1917 and 1948, Britain more than any other nation helped to lay the diplomatic, governmental, military and economic foundations for Israel.

Most of the Jews who settled in Palestine during this time were victims of the Nazi genocide, which the Zionist movement took advantage of to pursue the formation of Israel. Their legacies continue to be misused to justify the ongoing colonization of Palestine, which is actually driven by racism, classism, and imperialism. Many settler societies around the world have narratives that include escaping suffering and persecution. The somewhat obvious reality is that settler colonialism is not the only answer for refugees. We know that immigrants coming to the United States today (particularly nonwhite immigrants) are not afforded the privileges of settler colonialism; rather, they are incessantly othered and criminalized. It is white supremacy and power that manipulate peoples' experiences of migration toward colonial empires, such as the case of early Europeans settlers in the United States and Jewish settlers in Palestine.

The transformation of early immigrants into settlers and ongoing assimilation into whiteness is an important part of the progress of "civilization" in the history of the United States. "Progress" is often defined by a process of colonization and ethnic cleansing as is demonstrated in the rapid transformation of Jews from concentration camp survivors to settlers with political power. Palestinian American scholar Steven Salaita frames this complexity quite clearly in his book *Inter/Nationalism*: "When members of these groups or their descendants pick up guns and fulfill their army service they become implicated in a particular way in settler colonization. Nevertheless, these groups have mutable relationships with the colonial state and thus mercurial interactions with the Palestinians."[9] Salaita acknowledges that while settlers may have a wide range of histories and relationships the state, when they become active participants in the military occupation of Palestine, they become complicit with the settler-colonial state of Israel.

To continue connecting histories of colonization, we must see the broader systems at play. Palestinian scholar Edward Said refers to Palestinians as the victims of the victims. Within this understanding, Said makes way for a different kind of intervention within cycles of violence. He writes,

> It is inadequate only to affirm that a people were dispossessed, oppressed, or slaughtered, denied its rights and its political existence, without at the same time . . . affiliating those horrors with the similar afflictions of other people. This does not at all mean a loss in historical specificity, but rather it guards against the possibility that a lesson learned about oppression in one place will be forgotten or violated in another place or time. And just because you represent the suffering that your people lived through which you yourself might have lived through also, you are not relieved of the duty of revealing that your own people now may be visiting related crimes on their victims.[10]

Said's intervention requires compassion and understanding of a historical context while simultaneously being accountable for harm caused.

Jews fleeing pogroms in the early 1900s and then the Nazi genocide sought refuge in countries around the world, including the United States and Palestine. Some of these refugees were denied entry, some "successfully" settled in these new countries, and many were killed before they could immigrate. Over 60,000 Jewish refugees migrated to Palestine in the 1930s, and another 140,000 Jewish survivors of the Nazi genocide arrived in the few years between the end of World War II in 1945 and the official establishment of Israel in 1948.[11] The history of Jews seeking refuge from persecution is only a piece of the full story. Throughout this history, colonial and imperialist powers have determined the fate of people and land. During the Ottoman Empire in the mid-sixteenth century, Arab Jews made up 5 percent of the Palestinian population. In 1917, after the British drove out Ottoman forces, the Balfour Declaration was written and (soon after) adopted as the British Mandate for Palestine: promising Palestine as a "national home for the Jewish people."[12] In 1947, Jews (now predominantly European refugees and immigrants) made up 26 percent of the population of Palestine and owned approximately 7 percent of the total land.[13] By 1949 these figures had grown to had grown to constitute 80 percent of the population and

77 percent of the land. In this time Zionist militias consolidated to form the Israeli Defense Forces (IDF), expelling thousands of Palestinians from their homes and preventing them from returning. Other nongovernmental organizations, like the Jewish National Fund, participated in this displacement as well.

In debates about the legitimacy of the state of Israel and justification of Jews settling in Palestine, people pull on sympathy for the Jews seeking safety from persecution but also make biblical claims to indigeneity. In this context, the script is flipped, and indigeneity becomes a term used to justify further colonization. So, rather than basing indigeneity on subjective historical narratives or rights-based paradigms, we can understand indigeneity in terms of precolonial inhabitants: people colonized after the emergence of modern imperialism and militarism. In the case of Palestine, this means the distinction is not between the Jew and the Arab, it is between the Israeli settler and the precolonial inhabitant: Palestinians—including Jews, Muslims, and Christians. By situating Palestine as a part of broader analyses on settler colonialism internationally, we can expose Zionist messianism and exceptionalism. So often the colonization of Palestine is referred to as a "conflict" between Jews and Arabs. This is a way of individualizing the issue and diverting attention away from the powerful forces of Zionism and US imperialism that are foundational to the establishment of Israel.

In understanding some of this history, we can see that Zionism is a colonial project based on white supremacy and nationalism and has little to do with safety for Jews or combating antisemitism. In actuality, Zionism is predicated on the antisemitic idea that Jews do not belong in the places we live. Holocaust survivors have been outspoken about the misuse of our histories including as part of the "Never Again for Anyone" campaign launched by IJAN in 2010. Hajo Meyer, a then ninety-year-old survivor of the Auschwitz death camp asserted: "No injustice can be undone by a new injustice."[14] In his writing and activism, Meyer worked to expose the ways Zionism is connected to other forms of racism, including antisemitism. He also parallels the fascist regime he faced in Germany with the fascist nature of Israeli apartheid.

The Zionist Federation of Germany sent this letter of support to the Nazi Party on June 21, 1933: "A rebirth of national life such as is occurring in German life ... must also take place in the Jewish national group. On the foundation of the new [Nazi] state which has established the principle of race, we wish so to fit our community into the total structure so that for us, too, in the sphere assigned to us, fruitful activity for the Fatherland is possible."[15] Later that year, the World Zionist Organization (WZO) not only struck down a resolution calling for action against Hitler by a vote of 240 to 43 but also broke the boycott against the Nazi regime by issuing a trade agreement. The WZO then became the largest distributor of Nazi goods in the Middle East and northern Europe.

In addition, Fievel Polkes, a member of the Haganah (the predecessor to the Israeli Defense Forces) met with Nazi leader Adolf Eichmann and said: "Jewish nationalist circles were very pleased with the radical German policy, since the strength of the Jewish population in Palestine would be so far increased thereby that in the foreseeable future the Jews could reckon upon numerical superiority over the Arabs."[16] These powerful Zionists essentially encouraged Nazis to violently displace Jews from their homes in eastern Europe. The Zionist project abandoned Jews they saw as unfit to fulfill their agenda—such as anarchists, communists, and members of the Jewish Socialist Bund—in order to increase the Jewish refugee population and colonize Palestine.

These cycles of violence perpetuated by imperialism continue to function through Israel today. Yet, along with continued repression, there has been continued resistance to fascism in all its forms. During the brutal attack on Gaza in 2014, the "Never Again for Anyone" campaign (started in collaboration with Hajo Meyer), published a letter written by more than 350 survivors and descendants of survivors and victims of the Nazi genocide. Responding to Elie Wiesel's manipulation of the Nazi genocide in the August 23 edition of the *New York Times*, the letter declared: "As Jewish survivors and descendants of survivors and victims of the Nazi genocide we unequivocally condemn the massacre of Palestinians in Gaza and the ongoing occupation and colonization of historic Palestine. We further condemn the United States for providing Israel with the funding to carry out the attack, and Western states more generally for using their diplomatic muscle to protect Israel from condemnation."[17] Jewish survivors and descendants of the Nazi genocide, healing and reclaiming histories of trauma, interrupt the monolithic narrative that in order for Jews to feel safe we need the settler state of Israel. This false narrative that Zionism is what keeps us safe from forces like fascism is weakening. Zionism clearly perpetuates ethnonationalism and positions Jews as intermediaries and scapegoats in a broader imperialist agenda.[18]

From Jackson to Jabotinsky

> The discursive foundations of removal and the nakba, as exemplified by [Andrew] Jackson and [Ze'ev] Jabotinsky, are striking in their reliance on the same narrow mythos of progress.... This mythos even in its secular incarnation is fundamentally biblical: the settler is aggrieved, usually escaping persecution in the originating nation, and must be redeemed through a violent national rebirth.
>
> —Steven Salaita

Anyone who investigates the colonization of the United States or Palestine can see that the two are intrinsically linked. Building on Palestinian scholar Steven Salaita's work to expose the similarities between Andrew Jackson's role in colonizing the United States and Ze'ev Jabotinsky's role in colonizing Palestine, we will weave in and out of these narratives to build a political analysis that includes the unique conditions of the colonization of Palestine but does not see it as exceptional.

As president of the United States in the 1830s, Andrew Jackson enslaved nearly one hundred Black people and signed the Indian Removal Act, which displaced and killed tens of thousands of Indigenous people in an ethnic cleansing effort. Ze'ev Jabotinsky (1880–1940) was a Jewish nationalist and one of the founders of Zionism. In 1923 Jabotinsky wrote the now infamous essay "The Iron Wall." In it, he laid out the road map for Israel›s domestic and foreign policy, particularly the enforcement of ethnic cleansing through a powerful military force. The essay begins with an exhortation:

> Colonisation of Palestine
> Agreement with Arabs Impossible at present
> Zionism Must Go Forward[19]

This summarizes Jabotinsky's relentless commitment to the violent colonization of Palestine. He goes on to say, "Zionist colonization, even the most restricted, must either be terminated or carried out in defiance of the will of the native population. This colonization can, therefore, continue and develop only under the protection of a force independent of the local population—an iron wall which the native population cannot break through. This is, in toto, our policy towards the Arabs. To formulate it any other way would only be hypocrisy."[20] Today liberal Zionism is this hypocrisy. It uses tactics of normalization such as greenwashing and pinkwashing (explained later) to paint a picture of Israel as a leader of democracy in the region.

Foundational Zionist thinkers looked to the United States as a success story of colonization. Jabotinsky based his Zionist agenda on a blueprint of US colonization and was explicit from the beginning that Israel was a colonial project. He wrote, "We may tell them whatever we like about the innocence of our aims, watering them down and sweetening them with honeyed words to make them palatable, but they know what we want, as well as we know what they do not want. They feel at least the same instinctive jealous love of Palestine, as the old Aztecs felt for ancient Mexico, and [the native] Sioux for their rolling Prairies."[21] Again, unlike liberal Zionists, Jabotinsky was clear on the connection between indigenous struggles, though this understanding was fuel for his leadership in drumming up support from other nation-states toward the colonization of Palestine. Both Jabotinsky and Andrew Jackson had overt aims of ethnic cleansing through the genocide of indigenous peoples. Gyasi Ross, lawyer for the Blackfeet Indian Reservation, asserts that the conquest of the Americas became the foundation for displacement internationally, including the Zionist colonization of Palestine. The connections between Zionism and colonization in the United States are not only theoretical, they co-evolved and continue to inform each other.

The United States uses Israel as an imperialist outpost in the SWANA (Southwest Asia and North Africa) region, sending an average of $3.3 billion a year and providing ongoing military and police training specifically focused on repression. In addition to the central role of Zionism in both US and Israeli politics, Israel has also played a role in enacting US imperialism across the world. Israel has armed and trained apartheid regimes of South Africa, colonial regimes in the Middle East, dictators in Central and South America, and police forces in the United States.[22] One of the most egregious examples is Israel's role providing tactical oversight and material support in the genocide in Guatemala and El Salvador in the 1980s. General Efrain Rios Montt, the dictator responsible for Guatemala's 1982–83 genocide, considered Israel an indispensable ally in fighting communism and destroying Guatemala's Native communities. The Israeli Defense Forces (which would more accurately be named the Israeli Offensive Forces) continue to be turned to as a model for militarism, providing trainings and weaponry to the US military and police forces responsible for killing Black and Brown people every single day.

Political leaders like Jabotinsky and Jackson based their colonial, imperialist practices on messianic abstractions and mythology claiming that the progress of "civilization" required bloodshed and displacement. In this abstraction, the colonization of the US was justified, as was (and is) Israel's colonization of Palestine, in addition to Zionists' claim to the "Holy Land," further illustrating the messianic nature of their colonial project.

In *Inter/Nationalism*, Salaita offers the metaphorical grounding of iron deficiency,—fascinating from an embodiment perspective. He suggests that Jabotinsky perhaps chose the term "Iron Wall" cognizant of the fact that iron is an essential element for our survival, aiding in distributing oxygen through our bodies. "His exaltations of strength and steadfastness, after all, sharply contrast nearly all the connotations of anemia. The body of the Israeli state could not survive without this self-regenerating chemical."[23] To extend this metaphor across time and place, we see that after World War II there was the so-called Iron Curtain that separated communist and capitalist regions in Europe. This division was used to mobilize Jewish communities on the western side of the Iron Curtain to pledge their allegiance to the United States and Israel. Over sixty years later, the iron metaphor continues to represent brutal militarization and invincibility of the nation-state. In a 2019 statement, Israeli prime minister Netanyahu congratulated the United States on its purchase of Israel's missile defense technology (developed and named the Iron Dome in 2011), stating: "Israel has an Iron Dome and an iron fist. Our systems know how to deal with any threat, both in defense and in attack. I would not recommend our enemies to try us." This toxic embodiment of militarism has been a key part of the Zionist project from the beginning.

Contrary to settler narratives, before 1948 when the state of Israel was founded, Palestine was a vibrant place with a varied indigenous community of peoples whose traditions were deeply rooted in the land. Still today Palestinians practice a range of faith traditions, and many have deep relationship with the land through farming olive groves, maintaining their villages, and resisting the forces of colonization. The Israeli government, with US military and government backing, continues to expand its imperial reach and strengthen its Iron Wall. Excuses and apologies are made, while little has been done in either the United States or Israel to restore indigenous self-determination or sovereignty.

False Safety Narratives: The Misuse of "Antisemitism"

> From the body's viewpoint, safety and danger are neither situational nor based on cognitive feelings. Rather, they are physical, visceral sensations. The body either has a sense of safety or it doesn't. If it doesn't, it will do almost anything to establish or recover that sense of safety.
>
> —Resmaa Menakem

All my life I have experienced the ways nationalism, Zionism, and antisemitism and other forms of racism inform our sense of safety in our individual and collective bodies. I went to a Jewish school from kindergarten through eighth grade where we pledged our allegiance to the flags of both the United States and Israel every morning. We were shown Holocaust documentaries year after year linking the pain of our history to the importance of the state of Israel. We had ex-IDF soldiers who worked as security guards at the school. And I remember the first time we were on lockdown in kindergarten after receiving one of many bomb threats. I was steeped in the Jewish community in San Francisco, which in large part participated in movements for justice ... except when it came to Palestine. Despite being totally immersed in Jewish culture as a child, I felt disconnected from my Jewishness. The kind of Jewish experience offered at the school was rigid and based in fear and survival. It wasn't until I was in my early twenties when I was exploring different healing, spiritual, and political traditions that I began to really connect with my Jewishness as a rooted history and practice. As my connection to Jewishness grew, my understanding about the misuse of our histories, the Nazi genocide, and violent expressions of Zionism grew too. I became increasingly enraged at how many of us had been indoctrinated as kids to believe the myth that in order to be safe we needed the state of Israel. But Israel has created extremely unsafe conditions for everyone in that region.

If democracy is about ensuring safety and equity for all, then democracy cannot and does not exist when an entire population is stripped of their homes, their land, and any political power. First and foremost, the colonization of Palestine impacts Palestinians. To say that Jews are the only other group with a stake in the movement for Palestine would be Zionist in and of itself. We share our collective commitments to end systems of injustice oppressing people around the world. We share our humanity. Zionism has bred Jewish exceptionalism in ways that contribute to antisemitism such as holding Jews to a certain standard around anti-Zionism without holding non-Jews to the same standard. For example, it is antisemitic to not let a Jewish person participate in a space without proving their politics around Zionism when the organizers don't ask anyone else (non-Jews) to take a stance on Palestine.

The centering of Jewishness in the movement for Palestine is also a reproduction of Jewish entitlement to Palestinian space. This can show up in a variety of ways, including problematic uses of public Jewish ritual in moments of extreme terror and grief in Palestine. For example, during the 2014 attack on Gaza some Jewish groups held public vigils to pray and say mourners' kaddish for the thousands of Palestinians killed. This was meaningful for many participants, but in some cases these rituals failed to draw connections between international struggles (some even failed to contest Zionism) and instead collapsed into a whitewashed solidarity. In 2023 I participated in a civil disobedience action in the rotunda of the US Capitol in Washington, DC. During some of the ritual components, I found myself extremely uncomfortable as a circle of rabbis danced and sang in the center of the circle. There was a buzz of excitement and talk about how we had "occupied" the capitol for so many hours. The action was primarily for media optics, which is indeed an important tactic, but in the meantime we reified hierarchical ideologies and showed whose lives really mattered: by setting the rest of us up to protect the rabbis at the center showed how horrible it was that those "peaceful rabbis" were arrested. In the meantime, Palestinians were being targeted and killed by the minute. In these moments, I hoped both for more reverence and also for more boldness in our action. Jewish ritual around Palestinian loss is a precarious practice that without clear leadership from those most impacted can look like centering whiteness and the shame of complicity in oppression. That said, we can all benefit from a diversity of tactics, and there have been times when Jewish ritual has been used to bring in our broader community rather than just as a performance of solidarity politics. For example, many communities hold anti-Zionist Passover seders inviting both Jews and non-Jews to go more deeply into the liberation theology and offer material support through fund-raising for Palestine. Also, many of the "Hanukkah for ceasefire" actions in 2023 offered space for ritual candle-lighting that raised public awareness and encouraged passersby to rally their representatives for a ceasefire in Gaza. With a clear tone and intention, I believe there can *absolutely* be a place for

Jewish ritual in movements for justice. Whether through public ritual or other forms of Jewish-led action, we must stay connected to our shared humanity rather than falling into the traps of exceptionalism and Zionism by conflating Jewishness with the state of Israel or centering Jewishness in the Palestinian struggle (or both).

This kind of exceptionalism also arises when organizations feel they must invite a Jew to speak alongside a Palestinian, perpetuating the notion that there is a Jewish-Palestinian conflict and inhibiting the space for Palestinian self-determination. Another major place it shows up is with Jewish social justice funders that suppress expressions of political support for the liberation of Palestine by calling out grant recipients as antisemitic. One such instance was in 2016 when the Movement for Black Lives (M4BL) released its policy platform including a section on US divestment from apartheid Israel. Major sources cut off M4BL funding, and Zionist institutions such as the Jewish Community Relations Council and the Anti-Defamation League targeted M4BL and attempted to control the narrative. These are just a few of many examples of how the centering of Jewishness and the misuse of antisemitism can dictate our movements.

Given these realities, as Jews we have a particular and tenuous role to play in speaking out and taking action in the face of Zionist repression and the misuse of antisemitism. It is our role to show solidarity with the actions Palestinians take in their homelands as well as in diaspora—to support their calls for self-determination and Palestinian right of return. It is also our role to reclaim our histories and lift up stories of Jews living and resisting all forms of oppression in diverse, stateless communities around the world. It is our role to dismantle support for the political project of Zionism in order to redeem a liberatory Judaism rooted in diaspora. And it is our role to de-exceptionalize antisemitism and its history, which currently isolates Jews and overlooks the context from which antisemitism was born: white supremacy.

The Nazis set out to exterminate Jews as part of a broader political strategy of European white nationalism. In 1922 Adolf Hitler gave a speech in Munich and made a point strikingly similar to Jabotinsky's assertion of the need for force in the colonization of Palestine. Hitler said: "There can be no compromise—there are only two possibilities: either victory of the Aryan, or annihilation of the Aryan and the victory of the Jew."[24] One impact of Zionism is creating confusion about these origins of antisemitism and its connection to other forms of racism.

As we begin to disentangle Jewishness from Zionism, it is important to note that there are more people affiliated with Christian Zionist organizations in the United States (Christians United for Israel has 10 million members alone) than there are in the entire Jewish American population (7.6 million).[25] Christian Zionists are invested in the state of Israel as part of a broader white nationalism that includes antisemitism. Many Christians support the existence of Israel as a Jewish state and the immigration of Jews to Palestine because they wish to hasten the second coming of the Messiah and the dawn of the End Times.[26] Christian Zionists are not interested in supporting the safety of the Jewish people. On the contrary, they are invested in the messianic story that when the End Times come, the Jews will be sent to Hell for their failure to accept Jesus as the one true Lord and Savior. John Hagee, founder of Christians United for Israel, suggested in a sermon that Hitler was part of God's plan to get Jewish people "back to the land of Israel."[27] Christian Zionism is deeply interwoven with white nationalism in terms of its theology and its followers and is supported, of course, by white Christian supremacy.

Throughout history Jews have been positioned as the middlemen between dominant (most often white and Christian) regimes and the people they attempted to oppress. In 1903 *The Protocols of the Learned Elders of Zion* was published, a fabricated document purportedly representing an actual meeting of international Jewish conspirers. This antisemitic text—which despite massive protest remained on Walmart shelves until 2004—indicated that Jews were plotting to dominate the world. The gunman responsible for the massacre at the Tree of Life synagogue in Pittsburgh in 2018 acted on such white nationalist conspiracy theories, stating that Jews were culpable for allowing immigrants into the country. Just before going into the synagogue to murder eleven Jewish congregants, he posted, "HIAS [Hebrew Immigrant Aid Society] likes to bring invaders in that kill our people. I can't sit by and watch my people get slaughtered. Screw your optics, I'm going in."[28] The current rise of white nationalism draws on this history through alt-right propaganda fueled through online forums such as Breitbart, 4chan, and Gab. Eric Ward, civil rights strategist and political analyst, calls us to attend to the role of antisemitism in white nationalist ideology, writing, "American White nationalism . . . is a revolutionary social movement committed to building a Whites-only nation, and antisemitism forms its theoretical core."[29] White nationalism has always maintained an ideology that claims Jews manipulate policy to use nonwhite immigrants as a weapon against white people. Derogatory claims that Jews control the media, banking, entertainment, and even the US government, blame progressive politics (particularly around immigration) on Jews. Neo-Nazis chant "Jews will not replace us!"—referring not only to suppressing Jewish populations through ethnic cleansing but also to the conspiracy theory that Jews are responsible for immigration to the United States through financial and political support that threatens the white race. To be clear, Jews make up a large portion of progressive and radical movements relative to our small makeup of the general population. However, it is not because of a conspiracy to take over the world that we engage in movements for justice. It is because of our own histories of oppression, legacies of resistance, and embedded commitment to social justice through the practice of *tikkun olam*—a Jewish practice of social engagement and activism. ("Tikkun olam" can be translated as "repair of the world.")

Antisemitism is often confused with anti-Jewish sentiment. Anti-Jewish sentiment is rooted in an experience of a colonial Jewish state and differs from antisemitism and the scapegoating of Jews due to the difference in power, history, and context. For example, the Star of David on the Israeli flag used in the colonization of Palestine creates for many a negative connotation with this religious symbol. This negative sense is not antisemitism. Rather, it indicates the success of Zionism in conflating Jewishness with the Israeli apartheid state.

The old trope that Jews are cosmopolitans without any roots or loyalty to a nation (as was laid out in *The Protocols of the Elders of Zion*), became embodied as a foundational trauma resulting in people's investment in nationalism as the way to protect against antisemitism or another genocide rather than embrace statelessness and diaspora. This trauma is exploited in the false conflation of antisemitism and anti-Zionism. The portrayal of Israel as the national embodiment of Jewish culture begs a question: How do we as Jews embody an anti-Zionism that challenges this conflation and returns our traditions and legacies of resistance back to our individual and collective bodies?

Normalization: Greenwashing and Pinkwashing

Israel is understood as a place that provides safety and security for persecuted peoples—namely Jews, but it also claims to be a pioneer of environmentalism (such claims are known as greenwashing) and a haven for queer communities (in claims known as pinkwashing).

"Pinkwashing" is a term used to describe nationalist and Islamophobic tactics portraying the state of Israel as a safe haven for the LGBTQ community, which are—actually about gaining greater imperial power in the region.[30] Queer theorist Jasbir Puar developed the concept of homonationalism: the strategic fusing of queerness and US imperialism. Homonationalism is demonstrated through policies like "don't ask, don't tell" in the military, or through the assimilation of (mostly white) lesbian and gays into marriage and nuclear family systems set up to benefit capitalism. Homonationalism becomes a way for LGBTQ people to return to comfort—to assimilate their gender and sexuality into national norms so they can receive government and social benefits such as those that come with the institution of marriage or participation in the military. In recounting more recent examples of homonationalism, Puar talks about concurrent events that link LGBTQ policies to immigration and military policies. She points out that the dismantling of the Defense of Marriage Act (legalizing gay marriage) happened on the same day as the repeal of the Voting Rights Act. The repeal of the ban on homosexuals in the military (encouraging homonationalism) happened the same day there was a temporary halt to the DREAM Act that gave access to education and military enlistment to undocumented students. These are but two examples of how queer progress is predicated on support for the "war on terror," more aptly described as the war on immigrants, specifically Muslims and Arabs, and their homelands.[31] One of the more blatant examples of homonationalism in the United States is the co-optation of Pride parades. As many activists continue to assert, Pride was originally intended to celebrate the anniversary of a Black transwomen–led riot against the police. Today Pride parades have become a major expression of homonationalism, with police, military floats, and corporate sponsors.

Homonationalism also shows up in a particular way through the interlocking of Zionism and homophobia. Israel's gay male culture, fueled by pinkwashing, perpetuates toxic masculinity, femmephobia, and islamophobia. Contemporary images of white gay men are used as propaganda to encourage gay Jews to settle in Israel. "Muscular Judaism"—a term coined by Max Nordau at the first World Zionist Conference in 1897, when Muscular Christianity was increasingly prevalent—emphasized that colonizing Palestine would require radically reshaping Jewish body culture.[32] Superseding the stereotype of dominant Jewish women and weak effeminate men, there would be a hyper-masculinization of Israel via the formation of the Israeli army and the widespread portrayal of strong, powerful Jewish men. Pinkwashing also uses Islamophobic rhetoric, not only asserting that Israel is gay-friendly but also telling queer people they would be killed for being gay in a predominantly Muslim country. According to alQaws, a grassroots LGBTQ Palestinian organization, pink-washing pushes the racist idea that queerness is unnatural and foreign to Palestinian society.[33] The truth is that homophobia has no borders. Hate crimes against LGBTQ people in Israel peaked at 3,309 incidents in 2022.[34]

In addition to normalization through pinkwashing, Israel positions itself as a leader in environmentalism and green technology. Early on, Zionists boasted about the superiority of their agricultural practices, which exploited native land and introduced invasive species. The Jewish National Fund (JNF), a major Zionist institution and land acquisition agency, is one of many state apparatuses that aims to control and repress Palestinian bodies and land. They do so by portraying themselves as an environmental ("green") project with the slogan of making the desert bloom. In reality, the JNF, with the backing of the Israeli government, has destroyed indigenous landscapes, torn up thousand-year-old olive trees, and planted invasive species such as pine and eucalyptus. The JNF has been instrumental in major land grabs over the past hundred years, resulting in their ownership of 13 percent of the land in Israel. An additional 80 percent is controlled by the Israeli Land Authority, which has deep ties with the JNF, meaning together they control 93 percent of the land. Israel's dubious claims of environmental excellence are commonly referred to as greenwashing, a form of environmental racism[35].

For Palestinians, connection to their land, especially to the native olive groves, is instrumental to their survival and resilience. When inter-viewed by an International Jewish Anti-Zionist Network member, Umar al-Ghubari, a Palestinian organizer with Zochrot, from the village of Musheirifa said,

> The JNF will not admit that they administrate land of refugees. It's a terrible thing that you're taking lands of refugees. Of course, according to Israeli law this land was confiscated and the Israelis decided that it doesn't belong anymore to anyone. It belongs to the State. This policy doesn't make this true or fact. The fact that this land belongs to the refugees and most of the refugees even have papers. But again, papers isn't the only thing, the only evidence.

People can see the land and can remember that this place is their land and people can know each other and they know where exactly was the land of each family.[36]

Despite facing immense repression, Palestinians have continued to show their resilience through weekly protests in the West Bank, continued tending of olive groves, and organized resistance. For example, in the Great March of Return in 2018, Palestinians protested along the fence separating the besieged Gaza Strip from Israel and demanding the right to return to their ancestors' homes. In 2021 residents of Sheikh Jarrah drew international attention and support for their resistance to Israeli settlers' attempts to evict the majority of this Palestinian village in East Jerusalem. In 2023 Palestinians in Gaza returned to the wall, this time with a bulldozer, bringing it down and allowing them to break free of their open-air prison.[37] We know that what followed was the inevitable and relentless Israeli military invasion killing and displacing tens of thousands of Palestinians in Gaza (and the count grows as I write). While nothing makes up for loss of these homes and martyrs, Palestinians continue to show incredible force as they assert their right to resist under international law.

Reimagining Doykeit, beyond the Bund

We are cursed, and that curse is ourselves. When we were cursed, it was to wander—not just to wander, but to live forever without rest. And how little rest for the wicked there is. Back then, before the *shoah* and the *nakba*, home was "in the diaspora"—rather than existing in or as a physical place, home was in each other's hearts. For white Jews, it should be obvious that assimilating into whiteness killed the home in our hearts, building what was left into a number of physically bound structures that gave little respite for our hearts. Israel is a country gripped with an anxiety of othered humans—and here, in the diaspora, restless queer Jews move from gentrifying neighborhood to neighborhood, creating vacuums for developers to capitalize on. Our movement need be something different. We need to move from a Jewish guilt like white guilt and white tears to a queer Jewish action that has learned from the pitfalls of radical Zionism.

—Magpie Liebowitz

The concept of doykeit arose from the Jewish Labor Bund, a pre–World War II Polish labor group. Amid the rise of the Nazi regime in eastern Europe, the Bund organized Jewish community around cultural resilience and in opposition to fascist state power.

In an article about Bernard Goldstein's recently translated *Twenty Years with the Jewish Labor Bund*, Samuel Farber writes: "Unlike Zionism, the Polish Bund insisted, under its doctrine of 'hereness' (doykeit in Yiddish), that the right place for Jews was where they already lived. Trying to escape antisemitism by moving to Palestine—which, it reminded its members, was not empty land—and establishing a Jewish state would be unjust and provoke resistance. Instead, Jews had a duty to fight in alliance with the labor movement and with socialist organizations to establish a democratic republic in Poland."[38] In the face of extreme antisemitism and fascism, the Bund built a robust culture of resistance and resilience that encompassed all aspects of Jewish life, including programs for youth (Tsukunft), women (Yidisher Arbeter Froy), and children (Sotsyalistishe Kinder Farband—SKIF). The Bund responded to the political moment in which fascism was gaining momentum in eastern Europe, but it was also a visionary, generative social movement that brought together working-class people and facilitated sharing of resources and meeting people's basic needs. Today the concept of doykeit continues to be a touchstone for building opposition to a Jewish nation-state and gives historical precedent for nuanced ideas of diaspora and indigeneity.

Nationalism relies on a politics of purity and the idea that we should trace our roots back to where we are "really" from, as if there is a certain pure origin point for each of us. This also erases the experiences of people with mixed heritage whose ancestors come from a variety of places around the world. Some Jewish scholars and activists interpret references made to "the Promised Land" in the Torah as referencing the entire earth rather than only the land of Palestine as a way of breaking down border mentality in spiritual and religious traditions.

Today the concept of doykeit—rooted in Ashkenazi Jewish history—could be interpreted as a principle of embodiment, as an invitation to find home in the present moment, in our bodies. Rather than looking over there for some external knowing, we can look here, to the reality of our social, political, and environmental context, and draw from our embodied experiences a deeper knowing and political power. This does not disregard ancestral histories, but it builds on an embodied wisdom of living in interconnected ways and building cultures of mutual dignity and collaboration. Doykeit is about finding the breath and life in our bodies and in communities.

"Yiddishland" could also be understood as an example of doykeit. The often-overlooked Jewish writer and anarchist Baruch Rivkin (1883–1945) gave us a vision of Yiddishland. This vision was for a cooperative, diverse, anarchistic, egalitarian society. Because Yiddish was never associated with a nation-state or military, he posed it as the perfect language around which to form a stateless society. Yiddishland exists in the imagination of a decentralized diaspora without borders. Prior to the establishment of the state of Israel, Hebrew was used only for prayer and Torah. Jews otherwise spoke Ladino, Yiddish, Judeo-Arabic, and many other languages of the places where they lived around the globe. Hebrew was forced on the large Yiddish-speaking population of immigrants who came to the newly formed state of Israel, most having fled persecution in eastern Europe. The creation and use of modern Hebrew was vital in the initial formation of an Israeli national identity and erasure of Jewish cultures thriving elsewhere around the globe. When defending the eradication of Yiddish, Menachem Begin (a founding Zionist and the prime minister of Israel from 1977 to 1983) said, "With Yiddish, we could not have created any navy; with Yiddish, we could have no army; we could not defend ourselves with powerful jet planes; with Yiddish we would be nothing. We would be like animals."[39] Begin put it quite plainly: Yiddish and the culture developed around it would have stood in the way of the militarization of Zionism and colonization of Palestine. In fact, it did stand in the way, and it still does. Early Jewish American anarchists described Jews as a people defined by *Yiddishkeit* (Jewishness), not by a nation or a race.

Doykeit is an invitation to join with all oppressed peoples and build on legacies of Yiddishkeit, of a diaspora that rejects militarized borders and nation states. Solomon Brager writes, "Doykeit in a contemporary context implies a radical investment in the local communities that sustain us and an understanding that in a globalized society, solidarity politics must cross borders real and imagined."[40] In refusing to allow ancestral histories of trauma to be weaponized for the purpose of nationalism, we can get in touch with what is at the core of our humanity: interdependence.

As long as there has been Zionism, there has been Jewish opposition to Zionism. Jewish anti-Zionist organizing engages in a long history predating the Nazi genocide. These Jews engaged in resistance through communism, Bundism, or other forms of Jewish leftist anarchist organizing. Doykeit is not just a concept of the past, it is here permeating our communities. By developing a culture of collective care and safety, doykeit offers an embodied intervention against Zionism, white nationalism, and imperialism.

Queering Diaspora—Resisting Nationalism from the Body

> We can look at diaspora in that way: as upholding the sense of homeland and upholding this notion of the nation state and the ideals that come along with the nation state that are strict and binary and uninterested in narratives that move outside of these boundaries. So then, by queering this notion of diaspora we see diaspora as being the sort of anti-nation or moving away from nation state and figuring out this space in between nations or constantly in between nation.
>
> —Alexis Mitchell

From Turtle Island to Palestine, resistance to colonization comes from a deep well of knowing and belonging within the body.[41] Whether it is Palestinian children throwing rocks at Israeli tanks, water protectors camped out at Standing Rock, or Black folks at lunch counter sit-ins, when people put their bodies on the line, power is reclaimed. Listening to the bodies of those on the front lines supports not only their self-determination but also our collective liberation.

As noted earlier, Tara Williamson says, "The best way to demand self-determination is to be self-determining." This statement can be understood as a principle of embodiment and as a part of what it means to queer notions of diaspora; to prefiguratively embody the life and community you want to build in a way that demands people recognize your existence and respect your right to self-determination. When I say "queer diaspora," I refer to diaspora akin to doykeit and queerness that is beyond sexual and gender orientation, queerness that blurs the borders enforced by militarism and the nuclear family structures enforced by heteronormativity. In this way, a queer diaspora is a political intervention that shifts our relationships to each other and the land.

When I think about my role as a Jewish person challenging Zionism, or as a queer person challenging homonationalism, I think about how my body has been shaped by these systems and how reclaiming power in my body is part of my resistance to dismantling nationalism. However, it is beyond these identities that I find the most power in resistance—it is within my commitments to anti-imperialism and internationalism rooted in an ancestral history and connection to place. Jasbir Puar invites us to imagine homeland not as a specific, bordered nation-state but as something beyond: "The homeland is not represented only as a demographic, a geographical place, nor primarily through history, memory, or even trauma, but is cohered through sensations, vibrations, echoes, speed, feedback loops, recursive folds and feelings."[42] So when we talk about "queer diaspora," we are also challenging the limitations of binary conceptions of privilege and oppression, of indigeneity and who belongs where. "Queering diaspora" means taking down the borders and walls that separate people from land, from our bodies, and from each other. It invites us to look beyond identity politics and toward joint struggle, to envision cultures and places where all bodies belong and are dignified in their inherent worth.

In queer diaspora, we can reconceptualize diaspora not as ethnic or biological traceability but instead in terms of a queerness that challenges traditional structures of kinship. This reconfigures national and transnational communities into ones based on shared social practices and political commitments rather than place of origin or genetic ancestry. This also makes room to connect with queer ancestors: all those at our backs that make our lives possible.

The memory of belonging to a place, as well as the memory of having that place taken away from us, lives in our bodies. Hypothetically, most people could trace back their lineage and ultimately land in indigenous roots. Through centuries of displacement, colonization, and migration, these histories have been lost and distorted by systems of oppression. One by one, populations across the globe have either aligned with power, assimilated into whiteness, and/or been exploited and repressed in service of white supremacy.

Calls for decolonization are meant to hold colonial powers accountable and return peoples' rights to their lands and basic freedoms. Palestinian civil society calls for refugees right to return as stipulated in UN resolution 194.[43] Indigenous communities on Turtle Island call for land back ("Indigenous Lands back into Indigenous hands").[44] Black Americans call for reparations.[45] As Indigenous scholar Chris Finley writes, "Purposeful deconstruction of the logics of power rather than an explosion of identity politics will help end colonial domination for Native peoples."[46] Given the complexity of human relationships to land in the United States and organic movement of Indigenous communities across place and time, including the building of mixed-race families, there is no clear line to determine who does or does not belong in any given place, nor would drawing such a rigid boundary be aligned with principles of decolonization. Supporting Indigenous sovereignty can look a variety of ways, and it is important we don't get stuck in ideas of national purity that were actually the root of colonization in the first place.

Since the end of World War II, the German government has returned sixteen thousand objects taken from Jewish communities, paid over $87 billion in restitution, and offered citizenship to the descendants of victims and survivors of the Nazi genocide. In the meantime, Black, Palestinian, and other indigenous communities still await reparations and justice. A queer vision of a radical diasporic culture will not be satisfied until *all* oppressed people are restored access to their fundamental rights and ability to thrive.

Taking the state out of the body means honoring people's individual and collective agency to shape their own lives and communities; queer diaspora is a decolonial politic that allows for complex connections to home, land, and family; and doykeit is our charge as Ashkenazi Jews to resist ethnonationalism and recommit to solidarity with all oppressed peoples.

Embodied Practices

We must embody and enact decolonization in order to claim it. Decolonization is a generative and prefigurative process whereby we create the conditions in which we want to live and the social relations we wish to have—for ourselves and everyone else.

—Harsha Walia

You are invited to engage with these practices when the time is right for you and at your own pace. With everything, practice consent, self-responsiveness, accessibility, and mutual care. These practices are intended as applied learning and transformation—before entering, read through the content of the preceding chapter to better land the social, political, and/or ecological relevance of these practices. Also, you will need to refer to the author's note at the beginning–A Guide to Embodied Practice and Lineage–for a more comprehensive orientation and key to symbols.

- **Save Seeds:** Seed saving is both a practical and spiritual practice that spans both time and place. It is a form of cultural preservation and sustainability as we return the production of food and beauty into our own hands. Calendula, the flower used to show solidarity and indicate safe places for Jews in the Netherlands during the Nazi genocide happens to be a great plant for beginning to learn to save seeds. After they flower, they will dry into a cluster of brown seed pods. You can harvest the seed pods from flower heads in the late summer or early fall by simply plucking them off of the stem and drying them on a rack. Once they are dry, you can store them in a dark jar and plant again for years to come.

- **Body-to-Body Joint Struggle:** 𝅭 𝅭 ⏲ ⏲ ☆ The principle of this practice is bringing our communities into our commitments. It is meant to move us from an intellectual understanding of allyship towards a lived experience of joint struggle.
  1. Position yourselves in a row, side by side. Each person will take a turn being in the middle.
  2. The middle person will speak their commitment aloud (e.g., "I am committed to the decolonization of Palestine," "I am committed to safety and dignity for all").
  3. As each person feels that commitment move or inspire them, lift your arms and extend toward the space in front of you. Arms are parallel to the ground, palms face each other, elbows soft and relaxed.
  4. Practice letting in the experience of shared commitments to joint struggle.
  5. Debrief, switch roles, and repeat.
  Access note: This can be done seated or standing, and you can extend your energy without lifting your arms.

- **Pressure:** 𝅭 𝅭 ⏲ ⏲ ⏲ ☆ ☆ The purpose of this practice is to learn about yourself and your automatic responses under pressure (known as your conditioned tendencies). Conditioned tendencies tend to fall into one, or a combination, of three categories: moving toward, away from, or against. We have all been shaped to respond to pressure differently. These responses include the conditioned thinking, feelings, behaviors, beliefs, muscular contractions, and/or ways of relating that our bodies will produce under pressure, often developed as a way to take care of our basic needs. While these are wise and adaptive strategies, our conditioned tendencies can be limiting and get in the way of having the kinds of relationships we want and taking action in alignment with what we care about. For example, at a demonstration where there are counter protesters, or during a difficult political conversation, notice what sensations arise in your body. For an adapted somatic practice, follow the instructions below:

1. Each person thinks about an example of feeling under pressure or stress. To avoid overwhelming your system, adapt the intensity based on where you are at the level of relationship you have with your practice partner. I recommend starting with something that is a 3 or 4 out of 10 in intensity—don't go straight for the big pressures, especially if you are practicing without support.

2. Each person comes up with a short phrase that represents that pressure. For example, in the context of anti-Zionist organizing you might have them say "You are being antisemitic" or "You are a self-hating Jew." For lower intensity, you can practice with something like "Can we schedule a time to meet?"

3. Position yourself at a comfortable distance and orientation to each other.

4. Both people take a moment to center.

5. When Person A is ready, they will nod their head.

6. Person B will speak the phrase (in the tone and volume) Person A shared to them.

7. Pause, and notice what happens in your body. (You can use the reflection questions in the Guide to Practice).

8. Debrief, switch roles, and repeat. When you are switching, and at the end, be sure to shake off your roles.

Access and lineage note: This practice is derived from the "Grab" practice which was developed by the Strozzi Institute and politicized through generative somatics. It can be done seated or standing, and you can extend your energy without lifting your arms.

- **International Solidarity:** Acts of solidarity including direct action can also be practices of embodiment. We should not separate being present with our own bodies from being present to challenge injustice. Find a grassroots organization to get plugged into. If you don't know of local organizing projects, you can look for the nearest chapter of a national organization like Jewish Voice for Peace or Palestinian Youth Movement. When you go to your first meeting, bring a friend and tell someone you're new so you can get plugged in. Experiment with different risk levels of putting your body on the line. What role do you find yourself most connected to? It takes all kinds, so explore different roles, organizations, and movement locations to find where you can have the greatest impact.

CHAPTER 2

Redwoods: Collective Trauma

Rather than relying on singular taproots for their own stability, redwoods, like aspen, oak, and many other large trees, have shallow root systems that rarely go beyond twelve feet deep, but can extend up to one hundred feet, intertwining with surrounding trees. Redwoods grow in circles around their fallen ancestors. Through their intricate webs of underground roots, they support each other to heal and grow through each generation. Redwoods are thought of as living fossils, as the rings in their trunks tell stories of drought, fire, and growth through hundreds of years.

With the help of mycelia—a fungal network found in soil—the trees can communicate with each other and deliver the nutrients needed to support a healthy collective. When a redwood tree endures an injury, whether through a lightning strike or parasite, the trees next to it feel the impact and shape their bodies to support and heal together. It is the same for us as humans: when someone in our current or historic collective body experiences a trauma, we shape our bodies around that trauma.

Human biology evolved from early mammals with small brains (focused largely on sensory experiences) to Homo sapiens, with a neocortex (often called the thinking brain) taking up 80 percent of our minds. This shift does not necessitate disconnecting from sensory experiences. However, in more recent history, our minds have been subject to colonization in ways that prevent us from feeling these parts of our brains/bodies that support our ability to sense and feel. These evolutions and devolutions greatly impact our feelings of interconnectedness as well as our previously intuitive ability to follow our senses through an organic healing process.

Our bodies shape and reshape around ongoing trauma, leaving us with individual and cultural bodies of fragmentation, disconnection, and ultimately further perpetuation of violence. In order to traverse the realm of trauma and oppression with integrity, we must do the work to understand ourselves as part of broader collective bodies, like redwoods, with rings around our bodies that tell the stories of time and space.

Redwoods teach us about interdependence and collectivity—about widening our bodies to include the beings next to us, holding space for our ancestors, and growing together as a community, leaving nobody behind. So when we consider the connections between our traumas and struggles for liberation, we can call on the wisdom of the redwoods. The wisdom that shows how the fight for a free Palestine is distinct yet connected to the fight for Jewish liberation from antisemitism. Rather than putting peoples and lands at odds with each other, we can see the ways that our survival is interwoven and that defeating any form of violence is a win for all of us. Together, we can look to the rings around our redwood trunks and draw on our histories of rising up against fascism together.

"Collective trauma" refers to shared histories and experiences of violence, harm, and oppression that live in the body and get passed on through culture and between generations. Throughout time and space, collective bodies have faced colonization, imperialism, and genocide. The vast majority of people have experienced these forms of collective trauma, as did many of our ancestors, as settlers and perpetrators of violence and as people targeted by institutionalized and vigilante state violence. Our historical, intergenerational, and ancestral stories of trauma and resilience are embedded in our genes, tissues, muscles, and bones.

There is immense power and potential for healing that can be realized by locating experiences of trauma in a collective body. Understanding the collective nature of the origins of traumatic experiences—the social, political, and environmental contexts—is important in developing an approach to healing that trauma. If the trauma is addressed solely as an individual experience, we may miss the layers of pain that someone feels—that not only did someone experience a harmful thing, but so did their loved ones, family, or entire community. Also, by de-individualizing experiences of trauma, we can de-shame our adaptive strategies.

From the perspective of neuroscience as well as human instinct, not feeling alone in an experience is a critical part of healing trauma. That could mean something as simple as having your friend at your side through an invasive surgery, or something as nuanced as situating your own experience of sexual violence within broader systems of oppression by connecting with other survivors. While it can be incredibly painful to hold the breadth of collective trauma, this framework offers us the potential for shared processes that help heal the individual but also offer interventions to prevent harm in a collective body. For this reason, approaching trauma healing as a collective political practice ensures that our personal healing does not orient us toward adapting to the violent conditions of our lives and society but rather positions us to build power and resilience to uproot and transform harmful dynamics. This chapter explores how antisemitism, anti-Blackness, and settler colonialism from Turtle Island to Palestine have impacted all of our bodies, and it argues that acknowledging and addressing collective trauma offers a powerful alternative to white supremacy, nationalism, and assimilation.

As we enter the terrain of collective trauma, it is important to note that binary politics of privilege and oppression often leave out a more nuanced understanding of the inextricable ways we are all impacted by repressive systems and structures. There is a flattening of identity politics that is reductionist at best and harmful to our movements at its worst. Identity politics without a framework of intersectionality and joint struggle creates a hierarchy of oppression used to justify certain people's actions while canceling other people based on a myopic view of identity that is often rooted in shame. Ideally, we would be able to hold a more holistic, humanist, material understanding of relationships of power that account for collective and systemic impacts of oppression rather than reducing our politics to individual acts.

There are various ways community accountability can look: some strategies call people out or ostracize them from their communities, while others call people in.[1] An overall lack of accountability shows up on multiple scales, not just in interpersonal relationships but also when entire nations are unwilling to take steps toward reparations or other forms of accountability for institutional violence and harm.

Simultaneous to the flattening identity politics of privilege and oppression, there is an over-application of the term "trauma" that feeds white fragility and sidesteps accountability. This happens in part because of a conflation of discomfort, conflict, and trauma.[2] Hearing someone's anger about the impact you had on them is not traumatic—it is an opportunity (albeit an uncomfortable one) for mutual healing through accountability.

45

It's important to differentiate abuse and trauma from discomfort and hurt. What we know from somatic healing is that discomfort is a necessary part of the process—in order to transform we must reorganize our insides, and this is far from comfortable. For the purposes of this book, we will broaden how we define harm to include legally and socially sanctioned violence against collective bodies. As we hold this complexity, we must counter the ways that the language of harm and abuse are weaponized by people in power. For example, as Jews we push back against the misuse of the Nazi genocide as a justification for the colonization of Palestine, or as survivors of intimate violence we speak out against the misuse of our trauma to justify the prison industrial complex. In both cases, we exclaim, "Not in our name!" By holding an understanding of collective trauma, we can de-individualize instances of harm while also expanding our approaches to addressing harm.

The conflation of harm, discomfort, and the subsequent punitive responses also shows up in discourse on college campuses. Survivors of sexual violence and abuse have organized to make trigger warnings a common part of campus culture, included on course syllabi and event descriptions to flag topics that might be painful for those who have experienced trauma. Yet the language of "triggers" has become co-opted by students in a dominant or privileged position who feel uncomfortable. For example, at San Francisco State University, when Palestinian students spoke out about the impact of colonization on their homes and families, and Jewish students felt discomfort, it was called out as antisemitic hate speech and shut down by administrators.[3] This is where we can see the fields of political organizing and embodied organizing intersect. As anti-Zionist Jews our response must be to organize against the repression of Palestinian students as well as to organize our insides toward a sense of embodied safety outside of the state. When we hold the complexities of collective histories of trauma, we can facilitate processes in which people can understand their experiences of (and roles in) oppression while also disentangling their identities from structural power. We must account for individuals' experiences of (un)safety in ways that are not about policing but instead about being accountable to broader contexts of structural inequity.

Our lives are interwoven through the histories of our peoples, the memories of our brains, and the tissues of our bodies. Collective trauma is a vast expanse of intersecting bodies that tell stories of pain, suffering, and resilience. Collective trauma can have us organizing around ways of protecting against the past and get in the way of having a more updated, present attention to our ability to thrive. Understanding expressions of collective trauma is imperative in building internationalism through joint struggle. In this chapter, we will examine the myriad ways collective trauma is embodied, with a focus on US colonization, immigration, Jewishness, and antisemitism.

Rooting in Indigenous Struggle

Colonization relies on mythologized histories: in order to justify a colonized future, a new past must be invented. In the colonization of Palestine and the United States, settlers relied on the mythology of an empty landscape. There are many contradictions to being a settler on stolen land here in the United States. It is because, not in spite of, these complex histories that we can connect our struggles across time and place through stories of migration, trauma, and relationship with land. Parallel histories of repression and resistance as well as the contemporary narratives constructed to normalize the occupation of these lands link the colonization of the Americas to the colonization of Palestine.

The Zionist narrative regarding Israel's occupation of Palestine dictates that Jews came to a barren, uninhabited land and "made the desert bloom." Early Zionist leaders also referred to Palestine as "a land without people for a people without a land." These myths were popularized by the Jewish National Fund in an attempt to greenwash their colonial project. In the case of the European colonization of Turtle Island, history is also revised to paint a picture of a barren land with primitive, ignorant, Indigenous peoples. In a speech in 1830, President Andrew Jackson said: "What good man would prefer a country covered with forests and ranged by a few thousand savages to our extensive Republic, studded with cities, towns, and prosperous farms embellished with all the improvements which art can devise or industry execute, occupied by more than 12,000,000 happy people, and filled with all the blessings of liberty, civilization and religion?" This thinly veiled projection of industrialized civilization onto Indigenous lands demonstrates the values that guided the founding of this country: industries over forests, organized religion over decentralized spirituality, quantity over quality, and imagined communities over existing place-based cultures. Through these shared histories we can see that colonization across lands is both distinct and connected to colonization in other places, particularly where European and US imperialism are the driving forces.

Historic Trauma of US Colonization and Anti-Black Racism

Collective embodied trauma in the United States is rooted in a variety of histories and peoples. Volumes could be, and have been, written on the impacts of US colonization and anti-Black racism. In this chapter we will look at a couple of prominent examples.

The level of unresolved trauma that lives in our bodies and on this land has created a culture of amnesia and dissociation. The dominant narrative in the United States, engrained by the education system and federal holidays, is that the colonization of the Americas is a feat to be celebrated. We are steeped in pervasive historical narratives about white explorers "discovering" the Americas, "revolutionary" men founding a nation, and frontiersmen forging the way across the "empty" wilderness. We implicitly consent to these narratives through paying taxes and being citizens. All of this is a deluded attempt to justify the genocide of Native peoples and ongoing colonization. For those of us who are settlers in the United States, we must wake up to the trauma and violence of colonization and US imperialism. We must recognize that colonization is an ongoing process that occurs on land and in our individual and collective bodies.

We can start with the basics. What many of us know as "America" was originally referred to as Turtle Island. Turtle Island is the Algonquian- and Iroquoian-speaking peoples' name for this land before it was renamed after Italian "explorer and navigator" Amerigo Vespucci. Beginning with Europeans' initial settling on Turtle Island, the process of colonization meant replacing intact communities—Indigenous tribes and villages—with what Benedict Anderson, refers to as "imagined communities" of people who perceive themselves as part of a group based on a socially constructed racist ideology of nationalism.[4] This root of white supremacy meant that either you were able to assimilate into whiteness (an imagined community) or you were othered. We will come back to this later in discussing the pitfalls of identity politics as a reinforcement of a false monolithic culture of whiteness.

After the signing of the Declaration of Independence in 1776, US nationalism was written into law and later solidified by the Constitution and its amendments. These founding documents are riddled with racism, colonialism, sexism, ableism, and heteropatriarchy. For example, the First Amendment, affirming the freedom of speech, is more often afforded to neo-Nazis organizing white supremacist rallies in the United State than it is to Palestinian students speaking out against Israeli apartheid. The Second Amendment dictates the necessity of an armed militia for the security of the state and affirms citizens' right to bear arms. However, we know that this right is afforded to the military, police, and vigilantes, while women like Marissa Alexander are locked up in prison for defending themselves against their abusers, and Black children like Tamir Rice are killed for holding toy guns.[5] Since the beginning of this colonial project, the establishment of a nation founded in white male supremacy was pursued at the cost of all else, including the lives of 95 percent of all Indigenous people in the Americas—they were enslaved, raped, murdered, or lost to diseases to which they had no immunity.[6]

When it comes to the narrative of colonization in the United States, it is not that the historical facts or dates are incorrect, it is that the essence of how we approach the real origin story of this land is too often hidden. It is a story of plunder of land and bodies. "The history of the US is a history of settler colonialism, the founding of a state based on the ideology of white supremacy, the widespread practice of African slavery, and a policy of genocide and land theft," Indigenous writer and activist Roxanne Dunbar states in her *Indigenous Peoples History of the United States*.[7] Dunbar Ortiz invites readers to rethink what she calls the "consensual national narrative" that is told in the United States. A primary facet of the early colonization of Turtle Island was separating people from their land, cultures, languages, and communities. Early colonizers stole and privatized Indigenous land and murdered Indigenous people, and those who remained were displaced to reservations often far from their native homes. This land then became privately owned almost entirely by individual white men, and borders were drawn based on ownership rather than on the ecology of human, plant, and animal communities. Children were taken away from their families and sent to Native American boarding schools, under the guise that Indigenous mothers were unfit to parent. They were taught English and punished if they spoke their Native languages or engaged in any part of their traditions. Indigenous people were forced into getting a "civilized" education rather than learning what they were taught in their tribes, which was often more focused on tending relationships with each other and the land.

Another flaw in the US colonial narrative is the idea that explorers brought better tools and technology to these "primitive" communities. In reality, European settlers are often quoted as feeling inferior and lashing out when Indigenous communities continued to show their expansive capacity to enjoy the abundance of the land and thrive.[8] To make up for their ongoing lack, European settlers enslaved people from Africa to tend to the land and care for their families.

Black people whose ancestors were forcibly brought to the United States and enslaved experience the passing down of historical trauma through generations. Researcher and educator Dr. Joy DeGruy talks about "Post Traumatic Slave Syndrome" as "a condition that exists as a consequence of multigenerational oppression of Africans and their descendants resulting from centuries of chattel slavery—a form of slavery which was predicated on the belief that African Americans were inherently and genetically inferior to whites." She adds: "This was then followed by institutionalized racism which continues to perpetuate injury."[9] DeGruy's work painfully illuminates the ways slavery continues to live in Black bodies, Black families, and Black communities in the United States. The progression from slavery to lynching, sharecropping, Jim Crow, and now mass incarceration has been referenced by other writers, scholars, and activists, but DeGruy frames it in a unique way. She highlights the significance of the relentless nature of anti-Black racism throughout time. She describes the trauma in Black people's relationship to land and home, including through more contemporary examples of serial forced displacement such as sundown laws, redlining, urban renewal, mass incarceration, and gentrification. In an ongoing system of racial capitalism, Black people have not had the chance to heal and experience full freedom. But projects like the Nap Ministry are working to change that by uplifting Black rest as resistance; Black farmers like Leah Pennimen at Soul Farm offer pathways for reconnecting with tending land in liberatory ways; Black authors and somatic practitioners like adrienne maree brown and Prentis Hemphill model the ways embodiment is a part of antiracist practice; and Black organizations like Black Youth Project 100, Movement for Black Lives, Audre Lorde Project, and Black Organizing for Leadership and Dignity (BOLD) are doing the work to cultivate Black leadership. These are only some of many Black individuals and organizations leading the way in politicized healing and transformation. There is much more to integrate around Black intergenerational trauma, healing, and resilience than what is held in the scope of this book.

While resistance is ongoing and successful in many cases, living in a nation founded on the separation of family, home, and land is at the root of collective trauma both here in the United States and in Palestine. These processes are ongoing as indigenous people continue to fight to keep their families together in the face of intimate and systemic violence, from defending Native children's right to stay in their communities through the Indian Child Welfare Act (ICWA) to grassroots projects like the Sogorea Te' Land Trust on Chochenyo and Karkin Ohlone land. Sogorea Te' engages in extensive political organizing in what is commonly known as the San Francisco Bay Area: fighting for sacred sites, reclaiming access to land, inviting settlers to pay the Shuumi Land Tax, and joining with international indigenous struggles including the movement for a free Palestine.[10] As long as there is oppression, there will be resistance. Today Black and Indigenous communities continue to resist the state while also cultivating ancestrally rooted traditions around land and life.

The Cost of Assimilation and Privilege

Jews have long been considered white—yet this has never reflected the diverse reality of the Jewish diaspora, which includes not only Ashkenazi Jews (from central and eastern Europe), but also Sephardic Jews (originating in Spain and Portugal), Mizrahi Jews (from Southwest Asia and North Africa), and other Jews of color. Under the Naturalization Act of 1790, Jews were included as part of all the "free white persons" who could become US citizens. However, even for European Jews able to assimilate into whiteness, quotas were placed restricting their immigration. For those who successfully "naturalized," the racial and cultural status of Jews remained ambiguous, as many early immigrants lived in distinct and tight-knit communities. Many of these Jews spoke Yiddish, published their own newspapers, and followed their own calendars and holidays. Due to antisemitism, Jews were often excluded from certain jobs, clubs, and neighborhoods. Over time, largely dependent on class, many Jews began to assimilate into whiteness: those who could afford it fled to the suburbs, those who could access education took advantage of opportunities like the GI Bill, and those who were able integrated into different business sectors. Many of them stopped speaking Yiddish, stopped going to religious congregations, and distanced themselves from any markers of Jewishness. In just a couple of generations, Jews whose skin tone could pass, became white. Growing up, my sisters and I would argue with my father about how he didn't identify as white. He explained that even coming from a middle-class community in New Jersey he experienced blatant antisemitism and felt outside of the dominant culture of white-ness. Later on in his career as a civil rights attorney he was called a "spic lawyer" ("spic" being a racial slur against the immigrant populations he represented), and a newspaper article was printed with an antisemitic cartoon of his face with a big nose plastered on the front page. This image remained framed on his office wall until his retirement as a reminder to all of us of our connection to where we come from, what we have been through, and how our struggles are bound together. Today, while in some cases Jews remain racially ambiguous and vulnerable to individual acts of hate and bigotry, material antisemitism—including systemic discrimi-nation impacting people's access to basic needs—did not solidify due to a majority of Jews being able to assimilate into whiteness and a middle class. However, it is not a coincidence that as Jews have assimilated into white-ness and gained positions of power within the state, antisemitism has reemerged as an integral part of white nationalism, as demonstrated by the overtly antisemitic appointments made in the 2016 and 2020 Donald Trump runs for the presidency. This kind of antisemitism fuels racism and xenophobia, as Jews are held responsible for the organization of marginalized groups into popular social movements and seen as a secret evil that controls the media and the government. Thus, the security of Jewish assimilation is precarious, as we live in a white nationalist state with antisemitism having formed its theoretical core. Eric Ward, the afore-mentioned civil rights strategist, points out that historically, "in places where Jews were most assimilated—France at the time of the Dreyfus affair, Germany before Hitler came to power—they have functioned as a magic bullet to account for unaccountable contradictions at moments of national crisis." From the Hitler regime to the Trump presidency we have faced the impossible option of assimilation (if we have that "privilege"), being ostracized and forced out—or killed. During the Nazi genocide, the "Final Solution of the Jewish Question" ended policies aimed to force Jews out of the German Reich and other parts of Europe and replaced them with systematic annihilation. This "solution" was only possible because of the complicity of millions of people who were not immediate targets and saw themselves as separate from their neighbors. People may wonder what they would have done had they been alive in that time—would they too have been complicit? We don't have to wonder. There are genocides taking place today—from Gaza to Sudan and Congo—that are calling for our attention and intervention.

Assimilation requires complicity in existing systems of dominant power. In the United States, assimilation into whiteness has also often meant complicity in anti-Black violence. When you look at the faces of white civilians at lynchings in the late nineteenth-century, they seem beyond complicit—they seem to exhibit no remorse. Within capitalism and white supremacy, classism thrives on a strategy of divide and conquer. Its origins in the United States are deeply rooted in slavery, when white indentured servants were joining with Black enslaved people rising up against their "owners." In order to keep enslaved people under control, they divided them based on the lines of race, offering more benefits, including ownership of land, to white people. Furthermore, only certain white people—those with most desirable bodies, whether through strength or beauty—were granted this privilege, thus creating a divide on the lines of class. In *My Grandmother's Hands*, American author and psychotherapist, Resmaa Menakem offers a lens through which we can understand the embodied ways white supremacy was formed. He writes, "It was only in the late seventeenth century that white Americans began in earnest to formalize a culture of white-body supremacy in order to soothe the dissonance that existed between more powerful and less powerful white bodies; to blow centuries of white-on-white trauma through millions of Black and red bodies; and to attempt to colonize the minds of people of all colors."[11]

Every body contains multitudes of experiences on the spectrum of privilege and oppression based on our relationships to assimilation, power, and access to resources. Chris Finley elaborates on this complexity as it relates to the embodiment of a colonized, heteronormative, binary sexuality: "The colonizers may feel bad, stressed, and repressed by self-disciplining logics of normalizing sexuality, but Native people are systematically targeted for death and erasure by these same discourses."[12] Given the different ways trauma and internalized oppression impacts communities, the onus cannot be only on survivors of trauma and genocide to do the work of healing and transformation. Those whose ancestors perpetuated this harm have responsibility. The descendants of early settlers, slave owners, and other people on the forefront of land theft and colonization must examine how colonization continues to be embodied. For many of us, our roles in colonization here in the United States and our experiences of colonization in the places we come from have resulted in disconnection from our bodies, cultures, and traditions.

Many light-skinned immigrants coming from diverse backgrounds, ethnicities, and vibrant traditions assimilated into a monolithic race of whiteness after their arrival in the United States, leaving behind the ways our ancestors marked seasonal transitions, grieved death, blessed our food, built community, and otherwise connected with embodied culture. This assimilation came at a cost to the people assimilating but also to those who weren't able to access to the privilege of whiteness. White bodies had and have power over nonwhite bodies, creating a divide in service of racial capitalism.

These distinctions around assimilation, privilege, identity, and lived experience are an invitation into deeper accountability around the specific roles played in a broader colonial narrative. In my case, most of my family immigrated here in the early 1900s from eastern Europe to escape the pogroms—organized massacres against Jews that predate the Nazi genocide. While this history creates its own particular relationship to whiteness and being a settler, I still consider myself a white settler, as that is how I have always experienced the world and been afforded privileges accordingly. Also, while there is no record of my family ever enslaving people, some of them worked in the garment industry (as many Jewish immigrants did), including my paternal grandfather, who eventually became an owner of a lace and leather factory. I have not been able to find records that denote specific details, but given the time and the industry, we can assume they were purchasing cotton from former plantations in the South that used sharecropping practices or wage slavery. This role as middleman is very common for Jewish immigrants, particularly Ashkenazi Jews in the United States. It was part of the deal for assimilation that we become the intermediary face for repressive systems. In this way, my ancestors spun, wove, and sewed the cotton that simultaneously created the fabric of slavery in the United States and propelled my ancestors into the privileges of whiteness.

On my maternal side, my grandfather's story is yet another version of Jewish immigrants' assimilation allowing for greater economic opportunity. After returning from World War II, he started selling valves and fittings out of a car trunk with a friend of his. As my mother tells the story, it is one of our ancestors being able to pull themselves up by their bootstraps, my grandfather's business that started in a car trunk, that propelled our family into the white upper-middle class. I share all of this to illustrate that most of us have complex histories, and it is important to hold these contexts while also acknowledging that, as settlers on unceded land, we are still implicated in colonialism and connected to the struggles against it. How can we hold all of this without shaming ourselves or each other? This matters because of the detrimental impacts of internalized shame but also because the guilt of privilege can be an immobilizing force that creates more defensiveness and lack of engagement in dismantling racism. As James Baldwin writes in *Notes of a Native Son,* "I imagine one of the reasons people cling to their hate so stubbornly is because they sense, once hate is gone, they will be forced to deal with pain." When guilt, shame, or trauma goes unresolved, there is always a potential for it to surface in ways that end up harming oneself and others—through passive complacency regarding violence or through overt harm. Thus, in order to challenge and dismantle systems of oppression, we must start at the intimate level of healing trauma through connection—connection with our bodies, each other, and the land.

Refugees and Settlers: Cycles of Trauma

When I was growing up, my family had a weekly Shabbat practice. We said the blessings, ate dinner, and sat around the table for what seemed like forever at the time. Sometimes we argued, sometimes we laughed, and often my two sisters and I listened to my parents tell stories. My dad worked at a nonprofit civil rights law office in San Francisco and was often home late, my mom also worked full time, first as a civil rights attorney, and then for Jewish nonprofit organizations. Shabbat was a sacred time for our family to be together and rest. In the early 1990s my dad, Robert Rubin, took on a case that required him to travel a lot. Again, at the time his absences seemed to last forever. It turns out that the Shabbat dinners he missed those years were due to his work at Guantanamo Bay with Haitian refugees. He was involved in a case that changed him forever and became embedded in our family's story.

In 1990 Haiti's first democratic election resulted in a left-wing president, Jean-Bertrand Aristide, but only one year later he was removed by a military coup. The political unrest and persecution of Aristide supporters caused unprecedented numbers of Haitians to flee their country. In 1991 thousands of Haitians fleeing by boat were stopped by the US Coast Guard and detained at a refugee camp in Cuba's Guantanamo Bay. This number dwindled to 270 as most were sent back to Haiti. Those who remained were being quarantined due to their positive HIV status. When law students reached out to the Lawyers' Committee for Civil Rights to see if they could help, these 270 refugees became Robert Rubin's priority. He traveled to Guantanamo Bay several times over the course of a couple of years. During the refugees' hunger strike, one evening my dad was gathered with them on the open soccer field where they slept and was moved to share the story of the *St. Louis*. The *St. Louis* was a ship that left Nazi Germany in 1939 with almost a thousand Jewish refugees. Much like the Haitians, these Jewish refugees were sent back to Europe. Subsequently they were murdered—due to the refusal of the United States, Cuba, and Canada to admit them. In recalling this moment on Guantanamo Bay, my dad says, "Well, I get maybe halfway through this story, and I completely lose it. All lawyerly detachment and emotional objectivity is lost. I start seeing the faces of Haitians [alongside] the faces of Jews wearing striped uniforms with yellow stars. As a Jew it's obviously a very powerful experience for me because we swore, 'Never again' at the end of World War II; and yet here I was in some way a part of perpetuating the same gross injustice on the Haitians.... They see that, I talk about it, and we're sobbing." Two days later, Robert was kicked out of Guantanamo, and, as he was being driven off in an army jeep, some of the refugees gathered and began chanting: "Remember the St. Louis!" "It was very poignant," my dad said, "because they understood that this had happened to another people. There was a sense of solidarity."[13] The following year, the federal government finally let the Haitians into the United States to pursue their asylum claims. My dad waited on the tarmac in Miami and was the first to embrace them as they arrived. A solid bond rooted in care and solidarity had been formed.

There are many different stories that have shaped my understanding of migration, be it forced, such as in the case of Haitians, Jews, and other refugees, or as a part of a settler-colonial project such as early European and Zionist settlers. Without a broader context that makes room for the complexities of how people arrive on a certain land, settler colonialism often gets reduced to a binary understanding of indigenous versus nonindigenous peoples. While it is critical to be in right relationship with the indigenous peoples of any given land, we must also hold nuance in these histories. First, there are many different definitions of indigeneity. As we learned in the preceding chapter, one defining factor of indigeneity in the case of Palestine is precolonial habitation. Palestinians were the precolonial inhabitants before the Zionist settlers arrived. Another way to look at indigeneity is to situate regenerative relationships to land and place as a central component. That said, all of us can trace our predecessors back to land-based communities, and many frontline communities are forced to migrate due to climate crisis, political repression, or other traumatic situations. How did we get where we are today?

Let us consider the ways immigrants arrived from different lands. In the United States, African American people who arrived enslaved have a different relationship to being settlers than, for example, the descendants of European immigrants who came as early colonizers and slave owners. Also different is the journey of Ashkenazi Jews who fled to the United States from pogroms and the Nazi genocide, or Guatemalan refugees who came fleeing right-wing death squads that were aided by US and Israeli surveillance and military support.[14] The bottom line is that people move for reasons ranging from natural seasonal migrations to forced displacement, so along with being in right relationship with the indigenous people of any given land, we must also push back against nativist anti-immigrant ideologies rooted in a supremacist and homogenous flattening of relationship to time and place.

The landscape of settlers in Palestine is similarly complex. Some of the Sephardi and Mizrahi Jewish people living in occupied Palestine today fled there from their homelands in Yemen and Iraq as a result of Israeli-provoked violence and war. Ethiopian Jewish settlers in Palestine face brutal racism from the Israeli state, including the sterilization of women. Some Jewish settlers in Palestine are refugees and are descendants of people who experienced the Nazi genocide (which, despite common settler narratives, was a relatively small portion of the population).[15] Others are Jews from around the world who chose to come as settlers in Palestine. With the foundational understanding that those who are not indigenous to the land we live on are implicated in settler colonialism, we can engage in the complexities of collective trauma that lives in the bodies of those whose ancestors left their homes as refugees escaping genocide and seeking safety.

The Zionist project pushing settlers into Palestine is, of course, also responsible for the displacement of Palestinians. As of today, 1.8 million people in Gaza (close to its entire population) have been displaced just since the escalations starting October 7, 2023. This is not the first time there has been mass displacement of citizens due to unrelenting Israeli military attacks. During the Nakba of 1948, the founding of the state of Israel, at least 750,000 Palestinians were displaced. During the Naksa ("Setback"), in the 1967 war, another 430,000 Palestinians were displaced. There are now approximately 7.2 million Palestinian refugees and people displaced within the borders of Israel who have not been able to return to their homes and villages.[16] As many of us have now watched this ethnic cleansing and genocide unfold right before our eyes via social media, we are no strangers to the faces of immense trauma and suffering. The trauma of this kind of separation from family and place lives in people's ancestral bodies and is passed down through generations. The reverberations of this level of state violence will be felt for generations to come and, if history tells us anything, will only become fuel for further resistance.

Ancestral Trauma and Exceptionalism

The systematic targeted mass killing of Palestinians is genocide, yet there has been extensive pushback against using this term, which is seen as being reserved for the "good victims," the Jews. Jewish communities across the globe carry the trauma of the Nazi genocide, whether we had family members killed, family that escaped, or family that simply lived through that time and the trauma of antisemitism in all its forms. Ultimately, when this trauma is retained and unaddressed through multiple generations, it can become perceptible at the level of culture. In this case of intergenerational trauma, many Jewish people became protective over the experience of the Nazi genocide. Due to this survival response as well as Jewish assimilation into whiteness, the Nazi genocide is exceptionalized, while genocides of people in places like Palestine, Congo, and Sudan are made invisible. Over time, unhealed trauma gets compounded and can be visible through shifts in personality, family, and social norms. Resmaa Menakem writes, "Essentially, genetic changes train our descendants' bodies through heredity rather than behavior. This suggests that what we call genetic defects may actually be ways to increase our descendants' odds of survival in a potentially dangerous environment, by relaying hormonal information to the fetus in the womb."[17] This brilliant survival strategy, to protect and defend by any means necessary, is what has been cynically manipulated by US imperial interests and weaponized by Zionism. The echoes of trauma in our bodies are drawn out as we are told that the only way we can be safe from antisemitism or even genocide is to align with the state of Israel. The good news is that not only trauma gets passed down. So does resilience, and we can draw on that resilience to make different choices about how we keep each other safe.

A perhaps more benign example of how things are passed down through generations in the Jewish community is evident when people refer to food scarcity anxieties. This could be attributed to both the ancestral memory of sharing of abundant food as well as the ancestral trauma of starving in concentration camps. Or another example in my family is my mother's insistence that we keep a hidden stock of valuables that we could hide in our pockets in case we suddenly needed to flee—she reminded us that it was times in history when Jews felt most assimilated that the tables turned toward persecution and genocide. This kind of bracing and embodied terror has been passed on through each generation in my family, and I am determined to end it in my lifetime.

While trauma can be a powerful way of connecting and making meaning in our cultures, it can also distort present reality and limit our options to meet our collective needs for safety, belonging, and connection. Healing this ancestral trauma can move in multiple directions of nonlinear time. Through practices like ritual, somatics, or prayer we can make contact with our ancestors to heal our lineages and find the collective resilience that has been passed down through the cells of our bodies.

Along with spiritual traditions around ancestral trauma and healing, there is a vast field of science called epigenetics that looks at cellular and physiological traits as well as external factors that impact how our genes show up in our bodies. A researcher in the field of epigenetics as it relates to Jewish intergenerational trauma, Rachel Yehuda, has done numerous studies documenting the impacts of trauma in offspring of Jewish Holocaust survivors.[18] Yehuda expands what we think of when we talk about post-traumatic stress disorder (PTSD) to include the passing down of trauma through the genes and memories in our bodies. Yehuda used a sample of three hundred Holocaust survivors and their children and discovered a higher rate of depression, anxiety, and PTSD among the descendants. A primary marker for these conclusions was lower cortisol levels in the body, which is associated with PTSD in war veterans and other trauma survivors. Holocaust survivors and their descendants have become explicit demonstrators of the potential impacts of in utero trauma as encoding epigenetic markers on the next generation.

While Yehuda's studies provide a critical foundation for understanding intergenerational trauma, they also perpetuate the exceptionalization of Jewish trauma. If you start to look into research around intergenerational trauma, you will see that much of the funding and attention goes to understanding communities of Holocaust survivors and their descendants. This disproportionate focus on Jewish trauma reflects a broader dynamic of exceptionalism, in which the Jewish experience of the Nazi genocide is more significant than that of other people targeted by Nazis or other fascist white supremacist forces.

Even the term "Holocaust," which translates to "a burnt offering to God," simultaneously maintains Jewish exceptionalism while also justifying it, as if it were actually a religious offering. In this book, I use the term "Nazi genocide" as a way of acknowledging the many different groups of people targeted by Nazis, including queer and trans people, Romanis, people of color, and disabled people. This language can also help contextualize it as one of many genocides across time and place. Other common terms used include Shoah (Hebrew for "catastrophe") and Khurbn (Yiddish for "destruction").

Another leading researcher in ancestral trauma, Joy DeGruy, discussed earlier, focuses her research on "Post Traumatic Slave Syndrome." In an interview on PBS, DeGruy details the exploitation of enslaved young girls being raped and abused and refers to it as a holocaust. The interviewer stops her and says this word is used only in one context, and that is to commemorate the persecution and genocide of Jews. She responds powerfully to this exceptionalization by explaining that the Swahili word for holocaust is *Ma'afa*, meaning "the great catastrophe." When I heard this I was struck, because this is the same translation of the word Palestinians use to refer to the initial colonization and ethnic cleansing of Palestine in 1948, *al Nakba*. As DeGruy so poignantly illustrates, there have been many great catastrophes of a genocidal type, including the estimated eleven million Africans who died in the Middle Passage. Our Jewish histories of suffering and forced migration must be de-exceptionalized and recontextualized among other historical struggles.

In 2019, when Congresswoman Alexandria Ocasio-Cortez referred to the detention camps on the US-Mexico border as concentration camps, she received massive backlash from people asserting that this term too could only be used in reference to the Holocaust. She was shut down despite the fact that historians and political researchers affirm that a concentration camp is defined by "mass detention of civilians without trial," which is exactly what is happening at the US-Mexico border.[19]

Connecting these struggles is to insist on the recognition of colonization, militarized borders, genocide, and slavery in a way that counters the exceptionalizing of the Nazi genocide and expands how we think about cycles of collective trauma.

Not only is the history of the Nazi genocide disconnected from other struggles, it is also used as a justification for the establishment of the state of Israel through the colonization of Palestine. Rather than taking the lessons of the Nazi genocide to mean we must secure safety through militarization and nationalism, we should take it as a lesson to fortify our alliances in opposition to all forms of oppression. Throughout history, we can see the ways that bodies are separated by identity as an attempt to divide and conquer individual and collective bodies. By asserting the interconnection among different struggles, we can interrupt cycles of trauma and forced displacement here in the United States, in Mexico and Palestine, and across the globe.

Jewish Embodiment and Antisemitism

> No one was white before [they] came to America. It took generations, and a vast amount of coercion, before this became a white country. . . . It is probable that it is the Jewish community—or more accurately, perhaps, its remnants—that in America has paid the highest and most extraordinary price for becoming white. For the Jews came here from countries where they were not white, and they came here in part because they were not white.
>
> —James Baldwin

It is vital to understand how antisemitism relates to other forms of oppression and white supremacy. Ben Lorber, a Jewish researcher of the far right writes, "It is crucial for progressive movements to understand antisemitism, since it functions as a key weapon in the mainstream right-wing arsenal, and is used effectively to build and maintain power in political moments like our own."[20] We know from disabled scholar and activist Eli Clare that we cannot separate axes of oppression from each other: "Gender reaches into disability; disability wraps around class; class strains against abuse; abuse snarls into sexuality; sexuality folds on top of race . . . everything finally piling into a single human body. To write about any aspect of identity, any aspect of the body, means writing about this entire maze."[21] In this section, I add antisemitism to this mix to help us understand how Jewish bodies and identities experience oppression.

There are potential somatic distinctions between different forms of oppression, but they all share the principle that certain bodies have inferior corporeal attributes. The ambiguous racial, religious, and ethnic identities of Jewish bodies can be explored in a variety of ways, especially since Jews are a multiracial, multiethnic people. The dominant historical view of all Jewish bodies is that they are inferior.[22] Jews are depicted as animal, including images of Jews with horns. Jewish men are seen as effeminate and ridiculed for having small penises, Jewish women are seen as too masculine and overpowering, and queer and trans Jewish bodies are entirely erased. These are but a few of the prejudices that shape the Jewish experience. Some of these antisemitic tropes served as inspiration for Zionist leaders to portray Israel as a project of masculinization and militarization of the Jewish body, in an attempt to lure and exploit internalized sexism and antisemitism for the sake of an exclusively Jewish nation-state. Through assimilation into the United States *and* Israel, whiteness and Jewishness have been equated, offering both the privileges of assimilation as well as the struggle of repressed identity.

Revolutionary Marxist philosopher and psychiatrist Frantz Fanon made incredible contributions to the Black liberation movement, politicized healing, and the liberation of Palestine. In *Black Skin, White Masks* (1952), he makes distinctions between voluntary and involuntary markings (e.g., the involuntary nature of skin color versus the voluntary nature of wearing religious garments or traditional hairstyles such as payot— unshaven sidelocks. Fanon says that because the hereditary and somatic characteristics of the Jew are often invisible, antisemitism is distinct from other forms of racism since a Jewish person can at least attempt to hide their stigmatized identity and pass in dominant culture. While that wasn't true in Nazi Germany, today antisemitism is distinct from other forms of oppression in that white Jews in the United States do not face systemic oppression and have largely assimilated into the privileges of whiteness. However, this is complex and rapidly changing, as antisemitic white nationalists who rebuilt their base under the Trump presidency have been emboldened to commit mass violence, such as the massacre at the Tree of Life synagogue that killed eleven people in 2018. Historically, we know that mass violence is often the predecessor to state-sanctioned violence. Today we see the state and white nationalist vigilantes joining forces to condone antisemitism as a form of anti-elitism, as was done repeatedly in the attacks on George Soros (including by former president Trump himself), claiming he was responsible for the migrant caravan in 2018. White nationalists use people's frustrations about poverty, wealth inequity, and other symptoms of late capitalism to mobilize them against Jews. Immigrants are blamed for taking jobs, and Jews are blamed for bringing immigrants to the United States. In reality, it is both neoliberal and right-wing leaders who are perpetuating the economic crisis in the United States and furthering attacks on poor and working-class communities. This shows up not only in white nationalist communities but also in progressive movements, as antisemitism is dismissed because it is not as visible as other forms of oppression. Yet the claim of invisibility is founded in antisemitic tropes around secret Jewish conspiracies, the manipulation of Jews as intermediaries, and the use of Jews as targets for people's discontent with political conditions.

Additionally, there are a couple of underlying assumptions regarding the invisibility of antisemitism. First, there is the false assumption that Jews are white, which erases the bodies of Sephardic and Mizrahi Jews and Jews of color. Second, there is the assumption that Jews are able to hide their Jewishness, which—in terms of hereditary physical attributes, ritual practices, and religious ("voluntary") marking—is not always the case. Within this logic, one could say that queerness involves only "voluntary" markings, which would presuppose that trans people are making a choice that is causing their experience of oppression rather than acknowledging that queer and trans people have the right to live in their bodies without policing them for assimilation. Most people in the world contain a multiplicity of identities, which couldn't be separated even if we wanted to.

How (and why) for example, would one separate the experience of a queer, Jewish, trans woman of color from her experiences of racism, antisemitism, transmisogyny, and homophobia? This kind of identity politics is a slippery slope into a hierarchy of oppressions and single-issue politics. By engaging in these silos, we do the oppressors' work for them by turning targeted groups against each other. Claims about the invisibility of antisemitism also tend to overlook analysis around internalized oppression and the ways antisemitism continues to cause suffering in Jewish bodies around the world.

Instead, we can build on the work of feminists such as Kimberlé Crenshaw, Angela Davis, and Selma James to see that our identities not only intersect but also are inextricable, thus our movements must reflect the same kind of togetherness through joint struggle. By situating antisemitism in other forms of racism and oppression, we break through systems of isolation that keep people from joining together to fight injustice.

Over the course of my time organizing with the International Jewish Anti-Zionist Network, I helped run campaigns, supported direct actions, and contributed to research and writing that exposed the impacts of Zionism across the world. One such project was to create an educational primer that detailed the histories and described terms related to the movement for Palestine and Jewish anti-Zionism. This project was not completed, largely because of organizational dysfunction related to patterns already named in this book. The shaping of trauma guided our meetings and internal dynamics, and the relations of power between us left people feeling overworked and undervalued. That said, through my work with IJAN over the years, I built deeply important relationships that were foundational in my development of an internationalist, anti-imperialist political analysis. Below is one of the entries we drafted on antisemitism, working to highlight its violent history while distinguishing the ways it can be cynically manipulated.

What Is Antisemitism?
This section was written in collaboration with the International Jewish Anti-Zionist Network.

Antisemitism is the fear or hatred of Jews based on their Jewish identity. Antisemitism historically refers to a specific type of anti-Jewish racism that originated in Europe and is associated with state repression and violence as well as the interests of the ruling class.

Although the specific laws and practices varied by country and time period, anti-Jewish oppression in Europe was systematically enforced for centuries. Some notable expressions of antisemitism included state-sanctioned mass violence against Jews (the Russian pogroms), church-directed surveillance, torture and expulsion of Jews and others (the Spanish Inquisition), limitation of Jews' economic opportunities and freedom of movement (ghettos in Italy), and genocide (the Nazi genocide).

Historically in Europe, anti-Jewish racism served the interests of the ruling elites by positioning Jews as a scapegoat for their own misuse of power and the inequities of society.

The anti-Jewish racism that is now known as antisemitism shows the continuity between the medieval Christian tradition of Jew-hating. For centuries, Christian beliefs about Jewish inferiority bolstered Jewish segregation, expulsion, legal disempowerment, and subjection to violence. Through the process of Jewish emancipation from the seventeenth to the twentieth century, as Jewish people gained rights and freedoms, anti-Jewish discourse transformed from religious to racial "truth." New ideas about the Jewish body and mind mirrored religious beliefs but now flowed into the discourses of medicine and psychoanalysis, especially during the nineteenth century.

Antisemitic racism defined Jewish people's difference as bodily weakness and madness—both of which were powerfully represented in eugenics and Nazi "science" but also in mainstream medicine. Such "racial" definitions considered Jewish people to be outsiders to Christian Europe, with origins in the Middle East. These discourses also had a gendered and sexual component: as noted, while Jewish men were considered effeminate, overly intellectual, and weak in body, Jewish women were considered to be masculine (performing market activity, for instance, in public) and sexually aggressive—images that were synthesized in the popular figure of the "Jewess."

The state perpetuates and benefits from anti-Jewish racism in a variety of ways including through targeting communist and socialist movements by labeling them as "Jewish" or controlled by Jews as well as feeding into propaganda claiming a secret worldwide conspiracy of Jews. Hallmarks of anti-Jewish racism usually include the idea that Jews control governments, banks, and the media. These stereotypes became embedded due to the historical positioning of Jews (particularly Ashkenazim) as middlemen, scapegoats, or intermediaries so that when people take issue with the oppression of the state, Jews are a visible target and shield for those in power. In this way, Zionism has played right into these antisemitic tropes by using the guise of a Jewish state to cover a violent US imperialist project, therefore causing an increase in anti-Jewish sentiment.

A common strategy of Zionists is to use false charges of antisemitism as an attempt to assassinate the character of people who speak out for justice in Palestine. This is a cynical manipulation of the realities and histories of anti-Jewish racism.

Fear, Love, and Chaos

> I feel our nation's turning away from love . . . moving into a wilderness of spirit so intense we may never find our way home again. I write of love to bear witness both to the danger in this movement, and to call for a return to love.

> —bell hooks

White supremacy and nationalism encourage suspicion of deviant and "othered," bodies creating a fracture in trust and safety in our culture. This can become embodied as fear and show up in personal and political networks. Both nationalism and patriotism (a more cultural form of nationalism) espouse the language of love. This happens across the political spectrum with right-wing hate groups such as the Aryan Nation saying, "we hate in the name of loving our nation" and liberal Democrats saying "love trumps hate." Embodied experiences of emotions are weaponized to adhere to different forms of nationalism. Whether it is white nationalism, Zionism, or neoliberalism, love and hate are manipulated to support a settler-colonial government.

As the political climate shifts globally toward fascism, many people who have historically been a target of oppression (and perhaps still are) are experiencing a surge of activation of collective trauma. This is happening on an internalized emotional level as well as externally, as material conditions shift to make certain bodies less safe. Some manifestations of collective trauma are overt, and some are more subtle.

The echoes of collective trauma reverberated in the Jewish community as we watched neo-Nazis march the streets of Charlottesville, Virginia, in 2017 chanting "Blood and soil!"—a slogan originating in Nazi Germany expressing ideals of white Christian purity in the population (blood) and territory (soil). Going to synagogue for High Holidays the following year, I noticed I was carrying more fear of an attack, which was further heightened by the 2018 shooting at the Tree of Life synagogue—I was increasingly tracking my surroundings and felt a tight contraction in my stomach that at times would make me nauseous. Yet the response to our fears was to increase policing, which only made all our communities feel even less safe. In many ways, this feeling of collective unsafety is not new, particularly for Black people, people of color, queer and trans people, disabled people, immigrants, and refugees. But as the awareness and occurrence of violence and repression increase, there is an impact on our collective bodies. We must interrupt cycles of trauma and oppression in which one collective body's sense of fear or hatred (or both) justifies violence against another collective body.

In addition to the resurgence of fascism internationally, climate chaos has taken hold, instilling fear in millions of bodies, particularly in front-line communities across the globe. Humans, plants, and wildlife inhabiting the land are facing extreme conditions, from fires raging through the Amazon to hurricanes in Puerto Rico and the Bahamas. With record high temperatures, melting ice caps, and rising sea levels, people around the world face conditions that are already or will soon to be uninhabitable.

This sense of impending doom, whether through political or climate chaos, creates an extremely unsettled body, with specific impacts on our nervous systems. From a somatic perspective, fear can show up in many ways that shrink our bodies' freedom to move and disrupt our ability to connect. Our skin can remember the feeling of painful or unwanted contact, making us reluctant to give or receive touch. Our guts become twisted, inhibiting our ability to take in physical and emotional nourishment. Our hearts constrict and limit our ability to make centered choices. Our eyes lock and stay focused on the perceived threat, unable to take in new information. Our ears loosen to track more of the dangers in our environment disrupting our ability to hear the people closest to us.

While living in California, I was constantly anticipating when the next wildfire would burn. Each time the hot wind blew, I felt fear course through my body, causing my muscles to tense. As I talk with people in my community about political repression and climate chaos, I notice a collective, fearful contraction—our breath shortening, shoulders sinking, and chests caving. Our bodies are shaped by the fear of violent histories repeating, the love we share threatened by chaos, our anticipation of the future, and the reality of our present sensations. As we attune to this vast range of feeling, from love to fear, we grow our capacity to stay in connection with all life and land. Love is a sustaining force that can assuage fears and reclaim our power beyond the bounds of the state. As bell hooks says, "Love is an action, never simply a feeling."[23] .By taking love into action, we tell our bodies that even in the face of fear and hardship we can restore our rightful connection to ourselves and each other.

Addressing Collective Trauma through the Body

> Collective trauma [is] a blow to the basic tissues of social life that
> damages the bonds attaching people together.
>
> —Kai Erikson

Our bodies and histories can be the seeds for healing collective trauma and putting an end to ongoing state violence. Understanding the ways trauma is passed down through history is an important part of collective healing and liberation. However, building understanding is just one part of healing historical trauma. Because trauma impacts our reptilian brain—the most ancient part of the human brain, responsible for survival defenses—it is not something to be reasoned with. This is where somatic healing comes in. We can use our bodies as a direct line to healing our past and fighting for a different future. Somatic practices invite us to skip our cerebral cortex—where we might try to reason or intellectualize our way out—and go directly into our bodies to resolve a trauma response.

When we experience trauma, our nervous systems engage in fight, flight, or freeze responses as a way of seeking safety. Trauma stays in the body when the response freezes and we aren't able to relax back into ourselves. These stuck trauma responses can show up in ways that people come to believe are just part of who they are. For example, someone who walks with their head hanging down, not taking up space, or apologizing with their bodies could be coping with trauma-induced shame in the form of appeasing. Someone who has a hard time staying present and seems checked out could be in a frozen dissociative response. These trauma responses were effective at the time they shaped us. However, past trauma stuck in our bodies can limit our ability to show up for the present conditions of our work, our relationships, and our lives.

After a pro-Palestine action in which protesters faced escalated police violence, I was asked to support an affinity group related to that experience. One of the first practices I offered was the Walk About (detailed below in the Embodied Practices section). As participants moved around the room without talking, they organically found themselves back in a line with arms locked and bodies frozen, just as they were before the police broke them up. I was so moved by their collective body's knowing to return to the place where they got stuck. From there, rather than trying to convince them out of that shape, I invited them to lean into it, to feel the stuckness, to allow their muscles to contract and their breath to be shallow. Over the course of the next few minutes, I watched as their bodies cycled through this frozen reaction and came back to the present. I invited them to slowly look around, to see each other and see that they were safe. From there, their bodies turned in toward a big exhalation and embrace. In this two-hour group session we were able to heal and restore in the face of trauma—an experience that through individualized cognitive therapy might have taken years.

Due to the colonization of our minds, bodies, spaces, and resources, many of us repress our natural ways of discharging trauma or have lost touch with these instincts entirely. Colonization and other systems of oppression are not only the source of many of our traumas, they also inhibit our ability to respond to and heal from these traumas. Much of the research in the field of trauma healing is focused on individual experiences of harm or violence. For example, trauma specialist Peter Levine uses the examples of survivors of 9/11 and the Nazi genocide to talk about the impacts of their experiences of trauma on their individual bodies. In this, he fails to recognize the social and political context in which these events occurred. These events sent ripples of trauma and internalized oppression through the bodies of millions of people. Our responses to trauma need to address the different sites of shaping: individual, family, community, institutions, historical forces, social norms, connection with spirit, and landscape.[24] When we can identify the ways trauma compromises our ability to resist oppression, when we can heal and reclaim our people's histories, we can seize power from the state.

Embodied Practices

Emotions show us how histories stay alive, even when they are not consciously remembered; how histories of colonialism, slavery, and violence shape lives and worlds in the present.

—Sara Ahmed

You are invited to engage with these practices when the time is right for you and at your own pace. With everything, practice consent, self-responsiveness, accessibility, and mutual care. These practices are intended as applied learning and transformation—before entering, read through the content of the preceding chapter to better land the social, political, and/or ecological relevance of these practices. Also, you will need to refer to the author's note at the beginning—A Guide to Embodied Practice and Lineage—for a more comprehensive orientation and key to symbols.

- **Walk About:** 👤 ⏱ ☆ The principle of this practice is to bring awareness to how you move through space in relationship to yourself, others, and your environment. By yourself or in a group, walk or extend your energy around your space. Try changing the pace from slow to fast. Move together as different animals. Take on a protective shape. Take on an open, vulnerable shape. Move as if we have already transformed to embody the world we want to live in. Add in any relevant variations. As you go, scan your body and notice the impact as you take on different shapes: How do you feel? What does it feel like to connect from this place?
- **Morning Prayers:** 👤 ⏱ ☆ In Jewish tradition, the morning prayers are recited daily upon waking and are an invitation back into our bodies, with gratitude for another day and for breath. Morning prayers, Shacharit, traditionally involve four parts: (1) the psalms, songs, and blessings of P'sukei d'Zimrah, (2) the Shema, (3) the Amidah, and (4) closing prayers. Begin by opening your eyes, stretching your body, and giving gratitude to all your dimensions (length, width, depth, center) and all the directions (north, east, south, west). By coming into your bodies, you let energy flow through you, and you acknowledge that you are a porous vessel, inhaling and exhaling. The traditional Shacharit service can be found in most prayer books.
- **Centering with Ancestors:** 👤 ⏱ ☆ This practice is intended to connect you with the strength of your ancestors by resourcing you through the support of your back body.
  1. Lie down on your back or standing against a wall or in a supported seated position.
  2. Feel the parts of your back that are touching the ground or wall or chair.
  3. Focus on the depth of your body, opening your back body to what is beneath you. Feel the weight of gravity extending from your sacrum like a tail reaching towards ancestors chosen or blood. Include the contradictions and complexities in your

lineage and listen in for guidance toward right relationship. If you want, call in some of your ancestors who offer support in your path: you might imagine them lined up with their hands on each other's shoulders, leading all the way up to you. Give more of your weight to the back of your body. You may notice yourself shrinking or lifting away from your back, try contracting the muscles in your back and butt as you inhale and then release with a big exhalation out of your mouth. Listen for sensation (temperature, movement, contraction, etc.) and feel for connection to ancestral resilience.

4. Slow your breathing and get quiet.

5. When you feel more resourced, slowly shift to a seated or standing position and bring that feeling of resource with you.

- **Contradiction Practice:** ♌ ♌ ♌ ☉ ☉ ☉ ☆ ☆ ☆ The purpose of this practice is to learn how to see new possibilities when you're in a contradictory narrative or dynamic in your life. Each person thinks of a contradiction they are grappling with—meaning anything you find yourself stuck between, especially things that may seem at odds with each other. For example, you might talk about the complexity of being a settler on stolen land and also a refugee pushed out of your homeland; or you might talk about the contradictions of being committed to anticapitalism but still participating in capitalism and it's harmful extractive industries.

1. Person A share your contradiction with Person B and Person C.

2. Person A give the other two people a few phrases that represent what you are struggling with. Each person will take a different side of the narrative.

3. Person A stand with one person on either side of you; all are facing the same direction.

4. Person B and C start speaking, first one at a time, and then at the same time. Do this for several rounds.

5. Person A: notice where your attention goes, and feel the impact of the two different narratives. Pay attention to sensations in your body as they shift through the practice. Spend a few minutes here in the contradiction.

6. Person A: recenter by taking a deep breath, feeling your feet on the ground, and then taking one step forward out of the

binary of this contradiction. Spend a moment here in the new possibility.

7. Debrief: What new stories or possibilities emerge?

- **Dreaming with Ancestors:** At night, set a bowl of rose petals in water next to your bed. You can use leaves or petals from different flower if there's one you feel more ancestrally connected to. Before going to sleep, sit next to the bowl of water with petals or leaves and let them hold an intention for your dreams. Have a journal nearby so that when you wake in the morning, you can start writing first thing. What worlds do you feel connected to through your dreams? Did any ancestors visit you? What lessons are you taking away? Once you are done, empty the bowl onto the earth or in another ritual way, wherever you are. You can repeat this as many nights as you see fit.

- **Armoring Bands:** ♁ ◔ ☆ This practice is a way to learn where you hold unconscious muscular contractions (often held as a trauma response). By learning these locations, you can also start unlocking those tensions. To learn more about armoring bands, read section on Destigmatization of Touch.

  1. Find a comfortable position. Standing or lying down may be most conducive to observing the contractions.
  2. Move your awareness down the body, doing a body scan from head to toe.
  3. You'll move through horizontal zones or bands from top to bottom of the length of your body.
  4. Start at the eyes and the 360-degree band around the eyes and back of the head.
  5. Bring attention to the places in that band, both front and back, that feel contracted (armoring or protecting).
  6. Bring your awareness toward these by increasing or exaggerating the contraction or tightening, and then release or soften the area.
  7. Repeat steps 5 and 6, moving down the remaining bands at your jaw, your throat, chest, stomach, pelvis, thighs, knees, and feet (front and back of each band.
  8. What did you learn about where you contract and armor? What helped relax and soften those areas?

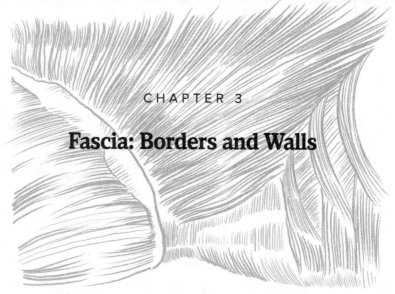

CHAPTER 3

Fascia: Borders and Walls

We are made to be permeable. Our bodies are not as rigid as we are made to believe through industrialized medical science. Our bones are actually soft, flexible, and full of blood. Our skin, the largest organ of our bodies, is a porous membrane. We are more fluid than we are anything else—around 60 percent water, with a cellular makeup most akin to the ocean.

Some people respond to the sensations of opening and fluidity by clamping down and putting up walls. Others might tend toward an overidentification with fluidity, not having any boundaries. Both of these tendencies at their extremes can lead to pain and suffering.

Fascia, bands of connective tissue, can help us find our centers. Fascia plays an important role in the support and function of our bodies by surrounding and attaching to all our internal structures. In a relaxed state, fascia has a wavy configuration, with the ability to stretch and move without restriction. There are also many layers to fascia: Deep fascia is associated with muscles, bones, nerves, and blood vessels. Superficial fascia is directly under the skin. Visceral fascia surrounds internal organs— for example, the pericardium surrounding the heart. The pericardium is a layered sac of fascia surrounding the heart and is a great teacher in centered boundaries. The space between the layers is filled with serous fluid that protects the heart from external shock or trauma and lubricates to allow for regular heart movement. It keeps the heart stable, maintains its structural integrity and acts as a barrier to infection. The pericardium prevents the excessive dilatation or overfilling of the heart. It also monitors the cardiac chambers and sets a boundary for the space of the heart.

We are all familiar with the heart, yet few of us are aware of this membrane of fascia that surrounds it and plays an essential role in regulation and protection. There is so much that goes into discerning what to let in, what to let out, and what to keep out. We open and close valves, create space, take up space, and move and extend our energy out into space.

When our bodies experience physical or emotional trauma, scarring, or inflammation, the fascia loses its pliability. It becomes tight, restricted, and a source of tension to the rest of the body. As early as the day we are born, fascia can get tightly wound and stuck though birth trauma. Healing, including our fascia, is not about returning to some perfect, natural, or normal state, it is about unwinding contractions to discover what our most centered and embodied self looks like.

"Fascia" comes from the same root as fascism: "fasces," meaning a bundle of limbs.[1] The etymology of "fascism" is rooted in a domination over togetherness (bundle) of bodies (limbs). "Fascism" also comes from the root "fasci": groups of men organized for political purposes. In all it's roots and limbs, fascism uses borders of the state to fracture these bundles of connection to separate us from our people, our lands, and our bodies. Living under a fascist regime causes the constriction of fascia through creating conditions of chronic stress, muscle tension, and hypervigilance. By expanding, healing, and integrating our fascia as we build collectively oriented movements, we can disentangle from the roots of fascism.

Palestinians [are] overcoming and overthrowing all of these colonial barriers that the Israeli occupation has created for us, be it the barriers that exist physically on the ground—the cement barriers, the checkpoints, the wall; or the barriers within the mind—the delusions that they have created for us.

—Mohammed el-Kurd

The militarization of borders and imperialist war machines required to back them is evident from Palestine to the United States and Mexico. On October 7, 2023, after sixteen years of surviving under a military blockade, we witnessed Palestinians in Gaza bulldozing through the Israeli apartheid wall to break free from what has been referred to as the world's largest open-air prison. In that moment, we felt the fragility of the wall—and the possibility of freedom, from the river to the sea. While that moment lives on in our collective memories of resistance, we also now carry the weight of Israel's immediate and brutal retaliation that followed. The fence was not just rebuilt, it was strengthened. The "threat" of Palestinian people being free was met with an extreme escalation of military violence, including blocking food, water, medical supplies, and any humanitarian aid from entering Gaza. As this physical and political wall is strengthened in Gaza, more Israeli settlements are being built in the West Bank that divert resources from Palestinian villages into Jewish-only settlements. During my time in Nabi Saleh in 2012, we marched to the wall surrounding the area's only water source; each time, we were blocked by Israeli army tanks and soldiers throwing sound bombs and tear gas to prevent Palestinians from accessing the water. The same company responsible for building these walls in Palestine is also responsible for building the wall along the US-Mexico border.

There are millions of people in Latin America attempting to cross the US-Mexico border each year as they flee from repression and conditions facilitated by US imperialism and climate change.[2] Many of these migrants are detained, torn from their families, and/or deported from their homes. Unlike the fascia in our bodies, or the natural borders of rivers and mountains, political borders are drawn to manipulate people and land in ways that serve those in power. With colonial-imperialist motives, governments make lines across land to repress people's power, limit access to resources, and deny people's freedom to move and freedom to stay. These borders are enforced to preserve and protect nationalism.

Nationalism breeds a false sense of community, dependent on militarized borders to keep people divided from the "other." Throughout history this "other" has most often been defined by authoritarian leaders who use lies and fear as a tactic for gaining control—fear of the dangerous black man, the witch doing evil magic, the queer who lives with the devil inside of them, the Muslim terrorist, or the Jew who controls the media and the banks. All of these discriminatory, bigoted tropes have been used to drum up fear and cultivate allegiance to the state as the entity to keep "us" (namely white Christian cis-het men) safe from the "other." This also often entails scapegoating groups of people, positioning others as intermediaries, and victim-blaming.

In this chapter, we will deconstruct the walls built to enclose, divide, and dissect our bodies from the land and each other. Like fascia, we will band together, and we will orient toward a kind of protection that is permeable and allows for an exchange of energy across boundaries. In

Undoing Border Imperialism, South Asian activist Harsha Walia defines border imperialism as "displacements as a result of the coercive extractions of capitalism and colonialism, and the simultaneous fortification of the border—often by those very same Western powers that are complicit in these displacements—which renders the migration of displaced people as perilous."[3] Alessandra Moctezuma and Mike Davis write, "All borders are acts of state violence inscribed in landscape."[4] These borders play out broadly and intimately, from the state to our relationships—and to our very own bodies.

Internally, these rigid borders can become embodied in a variety of ways, including through the enforcement of gender binaries and misdiagnosis and mistreatment in the medical system. There are myriad ways that bodies are crushed and stretched to fit in the bounds of "normal." Here I take inspiration from disabled author Eli Clare, who writes, "But how do I write about my body reclaimed, full of pride and pleasure? It is easy to say that abuse, ableism, transphobia, and homophobia stole my body away, broke my desire, removed me from my pleasure in the stones warm against my skin, the damp sponginess of moss growing on a rotten log, the taste of spring water dripping out of a rock. Harder to express how that break becomes healed, a bone once fractured, now whole, but different from the bone never broken. And harder still to follow the path between the two."[5] Through a rigorous and intersectional politics of disability justice, Clare blurs borders to show that the ways we are hurt are also often the ways we shine, and that our unique bodies are much bigger than the rigid identities the state requires us to conform to in order to access resources.

Our safety and access to the resources we need to survive are consolidated into borders that separate us from the land, each other, and ourselves. Walia and her coauthor Andrea Smith note, "Interrogating such discursive and embodied borders—their social construction and structures of affect—reveals how we are not just spatially segregated but also hierarchically stratified. . . . Whether through military checkpoints, gated communities in gentrified neighborhoods, secured corporate boardrooms. or gendered bathrooms, bordering practices delineate zones of access, inclusion, and privilege from zones of invisibility, exclusion, and death."[6] By defining safety as entirely dependent on external conditions dictated by the state, we become puppets of the prison industrial complex (manifest in all forms) playing out systems of punishment on ourselves. Instead of erecting walls, I invite us to take inspiration from the pericardium, that most incredible of fascia, which sets a boundary while allowing passage through.

From Turtle Island to Palestine to Mexico to Warsaw

> Yet no barricade or hinterland can separate the indigene from her homeland. Territory accompanies people across iron barriers and foreign landscapes. No colonizer can build a wall high or strong enough to separate a people from its own history. Nor can settlers fully remove a people from the land of its ancestors, even when the land falls under settler control.

—Steven Salaita

> Just as people have a right to their land, the land has a right to its people.

—Roxanne Dunbar Ortiz

The rhetoric and policies that the US government enacts against Central and South American refugees reflects the same closed-borders isolationism that led the United States to turn away Jewish refugees during World War II. Between the end of the war and the assimilation of Ashkenazi Jews into whiteness, there was a recognition of these atrocities, the loss of life, and the role of rigid borders. Subsequently, there was a refugee asylum system put in place that is now the same system that Central American migrants are appealing to as they seek safety within the borders of the United States. However, the Jewish refugee narrative was rewritten to accommodate an exceptionalized history of religious freedom and to conceal the connections between Jewish migration and contemporary immigrant and refugee issues. This manipulation was part of Jewish assimilation into whiteness and a perpetuation of isolating Jewish lives and struggles from those of other oppressed peoples. In addition to the racist nature of these immigration policies, there is a fundamental contradiction in the United States, in that these policies are being enforced by a settler government founded and sustained primarily by white European immigrants.

In the early 1800s, US government "Indian removal policies" pushed tribes to divide their land into personal private property. Indigenous peoples were told that by owning their own land, they would be more secure, and all they had to do in exchange was give up their commitment to land being held in common. Many Indigenous communities were displaced and/or destroyed through these policies. However, the Lakota people, along with other Sioux tribes, have continued to refuse to commodify their land. They have rejected the monetary offer of what has now accrued to over $1 billion from the US government to compensate for the land it stole. These indigenous communities want their land, not the government's money.[7] Since determination of landownership and inherent belonging shifted from depth of relationship to land to pieces of paper governed by the real estate industry, colonization and gentrification have continually reinforced private ownership and justified the fences and borders built to protect them.

While resistance was (and still is) successful in some cases, during the early years of establishing the colonial project that became the United States, the government and vigilantes gained control over massive amounts of land previously held collectively. Indigenous communities were split and moved onto separate parcels sometimes thousands of miles away from their homeland. Only one generation after many Indigenous people had been coerced onto individual plots of land, most of it had been stolen. The private property that was supposed to be their key to security was taken by ranchers and settlers who had a much easier time picking off families one by one than they did before, when Indigenous people held land in common. This devastating history has repeated itself across the world throughout time, since the rise of capitalism and imperialism, and serves as a reminder and motivation to redistribute land for public good as part of building collective power.

These histories of colonization and US nationalism mirror Israeli nationalism in a variety of ways, including the enforcement of borders and walls. Unfortunately, while many liberal Jews take issue with the border wall here in the United States, they don't extend this anti-border sentiment to the militarized apartheid wall in Palestine. This dynamic of people who are otherwise progressive not being willing or able to apply their politics to the situation in Palestine is so common that it has been given its own term: "PEP"—Progressive Except Palestine. Christian Zionists, on the other hand, are consistent with their white nationalist views that support both the strengthening of the US-Mexico border as well as the walls that define the state of Israel.

As noted in the preceding chapter, due to the Nakba (Catastrophe) of 1948 and ongoing Israeli colonization, Palestinians now comprise a huge refugee population, one of the world's largest. The borders in Palestine have been drawn and redrawn, exponentially shrinking access to land for Palestinians and expanding Israeli settlements.

In 2012 Israel constructed Saharonim Prison, which is now the world's largest detention center, holding up to eight thousand people. The prison is intended to incarcerate Eritrean, Sudanese, and other African asylum seekers for "threatening to change the character of the state" (according to Israeli prime minister Netanyahu in 2012).[8] This xenophobic rhetoric is familiar in the United States, as President Trump rallied a large swath of his voter base around calling immigrants rapists, murderers, and "an invasion of our country."[9] The Saharonim Prison exists because of a law that allows Israel to imprison asylum seekers for up to three years (amended from the law instituted to imprison Palestinian refugees trying to return to their homes after the 1948 Nakba). From the conception of Zionism at the First Zionist Congress in 1897 to the establishment of Israel in 1948 and the repression of the Great March of Return from 2018–2019, militarized borders have been instrumental in the colonization of Palestine.

Israel enforces borders in Palestine but also plays a role in border policing around the globe. Israeli exports in security technologies have almost quadrupled as migrant detention and border securitization have increased in the United State and internationally. In 2014 the United States gave the Israeli company Elbit a $145 million contract to expand the wall on the US-Mexico border.[10] The United States, India, and Israel, as three supposed democracies, together have built thirty-five hundred miles of border walls in the name of combatting terrorism.[11] Again, we can see here that the struggles against border imperialism in the United States, Palestine, and elsewhere internationally are not only rhetorical but also materially connected.

Fabricated Safety Resides in the State

Dominant culture in the United States is founded on an anxiety-induced fear. Cultures of fear and anxiety, where people feel they cannot trust each other, often translate into externalizing a sense of security, to be controlled by the state.[12] As Resmaa Menakem notes in *My Grandmother's Hands*, "The white body sees itself as fragile and vulnerable, and it looks to police bodies for protection and safety."[13] Rather than cultivating communities in which there is a safe place for everyone, the state becomes the mediator of safety. This plays out along the lines of race, class, gender, sexuality, and citizenship as entire communities and "othered" bodies are unilaterally deemed unsafe. Ultimately this gets reiterated and passed down through generations, creating a disembodied culture in which our nervous systems are distorted by the discriminatory nature of state violence. By putting our nervous systems in the hands of the state, we give the state access to manipulate our most basic emotions, including fear.

This is demonstrated by a tragic story representing many such stories—of George Zimmerman murdering a Black teenage boy, Trayvon Martin, because he felt afraid. Zimmerman's unfounded racist fear for his life held up in court and got him acquitted of the charges because of racist laws in Florida, like "Stand Your Ground." State and vigilante policing (like the neighborhood watch Zimmerman volunteered for) inscribe politics of fear onto Black, Brown, queer, trans, Muslim, disabled, and similarly deviant or "othered" bodies. The divisiveness of bigotry creates the other, and these others become the source of emotions, which in cases like that of Trayvon Martin, means agents of state violence are not held accountable for the actions that result from their emotions. In what was deemed "The Bread Massacre" in 2024, the Israeli army killed over one hundred people in Gaza waiting for flour to feed their families who were facing starvation due to Israel's military blockade. When interrogated, the soldiers' response was that they believed this crowd of people waiting in line for aid "posed a threat."[14] This racist war-driven logic creates a society in which those who are the least in danger are the most afraid.

Feminist writer and scholar Sara Ahmed teaches, "There can be nothing more dangerous to a body than the social agreement that that body is dangerous."[15] Wealthy white people are the most likely to call the police, while Black people, disabled people, and people with mental health struggles are the most likely to have the police called on them. In 2013, the Malcom X Grassroots Movement published *Operation Ghetto Storm*, documenting the disproportionate targeting of Black communities, reporting one Black person is killed by the state every twenty-eight hours. The report shows that in 47 percent of the incidents, police reported "feeling threatened" as a justification for shooting. The report also shows data from 2012 comparing Black, Latino, and white extrajudicial killings in five cities. For example, in Chicago, where Black people made up 32.9 percent of the population, they made up 91 percent of the people killed by police.[16] Statistical data, anecdotes, and lived experience all demonstrate the vivid and brutal reality that racism, classism, sexism, ableism, homophobia, and xenophobia expressed as fear translate into Black people being killed by the state (typically police and law enforcement officials), people with mental health struggles being criminalized, queer and trans people disproportionately incarcerated, and immigrants being detained and deported.

As we learned in the preceding chapter, when fear is internalized in the body it is vulnerable to exploitation. Depending on one's relative position of power and social conditioning, this could mean being more susceptible to experiencing harm or more susceptible to causing harm. Fear is manipulated by the state as a tool of repression to contain and restrict certain bodies while empowering other bodies to assertively take up more space. In describing the politics of fear, Ahmed writes, "The question of what is fearsome as well as who should be afraid is bound up in the politics of mobility, whereby the mobility of some bodies involves or even requires the restriction of the mobility of others." She notes, "Experiences of fear became lived as patriotic declarations of love, which allowed home to be mobilized as a defense against terror." These politics of fear can also then be transcribed as border anxiety.[17] Harsha Walia's concept of "border imperialism" refers to the phenomena of displacement as a result of extractive capitalism and colonialism while militarized borders are simultaneously strengthened, often by the same Western powers responsible for the displacement of peoples in the first place. This concept reaches across movements to expose how borders shape our bodies, communities, and our organizing. Border imperialism can be illustrated in many ways, including the current refugee crisis of Central Americans being displaced from their homelands due to climate crisis, globalization, and the rise of authoritarian dictatorships backed by the US government. Border imperialism also has a strong relationship with nationalism and militarism. In the aftermath of the September 11, 2001, terrorist attacks, the "War on Terror" was launched using rhetoric about keeping people—US citizens in particular—safe. The War on Terror actually became the war on Arab and Muslim bodies that were feared by people in power. This fear is externalized and projected onto bodies suspected of "terrorism" and used to justify the fortification of national borders and detention of these bodies.

Through this War on Terror, widespread campaigns funded by the Department of Homeland Security led to ads all over public transit systems and billboards reading: "See Something, Say Something." These were meant to encourage people to report "suspicious" behavior, leading to Islamophobic and racist policing. Keeping US citizens safe did not entail the safety of millions of Muslim citizens or the safety of the soldiers sent to Iraq and Afghanistan or the safety of Iraqi and Afghani civilians (hundreds of thousands murdered in the War on Terror). Under the guise of border security and patriotism, the United States effectively carried out its imperialist project through the destabilization and control of multiple countries—and their valuable resources, such as oil—in the Middle East.

Nationalism plays a critical role in the policing of borders and bodies. In order to protect the nation, the government puts immense energy and resource behind policing external or foreign threats to the state. While the US Department of State's list of terrorist organizations does not include many of the domestic white nationalist groups, it designates Al-Qaeda, ISIS, and Hamas as foreign terrorist organizations, reifying the narrative that terror resides in the outsider, and that outsider is primarily understood as Muslim or nonwhite. The legal and social designation of Hamas as a terrorist group has the power to completely sideline any conversation about Palestinian freedom and self-determination. Israel is actually responsible for the death of both Palestinians *and* Israelis, given that the Hamas October 2023 attack was in response to Israel's brutal military occupation and siege on Gaza. Yet any discussion of Israel's culpability is met by Zionists with the question "What about Hamas?"—as if Palestinians exercising their right to resist justifies the complete annihilation of a population.

While the terror the US military imposes around the world is granted impunity, the state weaponizes racialized fear through images and news of other governments' armed resistance that are at best de-contextualized and in many cases entirely untrue. Two examples: the *New York Times* reporting about Hamas's 2023 attack that was never fact-checked, and the fabricated campaign against weapons of mass destruction that was used to launch the war on Iraq in 2003.[18] In both cases the state misled citizens while also overlooking (or covering up) why Hamas or Saddam Hussein militarized in the first place: a result of US imperialism and militarism—and the void of leadership left in its wake.

Since after the 9/11 attacks in 2001, the FBI has expanded its Joint Terrorism Task Force to not only target threats outside of the United States but also to put the bullseye on social justice movements domestically, through designations such as the "Black Extremist Identity" and "Antifa." Anything that threatens the state is surveilled, repressed, and attacked.

The state reproduces what Benedict Anderson referred to as "imagined communities," and those deemed unfit are considered what Ahmed refers to as "bodies out of place."[19] In countries founded and developed through white nationalism (in the case of the United States) or Jewish nationalism and Zionism (in the case of Israel), safety and security are removed from an embodied experience and exploited to serve aims of ethnic cleansing and preserving purity of the nation.

Compulsory Heteronormativity as Nationalism

Ethnonationalism creates norms around sexuality as a way of controlling reproduction (e.g., eugenics) as well as controlling people's access to resources (e.g., health care via marriage). One of the ways the state impacts our experiences of our bodies is through sexual repression, including cisnormativity and heteronormativity. From a young age our bodies are forced to fit into check boxes of either "Male or Female" and "Gay or Straight." As more options such as "Non-Binary" begin to be offered on state documents, queer and trans people remain cautious to use them given how dangerous visibility in the eyes of the state can be. "Heteronormativity" refers to active assumptions regarding straight relationships and nuclear families. Heteronormativity is a tenet of white nationalism in the United States and many nations around the world. This kind of sexual normativity is not limited to straight people—as LGBTQ people have gained more rights through the state, some have aligned with dominant culture in what is referred to as homonormativity, which replicates models of a state-sanctioned nuclear family.

Ahmed bridges understandings of the nation and sexuality through her writing: "The risk of being a 'soft touch' for the nation and for the national subject is not only the risk of being feminine but also becoming less white by allowing those who are recognized as a racially other to penetrate the surface of the body."[20] Hetero- and homonormativity are indispensable to the hypermasculine militarized borders that enforce nationalism. Borders are a bulwark of a Christian hegemony, homophobia, transphobia, patriarchy, and white supremacy, which all serve to divide us under the guise of keeping us safe from the other. Compulsory heterosexuality instills shame in "deviant" bodies; queer and trans bodies are punished for straying from its binary borders.

Within our bodies, hetero- and homonormativity can offer a certain kind of empty comfort—distinct from authenticity or safety—that distorts who you are outside of how you are shaped by the world around you. Heterosexuality is assumed, and, if you are anything but that, you have to "come out" and often face ridicule, abandonment, and ostracization. Queerness, then, requires discomfort, a blurring of lines, a challenge to normativity. It means placing value on life beyond reproducing the nation through nuclear families and militarism.

Heteronormativity shows up in what anti-imperialist queer theorist Jasbir Puar calls "heteronormative penetration paradigms."[21] The land of the national body is the feminized body that is susceptible to penetration and invasion by the "other." Rhetoric and imagery of men (representative of the invader) penetrating women (representative of the nation) is used to validate globalization. In conversation with Harsha Walia's idea of border imperialism, we can see how immigrant bodies come to signify the invasion of "our" bodies: invading the borders of "our nation," and invading the borders of "our" white women. At the same time, the nation itself is sexualized, cast as a white women's body experiencing penetration from racialized migrants. Walia notes, "The victim of this criminal act is the state, and the alleged assault is on its own borders. The state becomes a tangible entity with its own personhood and boundaries that must not be violated.... Within this concept of sexualized nationhood, borders are engendered as needing protection."[22] This patriarchal narrative is enacted through the expansion of capitalism across borders, colonization within borders, and immigration policies that close borders. Heteronormative penetration paradigms are fueled by toxic masculinity that plays out through relationships to land, including the violence of resource extraction, assaults on feminized bodies, and contemporary expressions of white nationalism such as the War on Terror.

At the same time, queer loss is made invisible within "terrorist" and national narratives. Judith Butler talks about the necessity of lives that are "grievable" and lives that are "ingrievable" for the War on Terror. After 9/11, images and stories of widows grieving their husbands' deaths in the Twin Towers were used as fuel for the War on Terror, because they bolstered the narrative in which the heteronormative nuclear family is threatened and must be protected. It should be no surprise that gender and sexuality norms rooted in colonialism are not only inherently violent to our bodies but also bolster politics of invasion, imperialism, and nationalism.

The Enclosure of Bodies

Due to heterosexism and femmephobia, dominant culture has labeled permeability and vulnerability as feminine and therefore weak. This leads to an experience of boundaries that are rigid and impermeable: "masculine." When bodies are boxed into this narrow expression of boundaries, the inflexibility leads to boundaries being crossed. In some cases these boundaries are violated in ways that uphold existing power structures through exploitation and domination (e.g., prisons, sexual violence, and border policing). However, certain borders and binaries are meant to be crossed, and many of these crossings can be a subversive reclamation of our inherent fundamental rights.

The enforcement of borders relies on determining what bodies are worthy of being admitted through them and what bodies must be enclosed by them, based on discriminatory value judgements around what bodies are legitimate and whose bodies matter. These borders are enforced by the prison industrial complex, as undocumented people, queer and trans people, and people with mental health struggles are disproportionately incarcerated as "bodies out of place."

Progressive immigration reforms often endorse systems of detention and deportation. In advocating for changing policies of who is or is not allowed to enter this country, border imperialist politics are reinforced. This is perhaps one explanation for why we saw the most deportations in history under the Obama administration. There was a lot of rhetoric around reforming immigration policy, but ultimately it resulted in further policing and deportations. Because of diplomacy and respectability politics, Obama made concessions to the Right that cost many people their homes, families, and lives. In the article "Jewish Case for Open Borders," history professor Greg Afinogenov (2019) writes, "It was the center-leftists who made the concrete, and the fascists have only to pour it."[23] This embodied metaphor illustrates the rigidity of political borders and how that rigidity shows up across the political spectrum.

We don't need immigration reform; we need open borders. We don't need prisons, we need access to housing, education, health care, and transformative justice. The conversation about open borders exists outside of debates on immigration, just as the conversation about abolition exists outside of prison reform. They live in a visionary, yet possible future in which all people are free: free to move, free to stay, free to heal, and free to transform. Organizations like No More Deaths embody these principles of freedom and dignity by providing direct aid to people attempting to cross the border and documenting the abuses of border patrollers. Mijente and other grassroots base-building organizations embody these principles through longer-term campaigns against ICE and other forms of policing and surveillance that target Latinx and Chicanx communities. In these movements it is understood that the institutions behind border imperialism don't need reforming—they are working quite well to serve their purposes of anti-immigrant and political repression. Instead, we need practices of mutual aid and grassroots organizing, a rejection of militarized borders, and an analysis of the root causes of migration. With that, we can dissolve the facade of the state and its need to control and enclose our bodies.

Another way we see the state's attempt to enforce borders and binaries is through the targeting of queer, trans, and gender-nonconforming people. Our communities are disproportionately targeted by the prison industrial complex due to diminished access to resources, higher rates of mental health struggles, and the refusal to conform and assimilate into binaries founded in Christian purity (a Bible-based, sterile, abstinence-informed orientation to sexuality). There are currently policies on the table to make prisons "safer" for transgender people, but prisons are inherently unsafe for trans people and *all* people enclosed within them. Historically, men's prisons were designed to create more productive workers and more "masculine" citizens, while women's prisons centered around re-forming women's bodies to be better mothers, homemakers, and wives—those deemed unfit for these roles (often due to anti-Blackness) were frequently sterilized.[24]

The carceral system is set up to police people's bodies, including our expressions of gender and sexuality. This often begins at a young age, with things like gender-segregated learning and dress codes in schools. In my family, we have had our own experiences with these issues. I got in trouble at school all the time for dressing "inappropriately," while what was actually inappropriate was the way my principal looked at me as a child, or the way other kids would touch me without my consent. But, of course, it was "my fault" for distracting them with my belly shirt. One of my proudest memories of my mother is when a parent of one of the boys in my school called her to tell her that I should be punished for kicking his son. My mother's response was simple: "What was he doing before she kicked him?" She always had my sisters' and my back when it came to these matters. One of my older sisters experienced an inordinate amount of sexual harassment in middle school, which contributed to mental health struggles, including suicidal ideation and self-harming behaviors. One day, when she had had enough, she responded by stabbing with a pencil one of the boys who consistently harassed her. She was suspended. And what happened to him? Nothing, of course. This suspension resulted in her inability to attend the high school in our neighborhood because they had heard about what happened. For many students, particularly Black and Brown kids, being punished for their gender expression (or anything else for that matter) can put them on the school-to-prison pipeline. These are just some of the many ways that women, trans, and gender-nonconforming people experience punishment for the ways our bodies are a challenge to the heterosexist, transphobic state.

In cases of intimate partner violence, including different forms of assault and abuse, many people uphold the prison system, failing to see the connection between gender and sexual violence and the carceral state. Marissa Alexander, sentenced to twenty years in prison for firing a warning shot into the air to defend herself against her husband who was threatening to kill her, knew about the connection between gender violence and the prison industrial complex all too well.[25] The enclosure of bodies in prisons makes our communities less safe and reifies rigid borders around the "other." Rather than locking people up, resources should be invested in access to housing and health care and restoring a sense of safety, guided by the people most impacted by systemic inequities.

Rigid geopolitical boundaries are created and policed to keep us safe, it is said, when they are actually the cause of systematic trauma and oppression. This embodied oppression is passed down through generations and can impact a range of bodily functions, including how we see. At a juvenile detention center, Stanley Kaseno, a behavioral optometrist, tested the eyes of one thousand people, finding that 96 percent of them had abnormal vision. This he attributed to chronic stress and the need to have a constant narrow focus—hypervigilance resulted in pulling their eyes out of shape. Les Fehmi and Jim Robbins found that through glasses and vision training there was significant cognitive improvement but also that the recidivism rate decreased by 50 percent.[26] This was explained by the idea that when our eyes are relaxed and able to receive signs of connection, we are less likely to feel unsafe and thus act out violently. This is not to say that this is the root of why people end up in prison but rather that prisons and policing shape our bodies (some more than others) and engrain a felt sense of unsafety into our very own eyes. This research around how the way we see people shapes people is important in understanding the criminalization of certain bodies. Bonnie Badenoch, a teacher on relational neuroscience tells us, "We convey so much of our inner state in the quality of our looking and our gaze. If we saw eyes that were terrifying or vacant or anxious when we were very young, we experienced the whole-body upset that wounding eyes can bring. Adaptively we may become hesitant to share gaze with anyone. Over time, in an environment of safety, permission, and receptivity, we may begin to take little sips of nourishing gaze until these neural streams reclaim their birthright as portals of giving and receiving deep connection."[27] This capacity for seeing, whether through the eyes or otherwise, can ultimately impact people's access to everything from safe connections to basic resources such as housing, education, and health care.

There is also an intimate connection between our eyes, skin, and tissues that interact with the outer world and the deeper nervous system that processes this information and organizes our internal world. That said, we only take in a fraction of the information received by our retinas. "The ratio between what is received by the retina and what is processed by the integrative layer of the occipital cortex is about a million to one," Badenoch writes.[28] This perhaps accounts for at least some of the times that we have differing experiences of what we saw happen in a moment. When there is a sense of threat, our attention narrows and concentrates on specific details about the source of danger (using small parvo cells in the eye). When we are settled and calm, we are able to take in information about our environments more broadly, memorably, and cohesively by using the bigger magno cells in the eye. By shifting our eyes and nervous systems into more settled states, we create safer environments for ourselves and each other. This requires a different orientation to the width of our bodies, expanding and extending beyond a binary of self and other. By returning our sense of safety to our own bodies, we can challenge harmful borders—both intimately between people as well as systemically between geopolitical lines.

Messages are constantly being sent between our muscles and our brains. When we are stuck in a contraction, our tight muscles continue to send the message that we are in danger. The energy and stories held in our muscles are often rooted in the context of relationship, in response to a scary or painful experience. Offering contact with these tissues and muscles in a way that holds space for what is present, without trying to change or fix anything, has the potential to elicit a response of feeling safe in our bodies. Once our muscles have relaxed enough to feel safe and held, our bodies often know what to do and begin a process of releasing the stored trauma until our systems return to a more settled state.

The Walls between Us

> Because there was something in him that could not bend, he could only be broken.

> —James Baldwin

Political organizers and politicized healers alike are engaged in a practice of undoing borders in ourselves and between and around us. In movement organizations, we need to create ways of being with each other that do not replicate the hierarchies we experience within the borders of the heteropatriarchal and colonial United States. Border dynamics show up in movements through what is often referred to as "call out culture", in which people are publicly shamed for the mistakes they make.[29] By ostracizing people from their social and political homes, we reproduce militarized borders and policing. Cultures of disposability, whether enforced by the state or by our own comrades, are dehumanizing and strip people of their dignity. Drawing lines around who is radical enough, cool enough, queer enough, or fill-in-the-blank enough mirrors the binary divisions drawn between people who are "law abiding" and those who are not, between "victims" and "criminals," between "us" and "them." Thus, we end up reproducing state narratives on deviance and perpetuate the prison industrial complex. Carceral punishment is about profiting from the enclosure of people's bodies, not about accountability. True accountability can be reconciled in ways that don't require ostracization or permanently sending people away.

Another way rigid borders arise in social movements is in single-issue organizing where people get tunnel vision and fail to see the interconnection and interdependence between movements for justice. What is a climate justice movement without racial justice? What is a gender justice movement without queer and trans liberation? This disconnect can be fueled by the idea that identity is fixed and rigid rather than the reality that identity is fluid and intersectional. I have found this particularly in certain white anti-racist organizing spaces where people become overly comfortable and so over-identified with their whiteness that they fail to see potential points of connection. This doesn't have to be the case; there are many other groups that strategically organize white people or people with wealth to subvert power and redistribute resources. Building community and organizing around identity is also needed in some cases to support oppressed people's self-determination. For example, spaces that are exclusively by and for Black femmes as a counter to white supremacy and patriarchy is a critical contribution to collective liberation. Whether an identity-based caucus space or a mixed space, we can break down the walls between us. But when we fall into single-issue identity politics, we often fail to hold nuance and collaborate through principled struggle.

Centered Completion

The walls between us can also come up in intimate relationships, as breakups and breakdowns cause splits in our communities. Rather than doing the work to repair relationships, many people allow hurt and pain to rule their decision to cut someone out of their life and make their mutual friends choose a side. We need more resources on how to hold centered boundaries, end relationships, leave organizations, and grieve love lost. The avoidance of endings is part of a culture that has little capacity to embrace death as a part of life—and in which certain life is valued above all, resulting in social and ecological genocide. Embracing death, endings, and all the boundaries in between is a small but important part of decolonizing our relationships to each other and the land. For all of these reasons and more, our bodies and our movements must be part of dismantling borders and walls to be able to effectively participate in joint struggle toward collective liberation.

Embodied healing practices offer tools for us to use in coming into a centered relationship with setting limits and boundaries. This healing work can also happen collectively in a way that transforms not only our own bodies and personal relationships but also the way we engage with political struggles and issues such as borders. Embodying centered, permeable boundaries can more effectively challenge the creation and maintenance of border walls, white nationalism, and policing. By embodying interdependent, permeable membranes, we move toward more just and liberated relationships with each other and the land.

We can practice centered boundaries through somatics or other healing modalities, but more importantly we can practice in our daily lives. There are many opportunities to investigate how we relate to membranes, boundaries, borders, and walls.

Embodied Practices

Love is boundaries, not borders. Boundaries give us room to recover from harm, to realize what we must let go of in order to move forward, to act from real agency. But boundaries are not borders—walls of stone manned by armed guards, constructed by fear, never to be crossed. Borders perpetuate a myth of separation that is not true to how resources or life flow on our planet.

—adrienne maree brown

You are invited to engage with these practices when the time is right for you and at your own pace. With everything, practice consent, self-responsiveness, accessibility, and mutual care. These practices are intended as applied learning and transformation—before entering, read through the content of the preceding chapter to better land the social, political, and/or ecological relevance of these practices. Also, you will need to refer to the author's note at the beginning—A Guide to Embodied Practice and Lineage—for a more comprehensive orientation and key to symbols.

- **Boundaries:** 𝍩 𝍩 ☉ ☉ ☉ ☆ ☆ ☆ The purpose of this practice is learning to say no in a centered way. When we are first learning to set boundaries, we can be influenced by the rigidity of border walls as we are new to learning more relational ways to protect ourselves. We need to be able to set boundaries in a range of ways, including ones that maintain safety in connection and ones that are permeable and allow for a deepening of intimacy and growth in relationships. We need this in our organizing relationships, our romantic and/or sexual relationships, our familial relationships, our relationships with land, and our relationships with all the other beings with whom we share space. In this practice you can experiment with a range of boundaries. For example, there are the boundaries we set with the people we love, and then there are the boundaries we set with people we do not want in our lives.

First: *Notice and learn*

1. Partner A and Partner B stand about two to three feet apart, facing each other.
2. Partner B moves toward Partner A.
3. Partner A lifts their arms forward, elbows slightly bent and says "No," creating a physical and auditory boundary.
4. Partner B stops before making contact.
5. Partner A, notice your sensations as they approach and how it feels to make a boundary. Partner B, notice how it feels to receive a boundary.
6. Do one more round in these roles repeating steps 1–5.
7. Debrief: Share what you noticed after two rounds. What did you notice in your body and voice? Having said no to this, what can you say *yes* to? Were you able to tell your partner to stop when you wanted them to? How did you know where your boundary was?
8. Switch roles, and repeat steps 1–7, during which Partner B will get to set a boundary.

Second: *Add content and relevance*

1. Each person will share about a place in their life where they need to set a boundary.
2. Think of a short phrase your partner can say to represent that boundary (e.g., "I need you to help me with this").
3. Repeat steps 1–8 from round 1, except this time the partner who is walking toward the person setting a boundary will say the short phrase to make the practice relevant for their life.
4. Try this with a couple of different phrases that require a different kind of boundary. For example, the way you set a boundary with your exploitative boss is (ideally) different from how you set a boundary with your loved ones.
5. Debrief: What did you notice arise in your body before, during, and after saying no? What felt different about the different versions of boundary setting?

Access note: You can do this practice seated instead of standing. If you're seated, position the chairs so they face each other about one to two feet apart. When it is time to move forward toward your partner, slide forward in your chair.

- **Extending toward Each Other:** 👤 👤 🕐 🕐 🕐 ☆ ☆ Alongside the need to practice boundaries, we also need to be able to reach for each other across difference, conflict, and space.

First: *Notice and learn*

1. Partner A and Partner B stand about two to three feet apart facing each other.
2. Partner A stands with one leg in front of the other for a secure base.
3. Partner B moves toward Partner A, about two-thirds of the way.
4. Partner A slides forward and opens their arms to either side of their body, with palms face forward, chest open, and arms about 6–8 inches away from their body.
5. Partner B stops before making contact.
6. Partner A, notice how it feels to enter and extend. Partner B, notice how it feels to receive an extension.
7. Do one more round in these roles, repeating steps 1–5.
8. Share what you noticed after two rounds. What did you notice in your body? How does it feel to move forward? How does it feel to be met? Are you overextending or under-extending?
9. Switch roles, and repeat steps 1–7, where Partner B will get to enter and extend.

Second: *Add content and relevance*

1. Each person shares about a place in their life where they want to enter and extend.
2. Think of a short phrase your partner can say to represent that example (e.g., "Do you want to have quality time together this week"? Or: "Are you available to take on a role for the action on Saturday?)
3. Repeat steps 1–8 from round 1, except this time the partner who is walking toward the person entering and extending will say the short phrase to make the practice relevant for their life.
4. Try this with a couple different phrases that require a different kind of extension.
5. Debrief: What did you notice arise in your body before, during, and after extending?

Access note: You can do this practice seated instead of standing. If you're seated, position the chairs so they face each other about one to two feet apart. When it is time to move forward toward your partner, slide forward in your chair.

- **Goodbye Ritual:** 👤 ⏱ ⏱ ⏱ ☆ ☆ ☆ This practice is for completing a relationship with an ancestor, a loved one, or even a part of yourself you want to release.
  - When you are ready, you will extend your arms toward a tree, pillow, or anything else you want to represent what are saying goodbye to.
  - After making contact with your hands, share your gratitude (if applicable), and say out loud that your time together is complete.
  - Take your time to notice sensation, and then release your hands, turn around, and walk back in the direction you came from. Notice the pace at which you move, where you get stuck, and where you skip over. We all have different tendencies here; some of us might linger and struggle to detach, others might move so quickly that there is no time to feel the impact of the goodbye.
  - Allow the practice to come to a close, and then try another round after centering (see chapter 5 for full centering practice).
  - Reflect: How do you feel on the other side of this goodbye? What did you notice about your tendencies around goodbyes?
- **Width:** For those with sight, try bringing your two pointer fingers a couple of feet in front of your eyes, and then slowly separate them, moving out to the edges of your peripheral vision. Continue until they are at the edge of what you can see. With your eyes (and/or the rest of your body), extend into your width, stretching to include more of what's around you.
- **Maps:** Look at an outline of the continental United States, one without any of the state borders. Get curious about how your body responds differently to land that is not confined by state-imposed and patrolled borders.
- **Sukkot:** Pay attention to the spaces you inhabit and your relationship to the walls that do or don't surround you. In Jewish tradition, on Sukkot, we are invited to build, eat, and sleep in Sukkahs. The Sukkah is a wonderful demonstration of temporary, permeable structures, with three walls, lattice, and plants surrounding us as we celebrate the fall harvest.

- **Miklat:** Imagine what it's like to find refuge without any borders or walls. How can you find Miklat, a place of refuge, in your body?
- **Land Attunement:** ⚲ ⏱ ☆ Find a flower, a field, a mountain, or any kind of living plant. Take a moment to attune to these living beings. Notice their shape, their rhythm, their texture, their smell. See if you can match your body's shape, rhythm, et cetera to meet this other living being. Remember that the land does not belong to anyone but that we belong to the land.

CHAPTER 4

Vagus Nerve: Membranes
and Boundaries

One of the most influential theories of our time around the interplay of our bodies and boundaries is the polyvagal theory. This theory is a major evolution in understanding how both our autonomic and central nervous systems respond to signals from external environments as well as internal organs. The vagus nerve is one of the largest nerves in the body and has two distinct parts, the dorsal (back) and the ventral (front). The dorsal nerve is one of the oldest and is shared among many animals. It travels from the brainstem all the way down the spine and plays a role in the regulation of our lungs, heart, and stomach. The unmyelinated sub-diaphragmatic dorsal vagus is an ancient defense system associated with early vertebrates such as reptiles (hence references to the "reptilian brain"). This dorsal vagal nerve is meant to protect us from danger by disconnecting, shutting down, or freezing—akin to when animals play dead as way to survive an attack.

Unlike early vertebrates, we cannot survive for long periods of time without oxygen, thus these kind of defense responses can be lethal. For people who survive traumas in which their immobilization response was activated, it may be difficult to reorganize their nervous systems back into a settled, responsive but not reactive state. If the sympathetic system is overly aroused, the parasympathetic kicks in, and the dorsal vagus nerve shuts down the entire system, resulting in a freeze response. The ventral branch of the vagal nerve (a newer evolutionary development) affects body functioning above the diaphragm. This is the branch that serves the social engagement system. The ventral vagal nerve allows for activation in a more subtle and nuanced way, as opposed to the urgent and explicit quality of sympathetic activation. The ventral vagal nerve affects (1) the middle ear, which filters out background noises to make it easier to hear the human voice, (2) facial muscles and thus the ability to make communicative facial expressions, and (3) the larynx and thus vocal tone and vocal patterning, helping humans create sounds that soothe one another.

The polyvagal theory illustrates a more complex picture, in which all of the branches of the nervous system, or really the entire body, can be engaged in ways that are supportive and adaptive as well as defensive and destructive.

The polyvagal theory affirms the bidirectional connection between what we tend to think of as a separate mind and body by offering the science behind the peripheral nervous system. The peripheral nervous system (referring to all nerves and organs outside of the brain and spinal cord) is responsible for sensory information, movement, and unconscious processes such as heartrate, breathing, digestion and arousal. Polyvagal theory shows these peripheral organs impacting brain processes as well as our brain processes impacting peripheral organs. We recognize that our bodies are not made up of independent organs floating around but rather that all of our bodies organs and systems are deeply interconnected. Furthermore, through understanding the social engagement system we break through rigid notions of autonomy, separation, and othering and into more permeable notions of interdependence, connection, and co-regulation.

The embodiment of boundaries is all around us: from in the cells and fascia of our bodies, to the bark on the redwood and oak trees, to the ways we relate to each other and our movements. As opposed to mirroring walls and other rigid borders, we can embody discerning yet permeable membranes that allow for a liberated and consensual exchange of energy and resources. We shape boundaries with our own bodies and movements, and we are also shaped by the confines, borders, and walls we interface with. The way we are taught geography through colonial political borders, maps, and cartography heavily shapes our understandings of land. I remember when I was younger looking out the window of an airplane and wondering why the land was all divided into perfectly square plots, with fences and straight lines cutting through the landscape. I internalized this as the norm, when actually land has been cut, severed, and divided using arbitrary political lines in ways that interrupt the natural flow, rhythm and boundaries of rivers, oceans, and mountain ranges. Industrialization, including industrial farming, cuts through land with borders, roads, and resource extraction like mountaintop removal. All of these also etch lines through our bodies, as we are inseparable from the land.

Different bodies face different barriers. Due to patriarchy and the exploitation of women's and femmes' labor, including that of trans and gender-nonconforming people, we in those communities often face immense obstacles in understanding where our bodies end and where another body begins. There is an assumption that we will just keep giving, that our boundaries don't matter, that our bodies don't matter, and that we are here to serve and please white men. From family systems to movements for justice, we see the devaluing of reproductive labor resulting in exploitative conditions in which creating and maintaining boundaries can feel near-impossible.[1] Coming into a more centered relationship with boundaries is a radical feminist act of healing and transformation. The different ways we have been socialized impact how we are able to set boundaries—in our personal relationships, at work, in community, and in the weaving of our social political fabric. With an understanding of the harmful ways we have come to embody border politics and possibilities for more centered boundaries, we can reorganize, reconfigure and reshape our relationships with our bodies, each other, and the land.[2]

I have found that building an embodied understanding of the nervous system is critical in making these personal and political interventions—especially those that involve shifting from a survival response that elicits scarcity, extraction, and aggression, toward the social engagement system, where there is more room for healing, centered boundaries, transformation, and collective care.

Doctors, researchers, and medical schools working inside the medical industrial complex paint a picture of the body that is self-reliant, binary, symmetrical, and normative. It produces images and research that reify ableist, fatphobic, sexist, and colonial ideas about the body. Anybody who strays from these norms is shamed and pathologized. One of the ways this shows up is in how we have been taught to think about our nervous systems as internally and externally independent. Until recently, there was a seemingly unanimous agreement about the autonomic nervous system having two branches with opposite functions: the sympathetic being responsible for fight or flight, and the parasympathetic being associated with rest and digestion. With the emergence in 1994 of the polyvagal theory—a term coined by psychologist and neuroscientist

Stephen Porges—we now have access to research demonstrating how the vagus nerve interacts with the autonomic nervous system. This research presents a third branch of the nervous system, connected to the ventral vagus nerve, referred to as the social engagement system. This discovery radically changed the way neuroscientists understand the body, from individual to interdependent, from a closed circuit with walls to a porous membrane able to impact and be impacted by another nervous system.

The Three Branches of the Autonomic Nervous System (ANS)

Fight or Flight (Sympathetic)
- Response to danger through hyperarousal
- Increases heart rate, blood pressure, adrenaline and other defensive responses
- Decreases digestion, relationality, and immune response
- When facing perceived threat or actual danger, able to respond
- Could be within the outer edges or completely outside of our window of tolerance*

Freeze – Dorsal Vagus (Paraympathetic)
- Ancient defense system of unmyelinated pathways
- Increases endorphins to numb sensations
- Decreases heart rate, blood pressure, sexual responses, immune responses, breathing
- When facing perceived threat or actual danger, unable to respond
- Outside of the window of tolerance*

Safety – Ventral Vagus (Parasympathetic Social Engagement System)
- Evolved through the development of myelinated pathways
- Increases digestion, relationality, immune response, oxytocin, and breathing
- Decreases defensive responses
- Experience of safety and ability to stay engaged and open to new information and experience
- Within the window of tolerance*

* "Window of Tolerance," a term developed by Dan Siegel and Pat Ogden, refers to the level of intensity of emotion we can experience while remaining connected to ourselves and each other.

To understand the applications of the polyvagal theory, let us start with a brief overview of the limbic system. The limbic system is the part of the brain responsible for our survival response. It is activated in response to extreme stress, trauma, or threat. It is important to note that this can be either a real and present threat or one that is simply perceived. The response is automatic and subconscious, so it is not important to make such a distinction. When the limbic system is activated, it sets the hypothalamic-pituitary-adrenal (HPA) axis in motion, preparing the body for defense. Then the HPA activates the sympathetic branch (SNS) of the autonomic nervous system (ANS), which is our fight or flight response. The hormones epinephrine and norepinephrine are released, and our breathing and heart rate speed up. If neither fight nor flight is available, the limbic system engages the parasympathetic branch of the ANS, which is responsible for the freeze response and is connected to the dorsal vagus nerve. Once the traumatic incident is over, cortisol will stop the alarm reaction as well as the production of epinephrine/norepinephrine, which will bring the body back to homeostasis, and the ventral vagus nerve can be engaged along with our social engagement system. However, in some cases, the cortisol secretion is not adequate to stop the alarm reaction, in which case the brain and rest of the body continue to respond as if it is still under threat. This results in the trauma becoming embedded in the body, what is commonly referred to as post-traumatic stress. It is not yet known if the primary factor to cause the insufficient cortisol response is a continued perception of threat or insufficient cortisol previously existing. Either way, the limbic system continues to engage the hypothalamus, resulting in a chronic state of activation and/or dissociation.

One example of applied polyvagal theory can be found in understanding heart rate variability (HRV) and its relationship to healing trauma. When we have a neuroception of safety, our heart rhythm is responsive to the moment, creating a flexible variation in the time between beats. When we have a neuroception of danger, our HRV decreases and becomes more rigid and uniform. Low heart rate variability can be an indicator that a trauma has become embedded in our bodies and continues to impact our heart (and the rest of us) long after the memory leaves our conscious awareness. Extensive research has been devoted to strengthening circuits to increase HRV. However, under stress the implicit pattern always resurfaces and HRV decreases. But we can increase HRV in a way that more permanently holds by activating ventral vagal pathways and healing implicit memories (memories we unintentionally store) through embodied practices informed by polyvagal theory. This illustrates the somatic principle of transformation, in which we can embody what we call a "new shape" once we have fully held and healed our old shape. If we just place new patterns and practices on top of our current system, we will always resort back to our engrained patterns for safety.

The polyvagal theory emphasizes the importance of embodied, physiological states as influences on our behavior and social interactions. The theory provides an understanding of how risk, fear, and threat impact our bodies and how generating a sense of safety is not predicated on the removal of such threats but rather dependent on environmental and somatic social cues.

Mammals evolved to be able to shift from safe engagement into activation, dissociation, and immobilization responses as needed, but humans have yet to evolve to organically and efficiently shift back from immobilization to social engagement. The freeze response (dorsal vagal nerve) developed as a temporary numbing response, so that we feel less in case we are attacked and eaten by our predator. However, unlike other animals, humans have the neocortex, the thinking brain, which can get in the way of our natural ability to literally shake off trauma, causing us to move with walls of protection long past the traumatic incident. Peter Levine talks about this phenomena in his 2008 book *Healing Trauma*. He describes a predator chasing its prey: the prey activates fight, flight, or freeze, trying to attack the predator, outrun it, or play dead. Whatever the response, if and when the prey safely escapes, it will shake its entire body—discharging the trauma—and then return to its pack without any signs of PTSD. This research was foundational to Levine's development of understanding how we self-regulate and co-regulate through traumatic experiences. Due to a combination of (d)evolution and the colonization of our somas, many of us repress these natural ways of discharging trauma or have lost touch with these instincts entirely. When people are in activated or mobilized states, basic functions slow down, and the range of emotion they can express is limited. Levine's research helped to highlight the body's natural ways of discharging energy from a mobilization response. Whether engaging in activating conversations to organize people around anti-Zionism, or in healing your own trauma, somatic practices can support our bodies to discharge, activate, and move stuck energy so we have more agency in our lives and relationships.

In this chapter, we will talk about the ways that somatics, polyvagal theory, and politicized healing can offer an embodied experience of safety that does not rely on militarized borders, policing, or nationalism but instead offers opportunities for deeper mutual connection and community. Porges writes:

> By moving the defining features of "safety" from a structural model of the environment with fences, metal detectors, and surveillance monitoring to a visceral sensitivity model evaluating shifts in the neural regulation of autonomic state, the theory challenges our societal values regarding how people are treated. The theory forces us to question whether our society provides sufficient and appropriate opportunities to experience safe environments and trusting relationships. Once we recognize that the experiences within our societal institutions such as schools, hospitals, and churches are characterized by chronic evaluations that trigger feelings of danger and threat, we can see that these institutions can be as disruptive to health as political unrest, fiscal crisis, or war.[3]

These embedded institutions of the state and the repercussions of their actions (or lack of action) have a lasting impact on our experiences of safety and connection. I invite you to think about how you might apply the lens of embodied safety through nervous system regulation to having mutually supportive organizing networks, interdependent communities, and cross-movement connections.

Nonbinary Hemispheres and Bodies

Each part of the body is interactive and interdependent, not only with the other parts of the body but also with the surrounding people and environments. The two hemispheres of the brain foster different values and perspectives, influence the way we interact, and shape the kinds of systems and institutions we create. Due to binary patriarchal value systems, our culture tends to encourage staying within the left hemisphere, which prioritizes individual thought over collective experience and rationality over creativity. Within the right hemisphere, there is a greater capacity for embracing contradictions, whereas the left hemisphere seeks to categorize things as right or wrong. Physiologically speaking, the right hemisphere contains more white matter than the left because of all the interconnection of neurons allowing for information to pass with more ease, speed, and efficiency. Also, most new information flows in through the right hemisphere, as that is the part of the brain that is most available in the present moment. When new information makes its way to the left hemisphere it gets dissected into preexisting categories in the brain rather than right hemisphere being able to allow for different ways of knowing and being (including the more implicit and subtle experience that is otherwise available to us).

Living in our left hemisphere can cause us to become narrow-minded and concerned only with getting our individual or nuclear family unit's needs met rather than being able to hold a bigger vision of collective care. In *The Heart of Trauma: Healing the Embodied Brain in the Context of Relationships*, Bonnie Badenoch writes, "[The left hemisphere] values the explicit and distrusts the richer but never fully knowable implicit. It is the hemisphere of grasping and using, of autonomy, individuality, and self-reliance, of goal-driven movement, tasks, and behavior. The left concerns itself with algorithms, protocols, and interventions that can be broadly applied without regard to context or individuality."[4] It is within the right hemisphere that we are able to read people's faces and voices and meet them with empathy as part of our social engagement system. So, in a left hemisphere–centric culture we are constantly missing people's cues for needing reflection and compassion. To me, this sounds like a precise description of the dominant heteropatriarchal white supremacist culture in the United States. Capitalism requires us to spend so much time in our left hemisphere, whether through working in factory-like environments or through the stress of feeling that we must make all the "right" decisions in order to "succeed." In many cases, success simply means being able to financially and materially sustain ourselves, meaning the pressures of capitalism become wired into our survival response systems. As we are encouraged or forced to live in our left hemispheres, our bodies can become weaponized to sustain the divide-and-conquer strategies of capitalism and racism. Badenoch notes that the emphasis on left dominance "leaves us unable to even notice that we are in trouble because we are cut off from our body's distress signals, an adaptive strategy if the right hemisphere has become uninhabitable."[5]

It's probably starting to sound like the right hemisphere is good and left is bad—which is ironic, considering that would be a reflection of left hemisphere categorization and judgment. However, it is not that either is better or worse, they just need to be in conversation with each other. For instance, the right hemisphere can offer great visions, and the left is what grounds them. The left hemisphere can be the source of great intellectual discoveries and developments. I am drawing out the problematic nature of an over-engaged left hemisphere simply because it typifies dominant colonial cultures. Only engaging the right hemisphere would present its own set of concerns, but that is not the currently presiding dominant mode of thinking.

Our culture inhibits our ability to maintain a settled nervous system or a ventral vagal state, which has caused an adaptive shift into left-hemisphere dominance. When we are in a left hemisphere–dominant state, we are focused on task completion and control rather than being present and connected in relationship. From this state, we are less likely to form secure attachments with people, creating a cyclical pattern of dysregulation on personal and systemic levels. Recent studies show a significant favoring of the left hemisphere in people's brains resulting in a decreased capacity for empathy, and an increase of narcissism, and apathy.[6] As you can imagine, this has a massive impact on people's ability to form deep and meaningful connections, which is necessary for our immediate and long-term survival.

Badenoch defines trauma as "any experience of fear and/or pain that doesn't have the support it needs to be digested and integrated in to the flow of our developing brains."[7] This model of understanding emphasizes that there is no hierarchy of trauma and that aspects of our daily lives may be traumatic. It broadens our idea of trauma to include everything from the unseen and embedded to the seemingly insignificant to the immensely impactful. This perspective is not intended to diminish the experiences of people on the front lines of trauma and oppression but rather to close the gap between bodies that are seen as wounded and those that are not.

This offers an interesting point of view on the impacts of systems of oppression that are otherwise flattened into shallow identity politics (explored earlier). As an example, we know that Black people and other people of color are the primary targets of white supremacy, and we lose an important part of analysis when we overlook the fact that white supremacy is traumatizing for everyone on a certain level. In addition to targeting people of color, white supremacy demonizes queer and disabled bodies, props up classism through capitalism, and contributes to colonial and extractive relationships with land. Underlying each of these impacts is the reality that white supremacy robs us all of our humanity. I believe that all of us, in different ways, have healing work to do. We must work on our own transformation in order to dismantle systems without just replacing them with similarly oppressive systems. As we have seen, there is a cyclical nature to left hemisphere–centric culture and systems of capitalism and white supremacy. The polyvagal theory and related research that challenges the embodiment of binaries offer us ways into more fully inhabiting our humanity: to live in *both* hemispheres of the brain, *all* branches of the nervous system, and to embrace the interwoven, interdependent, magical unknown in the body. To further illustrate the nonbinary nature of the nervous system, the extreme downregulation of autonomic function through our ancient pathway of the dorsal vagus nerve (freeze response) can be fatal at worst, but the dorsal nerve is also part of the same system that is engaged in order for people to give birth and breastfeed. Our bodies are more brilliant than we often give them credit for, and the functions that we might label as wrong or bad are actually necessary for creating and sustaining life. The more we distance ourselves from our bodies (encouraged by white supremacy, capitalism, and colonization), the more we get stuck in trauma responses. Our trauma responses live in our nervous systems, so it doesn't necessarily matter if cognitively you can understand that you are safe now, or if intellectually you think that what happened to you "wasn't that bad" or that you are over it. If your body engaged a trauma response of mobilization or immobilization, you must address the trauma response by letting your body complete that cycle to heal and move forward. Simply put, this is done by literally shaking off the trauma as detailed in Peter Levine's work. When this hasn't happened naturally in the moment, it can still happen naturally later on—like in a moment of collective song, on the dance floor, or through new experiences of safety. With more extensive trauma, it is often supportive to do this work with a practitioner. This can look like being guided back into the moment, inviting more agency into the situation, choosing to fight or flee, enacting this through embodied practice (e.g., pushing, kicking, running) and then, once you feel complete, being guided back to the present where you can feel that trauma as survivable and that you are safe on the other side. There are more details on this practice later in this chapter.

Queering Boundaries

> The power of queer lies in leveraging the normalizing dynamics
> of nationalism, contesting their enclosures in ways that open up
> possibilities for modes of desire, embodiment, pleasure, associ-
> ation, and identification not constrained by the need to construct,
> legitimize, and manage a territorial and political entity.
>
> —Mark Rifkin

Queerness blurs the space in between, cutting through binaries of pain
and pleasure, allowing us to experience the vast spectrum of sensation
that lives within love and loss. Queering boundaries invites us into this
in-between space—guided into deeper and more nuanced relationships
with ourselves, each other, and the land.

Queer embodiment is a challenge to binary borders and policing,
as well as a profound example of the importance of self-determination.
The policing of gender and sexuality is one of the ways that borders and
surveillance are enforced on our bodies. These binaries imposed on plant
and animal bodies make it seem like there are only ever two choices,
which extensively limits possibilities for creativity and growth. From a
young age, in schools, at home, and on the street, kids are bullied and
forced to take on normative gender roles and fit within the binary. These
binaries rise out of the same systems that militarized borders do: white
supremacy, Christian hegemony, racism, and colonialism. The reality is
that queer and trans bodies have always existed and in many indigenous
traditions are actually revered as spiritual guides, teachers, and healers.
For example, in Cherokee tradition there are three gender roles including
one for two-spirit or "asegi udanto" meaning "other heart." Two-spirit
indigenous people are often trained in spiritual and traditional medicine
and held with deep respect. In Jewish tradition, trans identity and gender
nonconformity have a rich history in halakha—Jewish law. As trans rabbi
Elliot Kukla teaches, the word "androgynos" (referring to a person who
has both "male" and "female" sexual characteristics) has 149 references
in the Mishna and Talmud (first–eighth centuries CE) and 350 occurrences
in classical Midrash and Jewish law codes (second–sixteenth centuries
CE). "Tumtum"—referring to a person whose sexual characteristics do not
conform to the binary has 181 references in the Mishna and Talmud and
335 in classical Midrash and Jewish law codes.[8] These are just some of
many examples of how queer and nonbinary bodies have always existed

as a bridge between worlds or, to look at it differently, as a blurring of the boundaries and lies of normalcy.

In her book *Borderlands/La Frontera: The New Mestiza*, Gloria Anzaldúa illustrates the identities and experiences of people living on edges, margins, and borders. She lifts up the beauty and brilliance in border cultures as she describes the ways bodies, cultures, and land can become woven together when living in this space in between. The development of Borderlands Theory came out of Anzaldúa's experiences growing up at the US-Mexico border as a lesbian Chicana, yet it is expanded to address other forms of social, economic, emotional, sexual, and spiritual boundaries. Borderlands Theory constructs identity in a way that is fluid, nonhierarchical, and ever-evolving, based on the historical moment and context. This invites a deeply nuanced, expansive, and queer approach to understanding interlocking forms oppression as well as the ways communities build cultures of resistance together. Queering boundaries is critical in building regenerative relationships with our bodies, each other, and the land. Queer membranes bring the seemingly disparate parts of our individual and collective bodies together and allow for the reintegration of actual safety, agency, and dignity.

Poly Poly Poly: Boundaries from Polyamory to Polyvagal

Boundaries are the distance at which I can love you and me simultaneously.

—Prentis Hemphill

The way that we love is shaped by our bodies as well as by the state. So when we say "taking the state out of the body," what does that mean for how love? The dominant narrative in the United States is one of monogamy, of one person "forever," and of the repression of desires for anything beyond that. Yet in the openings of culture around queerness, polyamory, and nonmonogamy we find ways of loving that transcend the bounds of marriage, heteronormativity, and the state. That said, in many of these communities, we face the same struggles. We re-create norms and stigmas, and we re-create "shoulds" and hierarchies of polyamorous people being "more evolved," with monogamous people needing to work on their shit. What if, instead of creating more external rules for how we love, we create more internal knowing in our bodies about the kinds of love and connection we most deeply long for? To center the kinds of love that meet us where we are in deep, compassionate, and intimate ways. I don't mean relationship anarchy.[9] I mean love that has an order to it, order that can be found in the understanding of a different kind of poly: the polyvagal theory. The polyvagal theory indicates that our nervous systems are inherently inter-woven particularly through the social engagement system. It challenges the idea that what makes you feel safe in a relationship is your issue and yours only. For example, when my friend was feeling jealous about a date their partner recently went on, and their partner responded with "that's your stuff to work out," in a way, yes, that has some truth to it. But also, our bodies are constantly communicating cues of safety and attachment, so there is actually a lot we can do *together* to create conditions for secure attachment. Jessica Fern dives into this in her book *Polysecure*. She offers the framework of "HEARTS" as a guide to creating secure attachment in consensual nonmonogamous relationships: "**H**ere (being here and present with me), **E**xpressed Delight, **A**ttunement, **R**ituals and Routines, **T**urning Towards after Conflict, **S**ecure Attachment with Self."[10]

Somatically speaking, we can look at this fundamentally around finding the centers of our bodies: being present and connected to sensa-tion, communicating cues of safety through the social engagement system, sensing and feeling for the other person, committing to rhythms of prac-tice, centering amid nervous system activation for the sake of generative conflict, and being self-responsive. For example, if we are totally overex-tended in our front bodies, leaning all the way forward, eyes bulging, we are likely very focused on the other person. What are they feeling? What do they need? If we are collapsed into ourselves, caved backwards, shoulders turned in, chest dropped back, we might be able to feel parts of ourself but very little of the other person. When we find our centers, we find mutual connection, the place where we can simultaneously feel ourselves and another. In the terms of the polyvagal theory, this is when our social engagement systems are activated and we are in a state of co-regulation. In the terms of polyamory, this is when we are able to be present with our own desires and longings while also having space for the other person or people. Through a framework of polyvagal polyamory, we learn to practice boundaries, move toward our longings for connection, and make room for the impact of both of these practices in ourselves and each other.

Boundaries are critical for applying principles of polyamory and polyvagal theory. One of the best ways to understand and work with boundaries is through relationship. Bringing awareness to how we hold and receive boundaries in relationship can illuminate a lot about ourselves and the environments in which we were raised. As discussed in previous chapters, dominant culture pathologizes interdependence and glorifies self-reliance, relying on rigid borders and imbalances of power. These borders form around, and in, our bodies to keep us separate from each other and dependent on the state.

Boundaries can get distorted through experiences of trauma and oppression and keep us from the things we most long for. Many people set boundaries as a strategy to avoid repeating negative past experiences. We may find ourselves hardened and withdrawn, for example, when what we are longing for is intimacy and connection. There is a wisdom in this, to know from an embodied experience that certain situations are not safe and that you need to protect yourself. However, when this becomes automatic, it means we are reacting out of a trauma response instead of being responsive to the current moment. So, if you were hurt by a previous partner, it makes sense that you might have places where you are more rigid in protecting yourself, even if the person or people you are now with do not exhibit that same hurtful behavior. We can be more responsive to current, present-time dynamics by having a wide range of ways to set boundaries that allow us to engage with the wide range of people and experiences we face in our lives. Many of us feel we have only two options: either to stay in connection or totally shut people out. Having centered boundaries gives us more options outside of such binary extremes. If we look at some examples, we can see these extremes. Some people set boundaries as a cement wall—nobody and nothing can get in or out. In relationships, this could be expressed as communicating that even the idea of your partner being attracted to someone else is an unacceptable boundary crossing. This kind of rigidity and hypervigilance is often due to an unresolved trauma response—likely around attachment—and feeling the need to be armored to keep oneself safe. This can be evident in a locked jaw, tightening of the perineum (the space between the anus and genitals), distant eye contact (or lack of eye contact), or a number of other sensations depending on the body. Overextending and crossing our own boundaries is another example of an individual and collective trauma response. In relationship, this could manifest in making agreements around nonmonogamy in order to keep a partnership, even though it's not what you want. This can mean consistently putting other people's needs before our own in self-sacrificial ways, as can be evident in eyes bulging out, chest extended, leaning toward the other person, or other embodied cues of appeasement or fawning. While neither of these tendencies are necessarily wrong, when we aren't intentionally choosing them they can get in the way of maintaining our sense of self, developing positive relationships, and being effective in our work.

To give an example, I worked with a client who had a tendency to reach past their capacity —juggling multiple romantic relationships, always offering to take on next steps at the end of a meeting, picking up the phone when they were already doing two other things, and spending hours supporting a friend without tending to their own bodily needs. They had an automatic "yes" response, likely due to sexism and messages they received from a young age about what made them worthy of love and attention. This had a huge impact not only on their own mental health but also on their relationships and their organizing because they would inevitably crash and be unable to sustain trustworthy connections. We worked together to explore what was happening in their body and noticed they were always pitched forward, eyes open wide, and leaning away from their back body. Through somatic awareness, opening, and practice, we were able to build new pathways and muscle memory so they could feel their back more. Now when someone asks them to do something, they more often are able to breathe into their back, widen their gaze, and make a centered choice based on their capacity rather than on the ways they were conditioned through life experience.

Boundaries are the spaces we make in order to maintain connection. Living in a time that puts so much pressure on our connections, people are eager for ways of practicing boundaries that maintain the relationships in our lives. I have noticed in some communities that there has been a cultural pendulum swing from not having language or permission to create boundaries, to throwing up walls in every direction, calling each other out, and engaging in faux accountability processes that cut off connection entirely. These tendencies around setting boundaries are tied into individualized care models, in which we have to care for ourselves *before* caring for others. Instead, I believe that self-care and collective care must happen simultaneously. Honoring boundaries can be done in a variety of ways, including deciding to shift your boundaries to meet someone where they are. There is a quality to this that is different from that of self-sacrifice— and it is centered around the self-determination of boundaries. Being in mutual interdependent relationships shifts our ideas about what boundaries are needed and how to hold them. This practice counters dominant cultures of individualism that keep some bodies entirely separate from each other and other bodies overly dependent.

Understanding the ways we relate to the boundaries of our own bodies, and to the boundaries of other bodies, is a critical part of decolonization and reconnecting with the reciprocal interdependence of all bodies and the earth. For many people who have experienced trauma, regaining boundaries is a big part of healing and regenerating a sense of safety. Generative Somatics teaches, "Often during experiences of trauma, our ability to successfully defend ourselves is literally not possible. The situation, relationship or violence makes overt boundaries impossible and we shift to survival reactions. The soma can experience an intense state of helplessness. We often have to reintroduce and rebuild the competency to successfully protect or defend ourselves, and to have centered boundaries."[11] Often, we need to both rebuild an internal sense of safety and take care of material safety needs.

In addition to holding boundaries, we also must learn how to reach for our longing and each other. If we are moving toward expansive definitions of love and relationship, we are likely going to need to stretch. We need to breathe into the moments when we feel ourselves contracting, getting smaller, and choose to reenter into connection. When faced with a relationship that may seem like we are in competition, we can feel for our uniquely distinct edges while also extending to feel our interconnection. Boundaries help us define where we end and another begins. Extensions help us see where we can reach to cultivate the space that gets generated between two or more people. You can practice extension somatically by making a shape with your body energetically and/or physically in which you can feel an extension from your center (see Embodied Practice section in preceding chapter). These extended postures can invite other people into your center: what you care about and what you long for. While we may not physically enact this in a moment of connection, we can practice it so that when we face a situation that asks us to reach for the other person, there is a pathway in our bodies to know what it feels like to communicate that extension toward another. Having centered boundaries and extensions means that we are able to connect with other people and what they need, want, and desire, while simultaneously staying connected to ourselves within this connection. This alignment with individual and relational integrity is critical to building centered relationships, whether monogamous, nonmonogamous, polyamorous, or otherwise.

The polyvagal theory points to a different way of relating to boundaries, one that acknowledges our interconnection and requires malleability. Flexible boundaries do not mean that we bend ourselves into whatever shape works for other people; we are still grounded in a center that has structural integrity. Then too, just like fascia, we have layers atop that center that offer the capacity for protection as well as being impacted by our surroundings. Centered boundaries and extensions can change the shape of our somas by shifting our automatic responses and how we interact. Just as much as trauma can shape our bodies, so can our connections, and with agency and power we can shape our edges and ways of loving in ways that serve our deepest commitments.[12]

Attachment, Epigenetics, and Technology

If we allow ourselves to gaze at the culture that surrounds and implicitly infuses us, the situation for many of us at work and even at home isn't much different than that of the infant who is left to cry, except that we learned long ago the uselessness of our tears and so flee to our left hemispheres so we don't notice we are drowning in the sea of isolation and abandonment.

—Bonnie Badenoch

Forces of repression within the state contribute to a culture of left-hemisphere dominance and disconnection. In addition to these massive systems, early attachment issues, epigenetic factors, and the increased digital culture impact our ability to sustain presence with ourselves and connection with others. In the technology-heavy culture we live in, we are prone to lose patience and are constantly fostering an inability to stay present and give our full attention to something. To start, we should consider the fact that we take in eleven million bits of sensory information every second, including through the 24/7 news cycle, media, and advertising.[13] From this perspective too we can see that we are inextricably shaped by the cultures and environments around us. There is increasing research on the impact of technology on our brains—how people's dependent and excessive relationships with their smartphones impact our bodies and cultures, particularly through speeding up our pace and dividing our attention. The onslaught of stimulation and input also results in an embodied safety response of desensitization as we shift away from the right hemisphere, where we have more access to empathy and connection, into the left hemisphere, which keeps us distant and analytical. These shifts in our ability to connect with our bodies and each other is a trauma in and of itself—we have to contend with a reality in which our emotional survival requires us to withdraw from compassion and connection.

The intensity of digital culture begs questions: What are the lasting, epigenetic impacts of technology on our bodies? And how will these impacts be passed on to future generations? "Epigenetics" refers to shifts in the ways our genes are expressed in response to our life experience as well as the life experiences of our parents, grandparents, and even more distant ancestors. Thus, things we may not have personally experienced in our lifetime can still live in our bodies, shaping our perceptions, behaviors, relationships, and choices. Cellular biologist Bruce Lipton emphasizes that it is not necessarily the experience itself that shifts gene expression but rather our perception of experience. If we are afraid, our bodies produce cortisol; if we feel warmth and connection, our bodies produce oxytocin. As these chemicals permeate the cells in our bodies, we move into a state of protection or growth.[14] Thus, when trauma becomes embedded at a cellular level, our capacity for nourishment and growth is decreased and potentially passed on through generations. This intergenerational transmission challenges our perception of genes as linear or statistically randomized and shows that genes can actually be shaped, reshaped, and passed on based on the impact of survival hormones.

The way we are or are not able to receive nourishment through food and emotional support guides the emergence of epigenetic patterns that then play a role in our ongoing relationship with nourishment. Ingestive behaviors are an important part of understanding social engagement. This starts as a baby with nursing, and then as adults we eat meals together or go out for a drink as a way of socializing. Most people carrying embedded traumas and/or anxiety experience some symptoms in their gut or more broadly in their relationship to nourishment and nurturance. This can show up as conditions such as irritable bowel syndrome (IBS), eating disorders, or other digestive disturbances. Some experience a closing of the esophagus as an adaptive response to a stomach that is not going to be able to digest anything.

When we are infants, we often express our needs for nourishment through tears and a variety of other somatic signifiers of hunger or discomfort. If we are met by our parent or caregiver with warmth and reflection of our needs, we gradually learn to understand our need to eat food. If our caregiver does not answer our cries appropriately, we may develop a disconnect between sensations of hunger with the experience of being nourished.

There is a whole universe of wisdom around how we come into the world and the wisdom of birthing bodies. One example of our inherent capacity for nourishment is that right after birth, when placed on the birthing person's belly, an infant will instinctually crawl up to the nipple seeking nourishment. We come into the world expecting to be met with warmth and nourishment; it is through the embodiment of trauma that we come to expect to be mistreated, and it is through reestablishing secure connections that we can heal.

In addition to the involvement of epigenetics in passing on intergenerational trauma and resilience, we must consider the impacts of early attachment on people's ability to feel safe in connection. If we are met by our caregiver with warmth and curiosity in response to our needs, we become wired to expect this kind of nourishing relational experience,— setting us up to experience safety in future connections. In terms of early development, whatever part of us has experienced pain or fear develops in a disrupted way or stops developing entirely until we are met with sustained interpersonal connection and are given the space for these patterns to shift.

Porges talks about the "preamble" to attachment depending on signals of safety. "The social engagement system with the myelinated vagal pathway provides the neural platform upon which the attachment processes can occur."[15] Often when talking about theories of attachment, people try to pigeonhole you into one particular form: anxious (preoccupied with gaining others' approval), avoidant (preferring independence over connection), disorganized (fearing both intimacy and autonomy), or secure (being comfortable building and relying on interdependent relationships). Actually, attachment is an ever-shifting continuum, and people can have multiple attachment styles. The same person may embody different attachment styles depending on the relationship, and, within the same relationship or situation, different people will react differently. For example, in some families where connection has been disrupted, individuals will adapt anxiously, desperately reaching to reconnect. Other individuals may adapt to the same conditions avoidantly, resulting in a paradoxical internalization that being connected means staying separate. Attachment can become engrained when we are very young, but our connections continuously shape and impact what attachment styles show up most prevalently and how we show up to relationships. While I agree with what Porges proposes about forming safe connections through negotiations of social engagement, I don't think these phases have to be in succession. Instead, safe connections can happen in a rhythmic, nonlinear pattern in which we take risks outside our comfort zone and have experiences of physical intimacy that end up building safety.

Edges of Flora and Fauna

Boundaries in nature and in our bodies are mostly flexible and permeable. For example, consider our cellular structure. Each cell is contained in a membrane interspersed with passageways and pumps designed to bring in or expunge selected molecules in order to protect the cell's internal environment. Cell membranes protect and organize cells, moderate what comes in and goes out, and are responsible for communication. Cell membranes require the thickness and viscosity of fat as well as the fluidity of water. Our lungs have cilia that help filter the air we breathe, as well as layers of fascia—called pleura—surrounding them for structural integrity and protection. Throughout our bodies, from our cells to our fascia, we find examples of pliable membranes. Nowhere will we find the sort of cement walls that we see in militarized political borders.

Plant and animal bodies often have multiple layers and different kinds of boundaries. I find the best illustration of this principle in seeds. Some have thorny cages to protect them, others have husks or shells or, as in the case of stone fruit, are protected by a soft, juicy fruit. Plants such as stinging nettle, poison oak, and wild tobacco model another kind of boundary and defense system. Stinging nettle (*Urtica dioica*) produces tiny hairs on the underside of its leaves called trichomes, which when touched release a fluid causing mild to severe irritation of the skin of mammals. Seed-producing plants (referred to as "female plants" in binary botany) produce more of these hairs than pollen-producing plants ("male plants") to offer more protection for their precious seeds. Poison oak (*Toxicodendron diversilobum*) and poison ivy (*Toxicodendron radicans*) also carry a fluid toxic to mammals, urushiol, which causes itchy rashes. Both oak and ivy plants create boundaries to defend the land, particularly delicate ecosystems, which is why they both show up in areas where the soil has been heavily disrupted. Another example of plant boundaries is wild tobacco (*Nicotiana attenuata*), which is considered a sacred medicine to many Indigenous cultures in North America and used as a ceremonious offering to honor the land and ancestors and offer protection in a ritual container. Wild tobacco has more genes involved in environmental perception than most animals do. The seeds need wildfire to kickstart their growth and thus sometimes wait up to one hundred years before germination. When they finally emerge, they must face a totally new environment and thus have evolved a chemical, nicotine, used to poison any herbivore that tries to attack it. Each of these plants is sacred and embodies boundaries that keep them protected *and* thriving without inhibiting their own growth.

All of our bodies are different and need to hold boundaries in ways that are specific and responsive to our particular shaping and environments. We can learn from the plant bodies described above how to hold boundaries in a way that supports our ability to survive and thrive while also honoring the needs of the ecosystems around us. Lest we forget, we also have animal bodies that are much more integrated than medical science has led us to believe. Our bodies are often viewed as disparate parts of a disconnected system, when actually there is no part of our body that functions without relying on another part of our body. The medicalization of health and healing has resulted in a fragmentation of our bodies and a false dichotomy between mind and body.

The conversation between our muscles, belly, heart, autonomic nervous system and our skull-encased brain is bidirectional, with 80 percent of the information moving upward from the "body brain" to the "skull brain" and only 20 percent in the other direction. The brainstem filters what comes to our consciousness by selecting what is most relevant for the current moment. This process protects us from an overwhelming flood of potential thoughts and experiences, but it also means that in any given moment we should be aware that there is a vast realm of information we are unable to take into our awareness.

Reintegrating "mind" and "body" is important for therapists and other practitioners in understanding that our emotions don't necessarily need to be processed through our brains. It opens up possibilities to experience and heal emotional states through relationship without getting into the backstory. Until recently, a majority in the field of neuroscience believed that once implicit memories moved into long-term storage, they were completely locked in place. Around the beginning of the new millennium, research came out showing that these implicit synapses can be destabilized and reconsolidated to contain a changed implicit memory.[16] This research has major implications for how we practice healing therapies. Under the right conditions, we can open up these memories and offer what is referred to as a "disconfirming" experience. Put simply, if someone experienced something scary and felt alone in it, we can awaken the memory of feeling scared and alone and then ally with them so that they feel safe and connected. This has to be done in an embodied way. We are not just trying to override people's narratives by offering positive affirmations. We want to allow the memory to open in a way so that the trauma itself can unfold and heal. Badenoch writes, "It appears that at the moment embodiment meets embodiment, the neural net offers itself to receive new information and will reconsolidate about five hours later, bearing this precious healing cargo."[17] We can also have spontaneous experiences of disconfirmation and repair that happen outside of our conscious awareness. However, we can access these memories, consciously or subconsciously, if we meet them with compassion and connection, and give them the time and space they need to unfold, we are likely to see our bodies heal in sustained and powerful ways.

Safety as Treatment, Connection as Healing

Evolutionarily, biologically, and somatically speaking, being out of relationship, particularly through difficult experiences, is traumatic and even lethal. Unlike our ancient reptilian ancestors, we require social interdependence to survive. Given our wiring for interdependence, isolation and restraint are the most potent stressors for our social mammalian nervous systems. We need access to connection, but we also need it to feel part of a safe environment. Safety and connection together are necessary for basic biological functions such as sleep, digestion, and reproduction. The level to which we depend on connections for our survival should encourage us to prioritize the kind of environments we need to feel safety and belonging. The polyvagal theory recognizes that our needs for connection and co-regulation are a biological imperative and that, to fulfill on this need, we must strive to create environments and relationships where people feel safer.

Such environments and relationships are hard to come by, particularly in institutions in the United States, including those set up to offer health care, such as hospitals. The medical industrial complex understands bodies as independent machines—looking at each organ or system as separate from the rest like a cog on a wheel and each individual body as a separate wheel within the system. In this model, people who experience physical or emotional trauma—which from a somatic perspective, I would argue, always come together—are treated as damaged and need to be fixed.

Diagnoses comprise a slippery terrain, especially in the realm of trauma, addiction, and mental health. Diagnosis is part and parcel of the medical industrial complex since it is the primary way that doctors can bill insurance. Therapist Deb Dana notes, "Every diagnosis in the DSM is a dysregulated nervous system." It is important to ask when giving or seeking a diagnosis: What are we looking for? How might a diagnosis support or limit understanding of our pain and our healing? At times, diagnoses help give people a sense of what they are working with. Other times there are misdiagnoses, overdiagnosis, and racialized or sexualized diagnoses (e.g., hysteria). We must work against the stigma associated with certain diagnoses in a way that normalizes people's experiences while also seeking appropriate medical and/or alternative interventions and support in the framework of harm reduction. Harm reduction is a political practice that developed during the AIDS crisis and the rise in opiate over-doses beginning in the 1980s. It approaches injection drug use through the lens of decreasing harm with services such as needle exchanges. The principles of harm reduction can be expanded to meet people where they are in relationship to a variety of experiences of trauma, addiction, and mental health. To reframe diagnosis through a harm reduction and somatic transformation perspective means that rather than seeing people as being wrong, broken, or disordered, we see our bodies instead as wise, resilient, and adaptive. With understanding of the ways our bodies organically adapt to fear, pain, and trauma, we can see that there are no bad responses—we are simply trying to protect ourselves and maintain safety however we can in a given moment.

There are implications for this kind of approach to therapy and healing. Franklyn Sills, a well-established teacher in the biodynamic craniosacral tradition (more on this lineage later) introduced the idea of the "inherent treatment plan" based on listening to the wise and adaptive systems in patients.[18] In an inherent treatment plan, a diagnosis is not necessarily needed. Instead, we can see more of the wholeness of a person's body, life, and social and environmental context and we can trust that that person's body has the most information about how to heal.

A painful example of the way adaptive strategies manifest in the face of trauma is in the impacts of colonization on indigenous people. It was only after enduring the theft and extermination of their land, culture, and families that substance abuse and addiction became extremely prevalent in Indigenous American communities.[19] Substance use was survival strategy in the face of irreparable damage, to be able to dissociate and numb. This demonstrates the importance of supporting people struggling through addiction or other mental health concerns to understand the context in which they arose. In this case, supporting an Indigenous person struggling with addiction might entail harm reduction in tandem with addressing other impacts of colonization, including the enforcement of a culture that breeds individualism, competition, and isolation. At best, it also entails organizing to offer reparations (depending on the call from their community) and preventing further damage done by colonization. Many interventions are crafted in a left hemisphere–centric (patriarchal, white supremacist) way that is about control and can diminish a sense of trust, activate the sympathetic nervous system, and leave the person we are trying to support feeling more isolated and shut down. Whatever way we approach healing in addiction and other mental health struggles, it is important to meet people where they are, with an understanding of social context, and offer connection within a safe container.

There is one more implication to highlight that goes hand in hand with any kind of deep relational healing work, and that is the practice of transformative justice. If we understand the neuroscience behind how our bodies are wired to adapt to our environments and each other, then we must be able to challenge the ways our society deems certain behavior "criminal." With this understanding, people who are causing harm can be seen with more compassion. It is not that we necessarily need to forgive the people who harmed or abused us; in some cases this can be an important part of healing, in other cases stronger boundaries need to be drawn, and many times both boundaries and forgiveness are needed. However, if we truly want our relationships and broader culture to shift, we have to believe in the wisdom of our bodies and trust that we are all doing our best to adapt to the environments in which we reside. Badenoch writes about how 70 percent of our relationships are about rupture and repair, leaving only 30 percent for the warm, fuzzy, and easy parts of our connections. This means that reparative conversations and experiences, like those in transformative justice processes, are a huge part of building and sustaining relationships in our lives.

Integrating the Polyvagal Theory into Culture

Applying understandings of the nervous system can support working through political difference, taking strategic action, and breaking through cycles of violence. From my location as an anti-Zionist Jew, tools for nervous system regulation are helpful in variety of scenarios, including working with Ashkenazi anxiety (often referred to as a joke but also very real). Because of a particular culture and internalization of trauma, many Ashkenazi Jews struggle with anxiety. I think of Ashkenazi anxiety as a tension in our bodies regarding the different experiences of antisemitism that were passed down to us, in contrast to our current experiences of assimilation and freedom from material impacts of antisemitism. This contradiction leaves us constantly tracking for danger even when we are safe. This can show up as fear around there not being enough food, raising children with an extreme level of criticism, , or social anxiety around being left out or othered--all of these experiences can touch on an intergenerational trauma of being ostracized and systematically killed. Another example of the importance of nervous system regulation is in confronting Zionism in Jewish communities. We need to be able to deescalate in moments of extreme activation around antisemitism and recenter around shared commitments to justice, including in Palestine. Over the years I have used principles of the polyvagal theory to find ways to co-regulate with family members or other Jewish community members when confronting them around Zionism.

Porges's polyvagal theory not only offers a critique of the current mainstream society in the United States, it also offers a way forward—a way to move through trauma as individuals and collectively. For example, we know that cultures throughout time and place have used song as an avenue for healing. The polyvagal theory affirms the healing capacity of song through the expansion of the lungs, extending the duration of exhale, and a subsequent increase in the effectiveness of the myelinated vagal efferent pathways on the heart. It also increases the neural tone of your middle ear muscles and the neural regulation of your laryngeal and pharyngeal muscles. When we are listening to someone speak, we are listening to the meaning of words but also to the prosody (pitch, volume, and rhythm) for cues about whether it is safe to settle into relationship or whether we need to attend to possible danger.

In the inner ear, there is a muscle called the stapedius, which is less than one millimeter long and influences whether the sound entering our ears transmits safety or fear to our higher processing centers. When our sympathetic nervous system is aroused in response to fear, the stapedius muscle relaxes to allow in low-frequency ambient sounds so that we can orient to the environment and track the potential danger. If we are in a ventral vagal state with a neuroception of safety, this muscle tenses, allowing us to focus on human voices, the meaning of words, and connection. People who have unintegrated experiences of trauma may appear to be easily distracted, as their system is still anticipating danger and listening for signals of threat, or they may seem helpless and dissociative as they are unable to listen for or track their environment at all anymore. In connecting with people with unintegrated trauma (which is most of us), the more we are able to stay in a nonjudgmental, receptive state, the more we can modulate our voices to communicate safety and connection. While singing with others, we are literally engaging our social engagement system, thus soothing our nerves and creating experiences of safety in connection.

Another important takeaway from the polyvagal theory is that engaging in play is critical in nourishing the social engagement system. In modern technology-heavy cultures we have replaced play with video games and other solitary, screen-oriented activities. However, the most important part of play is the feedback of face-to-face, body-to-body interaction, in which we are activated but safe. This sort of communications technology is being introduced to children at a younger and younger age, impeding their ability to develop neuroception or self-regulation. Giving children—and people of all ages—access to safe environments for in-person play is part of keeping our nervous systems intact.

Along with the importance of social interactions, the polyvagal theory places significant attention on the role of physical environments in supporting settled nervous systems. In industrialized civilization we often find ourselves in enclosed spaces, around loud sounds, and inundated with information and stimuli. Porges talks about changing classroom environments to support children in feeling safe—inherently supporting a better learning environment. The impacts of acoustics and light on nervous systems are important to pay attention to, particularly in institutions where learning and healing are supposed to happen. Porges helped design a school building for children on the autism spectrum, intent on reducing background noise, providing ambient light, putting windows five feet off the ground so there was natural light but not distracting visual stimulation, and installing sound-absorbing ceilings and carpeted floors. Can you imagine what our institutions would look like if they took into account this research on understanding how to create supportive environments where more, if not all, bodies feel safe?

Often, when we are stuck in a state of feeling unsafe, we develop complex narratives to justify the physiological responses we are having to fear and trauma. At any point in our development, our nervous systems may end up detecting risk when there is no present risk. We then make meaning through a narrative that justifies our experience of not being safe, loved, connected, or able to trust. This can also go in the other direction, where people's nervous systems are stuck in such a way that they are too readily trusting and feel safe in situations that are unsafe. This discernment of safety involves two processes that Porges identifies as interoception and neuroception. "Interoception is the process describing both conscious feelings and unconscious monitoring of bodily processes by the nervous system."[20] Interoception includes sensors located in internal organs, to evaluate internal conditions, and pathways to convey and regulate information between organs and the brain. Interoception sometimes involves a conscious awareness of a bodily response, whereas neuroception occurs outside conscious awareness. When there is a sense of risk or safety, interoception occurs after the process of neuroception. "This automatic process [neuroception] involves brain areas that evaluate cues of safety, danger, and life threat. Once these are detected via neuroception, physiological state automatically shifts to optimize survival. Although we are usually not aware of cues that trigger neuroception, we tend to be aware of the physiological shift (i.e. interoception)."[21] These shifts can be described as a gut feeling or tenderness in the heart or an intuition or instinct. Neuroception also facilitates a somatic experience of trust, allowing for social engagement behaviors and building strong relationships.

It is important to note that neuroception is not always accurate. "Faulty neuroception might detect risk when there is no risk or identify cues of safety when there is risk."[22] If we know that our bodies are in an ongoing process of neuroception, what does that mean for our biases formed through systemic privilege and oppression impacting our capacity for clear neuroception? Histories of anti-Black racism, homophobia, fatphobia, Islamophobia, antisemitism, and sexism (to name just a few of many forms of oppression) demonstrate the ways certain bodies are viewed as an object of disgust, sin, pity, terror, or inferiority, inherently flawed and irremediable. Within these contexts, we are inhibited in our ability to perceive (through both neuroception and interoception) and be perceived with a sense of curiosity or respect for different bodies. This is one of many applications of the research behind the polyvagal theory that offers insight into different approaches to unlearning systems of oppression from within our bodies and relationships.

The polyvagal theory contributes importantly to a political analysis of social, medical, and governmental institutions and how they define safety. It asserts that we must deconstruct systems that are a threat to people's safety, and that the cost of living in an unsafe world is far too great. For example, police carrying guns, as the government's approach to safety, does not actually create a settled nervous system—with unsettled nervous systems we actually increase incidents of unsafe interaction. Another example: hospitals full of loud beeping and low humming machines that put our nervous systems in a constant state of alert. (It's bad enough that the medical industrial complex dehumanizes its patients and leaves little room for healing connections, even when the provider wants that.) Understanding that social interactions use neural pathways that support health, growth, and restoration is extremely important in how we look at health-care systems. If our institutions and society as a whole were to embody the principles of the polyvagal theory, we would be living in a world with accessible education, no jails and prisons, and safer environments for healing and recovery.

In so many ways, the polyvagal theory affirms survivors of trauma, in that our bodies are adaptive and have helped us survive. We also have to be able to recognize when it is time to let go of the survival strategy—when it not only doesn't serve us anymore but is actually getting in the way of our ability to thrive. In therapies that arise from integrating the polyvagal theory, supporting people in feeling safe in their bodies becomes the treatment. We have to shift from pathologizing behavior to understanding whether or not the behavior is adaptive in the current context. This is vital in lifting the stigma from trauma and mental health. The polyvagal theory offers insight about healing on personal, interpersonal, and collective levels. Incorporating these understandings of the nervous system can be part of the shift from relying on militarized borders and policing for safety to being able to have an embodied sense of safety in our communities and environments.

Isolation is trauma, interdependence is survival. Safety is treatment, and connection is healing.

Embodied Practices

> Emotions shape the very surface of bodies, which take shape through the repetition of actions overtime, as well as through orientations toward and away from others.
>
> —Sara Ahmed

You are invited to engage with these practices when the time is right for you and at your own pace. With everything, practice consent, self-responsiveness, accessibility, and mutual care. These practices are intended as applied learning and transformation—before entering, read through the content of the preceding chapter to better land the social, political, and/or ecological relevance of these practices. Also, you will need to refer to the author's note at the beginning—A Guide to Embodied Practice and Lineage—for a more comprehensive orientation and key to symbols.

- **Shaking It Off:** ♁ ☉ ☆ ☆ As we learned in this chapter, all animals have a natural instinct to shake their bodies free of the stress and contraction associated with a traumatic experience. Remember, humans are animals too! So, after an activating experience, or as a resilience practice, try moving from head to toe shaking each part of your body. Start slowly. You can roll your head around, open and close your jaw, shrug your shoulders up and down, and gently bounce letting your muscles relax as gravity holds the weight of your body.

  Access Note: You can do this seated, especially on a chair that has some bounce or give to it.

- **Plant Protectors:** When walking by a plant that is flowering, look closely and see if you can identify where the seed is and how it is protecting itself.

- **Automatic Responses:** Our automatic responses under pressure and relationships to power and the state (e.g., around race, class, and gender) can impact our level of comfort around saying yes, no, or maybe. Kai Cheng Thom offers a spectrum of consent: Enduring (this is hurting me, but I don't feel able to say so), Tolerating (this is something I am putting up with), Willing (this is something I am neutral about), Wanting (this makes me feel good). Spend time in reflection and/or journaling:

- When you are under stress or pressure, do you tend to move toward someone (getting close for safety, being overly nice and appeasing), away (fading into the background for safety and avoid conflict), or against (being defensive or challenging and fighting for safety)?
- Do you have more of an immediate "yes" response, or are you more likely to say no?
- Where do you often find yourself on this spectrum of consent?
- You can also refer to the Embodied Practices in chapter 1 to learn more about automatic responses and conditioned tendencies or those in chapter 3 on boundaries and extension to learn more consensual and interdependent ways of relating.

- **Containment:** ♁ ⏱ ☆ This practice can help regulate your nervous system and transition out of an activating experience. You can do this practice on yourself or invite someone else into consensual touch. Using your hands, press up and in toward your center, along the sides of your skull, shoulders, ribs, hips, and thighs. This gives your body a sense of its edges and also permission to allow any contractions for safety.

- **Co-Regulation:** ♁ ♁ ⏱ ⏱ ☆ These practices activate the social engagement system, allowing our bodies to sync with each other. Many may feel familiar just from your experience living and being in a body.
  - Mirror your partner's motions. This can be done seated or standing, with however much or little movement works for both people.
  - Sit or stand back-to-back and feel the inhalation and exhalation of your breath together.
  - Lie belly-to-belly in a circle of friends to feel the rising and falling of each other's bellies with each breath. It can help if there is play and laughter in this one!
  - Sing. Dance. Both of these done collectively are incredible practices of co-regulation that engage many systems of the body.

CHAPTER 5

Oak: Individualistic Embodiment and the Colonization of Healing

When Hurricane Katrina slammed into the Gulf Coast, almost everything lost its footing. Houses were detached from their foundations, trees and shrubbery were uprooted, sign posts and vehicles floated down the rivers that became of the streets. But amidst the whipping winds and surging water, the oak tree held its ground. How? Instead of digging its roots deep and solitary into the earth, the oak tree grows its roots wide and interlocks with other oak trees in the surrounding area. And you can't bring down a hundred oak trees bound beneath the soil! How do we survive the unnatural disasters of climate change, environmental injustice, over-policing, mass-imprisonment, militarization, economic inequality, corporate globalization and displacement? We must connect in the underground, my people! In this way, we shall survive.

—Naima Penniman

Each and every part of the oak tree is critical, not only to its own survival but also to the survival of other beings dependent on it for food, warmth, play, and connection. Oaks have a special relationship with jay birds, which spread their seeds in greater volumes and distance than squirrels do. Jays rely on the oaks for food, and the oaks rely on jays for reproduction through seed dispersal.

Oaks are the heart of many ecosystems around the world. In some regions of North America they are also a primary food source for Indigenous peoples through the dropping of their fruit: acorns. For thousands of years

Indigenous people have tended to the trees, including through controlled burns to clear out brush and encourage widely spaced trees with large canopies. Oaks have been used for food, basketry, tools, ritual, and much more. Due to the colonization of Indigenous peoples, lands, and their traditions, oaks are now endangered by invasive species, pests, disease (including Sudden Oak Death), and raging wildfires in part due to the repression of Indigenous fire practices.

The COVID-19 pandemic has been a painful reminder of what oaks and jays have known for a long time—our survival is interdependent. It has also exposed the downfalls of relying on a single person or nuclear family unit, as we have been forced into isolation in our "households." This isolation has led to breakups and breakdowns across many communities. In this time of grappling with the impacts of individualism on our bodies, I have been sitting with what I see as a transformative reckoning. One day, amid the oaks and redwoods, I wrote:

> Our bodies were not designed to survive alone. We lean on each other. Get nourishment from the soil beneath us, feed off of each other's blood, milk, sweat, and cum.

> Our bodies were not designed to survive alone. People who live through solitary confinement, who are torn from their families, isolated due to disabilities and/or chronic illness . . . all know this truth all too well.

> Our bodies, our fluids, our muscles, our tissues . . . exist because another exists. So, for those of us finding this isolation unbearable, for those of us whose bodies are telling us this is not survivable—there is wisdom there. Let's listen. Let's listen to our bodies' intolerance for isolation and start there. Dream up visions for our lives, our communities, and our movements from a place of understanding that we are inseparable.

> This is a time of contradictions. We are being told that isolation is what will keep us safe, when we know in our bones that isolation will ultimately kill us. And it already has for many. For the people in our communities experiencing acute mental health crises, incarceration, homelessness, and for everyone who is isolated from the

resources and connections we need to survive, we know this to be true. Our bodies are not meant to survive alone.

I do not know the way forward together through this time when we cannot physically gather—share a meal, hold hands, have hot queer sex—other than to cry, just as the rain falls from the sky, onto the trees and onto the forest floor. What I do know is that our bodies are wise when they tell us this isolation is unbearable.

So I sit in the forest listening. Not trying to change how I feel or talk myself out of it. And this is where I find the most comfort, in allowing the grief, fear, rage, and pain of this moment to be true and real— because it means we need each other. And that, our inseparability, the inherent interdependence of our survival, I hope we never forget.

Over the past four years, from the mass disabling impacts of the COVID-19 pandemic to the uprisings for Black lives in 2020 and to the escalation of the genocide in Gaza in 2023, we have been pushed to widen our definitions of community, to thaw from the isolation of the state and feel for our interdependence.

When I was eighteen, I was diagnosed with an aggressive strain of the Epstein-Barr virus. At the time, I thought this would be an acute case of mononucleosis, something I would heal and move on from. However, it turned out to be a long-term chronic condition much like long COVID that I still struggle with today. While my chronic illness has been the source of a lot of pain and suffering, it has also been a window into my resilience, my boundaries, and my interdependence. Building community with other sick and disabled people changed my life and how I see the world. From learning to negotiate conflicting access needs, to finding joy in the times we cannot leave our beds, I have learned some of the most important lessons about what it means to show up for your people. When the novel coronavirus hit in 2020, my community was more prepared to navigate a pandemic than the able-bodied population was. There was also overlap with nonmonogamous and queer communities in which we had already built skills of contact tracing and communication. We knew what it meant to practice boundaries, harm reduction, and consent.

The early days of the pandemic called for a shift from individualism to collectivism—to really consider each other in our decision making. It was a time that called for centering those most impacted. And it was a time that required us to notice our trauma responses and find our way back to ourselves and each other.

From my own personal experience, as well as working as a somatic practitioner throughout the pandemic, I watched many different dynamics play out. One was differences in how people were conditioned around individualism and collectivism—through our families, cultures, environments, and worldviews. The other was the dissonance between peoples conditioned tendencies—towards, away, or against (see the Embodied Practice section in chapter 1 for full descriptions). I saw that some people responded to the intensity of the pandemic by moving in closer step with the people in their homes and/or pods, spending most or all of their time together; others responded by taking more space, flying solo; and yet others were more antagonistic, focusing on the places they bumped up against others. We were bound to find dissonance. There isn't one right way to approach moments of pressure. Our approaches are rooted in our wise protection and survival strategies as well as our personalities and cultural shaping. However, we still must communicate and connect in ways that honor these tendencies while also co-regulating toward more grounded and safe ways of being connected. This is no easy task, and it is part of what we can explore through embodied theory and practice.

Conditioned tendencies of self-reliance and individualism can also show up in collective bodies, such as in social movements and healing practices. For example, mainstream environmentalism perpetuates hyper-individualism by focusing on individual acts such as recycling, getting an electric car, or other modes of what some people call "conscious capitalism." In general, there has been a tendency in US movements toward single-issue politics that fail to integrate the ways our bodies, identities, lives, and relationships are impacted by the same systems. While it can be difficult to build embodied and intellectual capacity to hold all the different intersecting struggles, individualizing struggles is a danger to our collective liberation. By isolating movements we leave each other more vulnerable to backlash and repression.

In regard to healing practices, these tendencies rear their head through the commodification and individualization of what were once held as sacred, collective, communal practices. On bulletin boards at local co-ops and cafés, poster after poster advertises one-on-one healing, usually costing an exorbitant amount of money, and massage therapy, yoga retreats, bodywork, and other spiritual healing traditions led by people outside the cultures in which they are rooted. Many of these healing modalities that have gained mainstream popularity have been stolen, appropriated, commodified, and co-opted from indigenous traditions across the world. Not only does this disrespect the peoples who developed these traditions; by taking them out of their cultural context, they lose their full dimensionality. An obvious example of cultural appropriation is in the practice of yoga in the United States. What we talk about being yoga actually references only one of the eight limbs of yoga, which, in and of itself, is only part of the layered history of yoga philosophy. The first two limbs, before you get to asanas (the physical postures) are about morals, ethics, study, and spiritual observance. Millions of white people and now entire corporations in the United States have taken what could be capitalized on and effectively diluted the tradition to an individual, physical practice. The commodification of healing has also begun to happen as the field of somatics and embodied healing have gained traction. A modality that, from the beginning, was about using our bodies as a tool for resistance has been reduced to expensive one-on-one healing sessions, graduate school programs, and culturally ungrounded practices.

When we honor the lineage of the modalities we practice, we regain the political and relational depth in which they are rooted. For those of us who are Jewish, we have our own lineages of somatics in more recent history as well as the anciently rooted traditions of embodiment such as the wrapping of tefillin (prayer boxes tied to the body with leather), immersion in a mikvah (ritual bathing), and davening (praying that can include rocking the body). While this chapter highlights the more modern Jewish legacies of somatics, this book as a whole works as an invitation for all of us to honor and recover practices that have been lost or destroyed. Whether in personal relationships, social movements, or healing lineages, the embodiment of individualism is a threat to our freedom, while historically rooted collective traditions restore our joy in connection.

Embodiment Lineage

Along with the overt impacts of colonization on indigenous lands—like the development of border walls, militarism, and policing—there are insidious ways that colonization impacts our bodies, our healing, and our movements through mechanisms of individualization. The individualization and commodification of health and healing has grown immensely in the last few decades as people continue to seek wholeness and belonging. Many people are seeking to restore that which has been fractured through colonization: connection with self, culture, lineage, and land. In the case of Jews, Zionism preys on these fractures of belonging, which further increases the need and implications for politicized healing. Rather than perpetuate harmful ways of relating to land, lineage, and life, we can restore these fractures through embodied movement building that integrates our individual and collective healing and transformation. When possible, connecting with our own lineages and cultures of healing can restore a sense of connection and interdependence.

While the term "somatics" was coined in 1972 by a white man, Thomas Hanna, many of us are working to retell the histories of embodiment to honor the foundational contributions of Black, Indigenous, Jewish, and Asian lineages, from the aikido practices taught by Morihei Ueshiba and to the meditation practices led by Charan Singh and Chögyam Trungpa Rinpoche to body work practices rooted in traditional Cherokee medicine.[1] These lineages range along a great expanse of time and place, from a traditional Chinese medicine text over four thousand years ago that referenced the art of "listening and calming [the heart]" through bodywork to the Vedas text from the 1500s in India detailing the chakra system to the twenty-first-century conception of healing justice developed by the Kindred Southern Healing Justice Collective. Generative Somatics (gs), an organization dedicated to bringing politicized somatics into social and ecological movements for justice, emerged from Generation Five (gen5), an organization dedicated to ending child sexual abuse within five generations. Generative Somatics started as an experiment in applying tools developed for personal and interpersonal healing to social movements. Practitioners and organizers from both gs and gen5 were the first to teach me about the history of somatics thanks to a living lineage document developed by Nathan Shara, Vassi Kapali (Johri), Staci Haines, MawuLisa Thomas-Adeyemo, and Elizabeth Ross.[2] I have continued to learn about many of these different histories from the Embodiment Institute's series on the lineage of Black and Brown leaders and practitioners, Marika Hendricks's work on reverence and repair for white people practicing somatics, and *Healing Justice Lineages*, by Cara Page and Erica Woodland.[3] Susan Raffo—another writer, cultural worker, and bodyworker at the intersection of healing and justice—offers a protocol for healers involving right relationship to the history of your practice, right relationship to all the people where you live, and building collective power.[4] The decolonization of the field of healing justice and somatics is ongoing and requires all of us practicing to investigate, uplift, and honor our own— and each other's—lineages.

One of the origins of the field of somatics as we know it today comes from practitioners living in Europe in the 1930s including Moshe Feldenkrais (founder of the Feldenkrais method), Elsa Gindler (somatic bodywork and sensory awareness practitioner), Laura and Fritz Perls (originators of Gestalt), and Wilhelm Reich (Freudian psychoanalyst). These practitioners had a range of relationships to Jewishness and Zionism and yet it wasn't later, when I did my own research, that I discovered all of these commonly cited innovators of somatics were Jewish. Moshe Feldenkrais emerged from his experience of European antisemitism by aligning with the Zionist movement and moving to Israel at a young age. He collaborated with the Israeli army and offered lessons in body awareness to the Israeli Prime Minister at the time, David Ben Gurion. Wilhelm Reich on the other hand, used his experience of living under a Nazi regime to show the impacts of fascism on the body, particularly around sexual repression. Reich was one of the more prominent leaders in the field of embodiment and psychoanalysis at that time, was raised by Jewish parents who, within the context of the pogroms in eastern Europe and rise of Nazism, decided not to raise their children as Jews and forbade them from speaking Yiddish. As an adult, Reich became a Marxist and part of the Freudian Left, building a more politicized version of psychoanalysis. With Hitler rising to power, Reich began to use his background in psychoanalysis to expose the underbelly of fascism. He took the political analysis formed by Karl Marx and the psychoanalysis formed by Freud to show the ways dominant ideas get engrained in the body. He talked about how muscular patters of repression (see chapter 3 on the restrictions of fascia) impede our capacity for revolutionary action and, thus, the body is a critical site for transforming social, political, and material realities. Many somatic practitioners will talk about the "shapes" we embody, which is language that originates with Reich. He worked with another prominent influencer on somatic bodywork, Elsa Gindler, who explored everyday movements such as sitting, breathing, walking, and standing to build sensory awareness. She also used her understandings to support her Jewish students who were being persecuted by the Nazi regime. Reich said: "What has to be explained is not the fact that the man who is hungry steals or the fact that the man who is exploited strikes, but why the majority of those who are hungry don't steal and why the majority of those who are exploited don't strike."[5] Through Reich's work, he began to see that the repetition of people's embodied patterns were limiting their ability to experience the world, including the ability to fight back against exploitive bosses and repressive regimes. As his practice diverged from Freudian psychoanalysis to include critiques of sexual repression, classism, and society writ large, including a book titled *The Mass Psychology of Fascism*, he was excommunicated from the field.

Reich went on to develop a nuanced healing philosophy around patterns of muscular holding. He was making a significant contribution to antiauthoritiarian healing and transformation of all oppressed peoples that the world he was living in was not prepared to accept. "The goal of sexual suppression is that of producing an individual who is adjusted to the authoritarian order and who will submit to it in spite of all misery and degradation. Initially, the child has to submit to the structure of the authoritarian miniature state, the family, which process makes it capable of later subordination to the general authoritarian system. The formation of the authoritarian structure takes place through the anchoring of sexual inhibition and anxiety."[6] In 1956 the FBI raided his institution, forced him to destroy all of his equipment, and literally placed a US flag on top of it. Later that year he was arrested for the second time by the FBI for his experiments and equipment developed to heal sexual repression, and he later died while serving a sentence in prison for violating a court order. His books were burned, and his reputation was tarnished until the social revolutions of the sixties and seventies revived his work and other politicized and embodied healing practices.[7] Around this time, revolutionary Marxist psychiatrist Frantz Fanon built on these legacies of radical psychology and wrote poignantly about the psychopathology of racism and colonization. One of Fanon's most famous quotes might be understood differently if seen through the lens of embodiment: "When we revolt it's not for a particular culture. We revolt simply because, for many reasons, we can no longer breathe."[8]

Unfortunately, with its growing popularity, somatics has not only lost connection to the Black, Indigenous, and Asian lineages it draws on, it has also lost its roots in resistance to fascism. Instead, it has developed within the context of racialized capitalism in the United States. It has become privatized, isolated, and splintered into different organizations and companies. In this vein, somatics is not only a tool for supporting movements for justice but also a movement itself in need of liberation.

By taking healing out of a social and political context, we limit possibilities for transformative collective healing. As healing modalities get co-opted and mainstreamed, they are put into tidy boxes, and the wisdom once held in our bodies and communities is sold back to us. Individualized and ahistorical healing practices are Band-Aids in a system that needs an entire overhaul. By honoring and rooting into our own lineages of dynamic, embodied, and land-based practices, we can recover a sense of safety and belonging that overhauls the confines of the state.

Destigmatization of Touch

Somatic bodywork—hands-on embodied practice—pulls from a range of different modalities, including polarity therapy, craniosacral, and Rolfing. As is true more broadly with the field of somatics, these modalities draw on Black, Indigenous, and Asian healing traditions.[9] At its core, somatic bodywork is organized around healing and releasing what are referred to as "armoring bands": common places that muscles and tissues contract. Armoring bands mirror what has already been shown through traditions around the world, such as the chakra system (India), the meridian system (China), and Yoruba healing traditions (Nigeria, Togo, and Benin). On Turtle Island, bodywork approaches draw from many Indigenous traditions. The Shawnee bodywork practices inspired American osteopathy and later, craniosacral therapy as one of their originators, A.T. Still (who himself had Lumbee ancestors), served as the Shawnees physician for over twenty years.[10] Zuni practices focused on setting the neck and spine become popularized as chiropractic medicine, and the Hopi word *hakomi*, which translates to "where do you stand in relation to these many realms?," was used to popularize hakomi massage (a mindfulness-based somatic approach developed by white men and rooted in Buddhist and Taoist practice).[11] Any bodyworker today should seek to honor these lineages and be in right relationship with the ancestors and elders of the healing traditions we practice. This is a critical part of decolonizing our relationships to healing and touch.

One thing you will notice in most, if not all, of these traditional healing modalities is the integration of mind, body, and spirit—these connections are otherwise typically separated and disregarded by modern Western medicine. "Soma" comes from a Greek root word for body and refers to the living organism or body in its wholeness. Somatic bodywork reaffirms this inseparability and is a powerful way to work with tissues around issues of attachment, boundaries, and other internal states.[12] There are many kinds of bodywork that hold potential for healing, but somatic bodywork is distinct in its commitment to addressing the root of what is causing the body to contract, feel pain, or numbness in the first place. Through the repression and colonization of Indigenous healing traditions, the connection between our bodily ailments and our emotional, spiritual, and mental health was lost. In today's realm of bodywork in the United States, people most commonly seek out different variations of deep tissue massages. At times, especially with a good practitioner, this can be a great fit and allow the muscular system to heal and restore. Often, however, this kind of muscular manipulation stems from a framework of someone else being able to remove pain from our bodies without our participation. The issue is that when it comes to the impacts of stress and trauma on the body, our muscles will often just go right back to contracting if we don't address the root cause of why they are tight to begin with. In cases where the practitioner isn't able to be present with the unraveling of trauma in their client's body, it can actually solidify the contraction, as the client's experience of feeling isolated and unsafe is reified. Somatic bodywork and other trauma-centered healing offers space for our bodies to unwind, move through, and resolve the traumas stored in our tissues. For example, when we stretch the eyes, widening our gaze to include places that our eye muscles have been trained to skip over, we reengage both hemispheres of the brain and open our entire somas to healing. Through mindful touch and following the body's natural impulse to move and heal, we can access generations of embodied histories and allow whatever part of us felt unseen, alone, and unsafe to be held and restored.

From a neurological perspective, bringing open, compassionate, and curious attention to our muscles engages our prefrontal cortex and limbic system, soothes our autonomic nervous system, relaxes the midbrain, and shifts neurotransmitters and hormones from chemicals of danger to those of safety in connection. Every part of our neural system is impacted by simply offering present and attentive touch. Through the professionalization of mental health services, we often lose the use of touch as a critical component of healing. Due to licensing, insurance, and liability issues, mental health professionals are specifically prohibited from using touch for the sake of protecting clients and preventing sexual assault or otherwise taking advantage of a vulnerable power dynamic. While this kind of protection is absolutely necessary, it is enforced in a fear-based way that eliminates the possibility for transformative healing touch. Beyond the importance of touch in a therapeutic relationship, we know that touch is vital to our survival. Studies have shown that without enough touch, infants don't develop properly, and in some cases this lack of touch is correlated with infant fatality.[13]

White Eurocentric societies relegate touch to sexual acts meant only for a married man and woman. Dr. Ken Cooper conducted a study on how frequently people spontaneously touch each other over the course of an hour-long conversation in different countries, and the results were: Puerto Rico, 180; Paris, 110; Florida, 2; London, 0.[14] I believe this rigid orientation, not touching others, is rooted in shame produced by Christian hegemony and the colonization of our bodies. Throughout time and place, Christianity has been an evangelical and colonial religious practice that instills shame of people's own bodies through the idea of sin. A potent example of this is in the Christian boarding schools set up in Native communities where—as Indigenous scholar Chris Finley describes— sexual shame took root. Fundamentalist Christianity purports that God is a disembodied, untouchable spirit, condemns self-touch/masturbation, and enforces a standard of purity on people's bodies. In addition, Christianity and Western society's emphasis on chastity, fidelity and the criminalization of sodomy has instilled in our bodies the message that our desires are sinful and shameful. This message is then reified through the state with anti-queer and anti-trans legislation and the criminalization of extramarital affairs (in some states), abortions (many states), and sex work. These religious and political practices have seeded a culture that is largely disconnected from embodied touch. There is good reason to have boundaries around touch given they ways it can become exploitative or violating. Unfortunately, without a proactive culture of consent, centered boundaries, and sex-positivity, shame can stand in the way of choice-full relationships to touch. Shame creates a breeding ground for harm, as people don't feel able to ask for and receive the kind of pleasurable, healing, or otherwise connecting touch they desire. Depending on someone's shaping, they may respond to harm by internalizing this shame rather than projecting it, making them feel unworthy, depressed, and/or isolated. These ongoing unmet needs combined with exertions of power and toxic masculinity create a rape culture that inhibits everyone's ability to access safe touch.

The trauma of nonconsensual touch lives in our bodies, as does the potential for healing through touch. Within our experiences of touch lies a full spectrum: from violating experiences of assault to pleasurable experiences of connection. This spectrum covers a range of different qualities of touch that our bodies pick up on. We can recall the feeling of a doctor's cold hands or latex gloves—the poking and prodding of medicalized touch—or being searched and patted down by airport security. Some of us may remember the likes of being told "you have to hug our uncle," even after we repeatedly said no. Throughout our days we experience these different qualities of touch. Through the destigmatization of touch we can restore access to healing through touch.

Deconstructing Self-Care

> If we let ourselves be caught up in the discussion of self-care we are missing the whole point of Healing Justice (HJ) work. . . . Too often self-care in our organizational cultures gets translated to our individual responsibility to leave work early, go home—alone—and go take a bath, go to the gym, eat some food and go to sleep. So we do all of that "self-care" to return to organizational cultures where we reproduce the systems we are trying to break.
>
> —Yashna Maya Padamsee

The capitalist conception of commodified and individualized healing and self-care is based on the consumption of self-care products and experiences formulated with the purpose of preserving oneself so that one can produce more. Because of this, class plays a big role in how people are or are not able to access care. People working nonprofit jobs might be encouraged to take a spa trip on their day off, largely because employers want their employees to be rejuvenated when they return to their cubicles. Many tech start-ups are offering what seem like incredible benefits, such as endless buffets of food, showers, yoga rooms, and child care—but all of this is done to keep workers at the office for longer hours and continually situate their jobs as the center of their lives. To add insult to injury, this is only done for "higher-up" employees and is not extended to service workers such as janitors, who keep these tech facilities clean. Those of us who are middle-class and professional workers—along with people in the owning class—are afforded these shallow means of self-care, while poor and working-class people are pushed to work long hours, often without any benefits and breaks, and with limited access to time off for any kind of self-care. In *Care Work*, Leah Lakshmi Piepzna-Samarasinha writes about poor- and working-class-led models of "sustainable hustling for liberation."[15] She problematizes the romanticization of poor people as such hard workers in ways that perpetuate the idea that certain bodies do not need care.

Systems of oppression take away our ability to recognize dignity and love in ourselves and each other. It is the job of the healing industrial complex (also made up of people working for corporations trying to make money) to sell dignity and love back to us in a way that looks just enough like the real thing to keep us complacent while they maintain structures of privilege and power. In social justice movements, these patterns are replicated with the glorification of "busy," a constant state of panic, and the pace of urgency that leaves people behind, especially disabled folks, poor people, and parents. In some cases, this urgency reflects a survival response frozen in a time when our material conditions left us with impossible choices. Through my years doing political organizing I saw this overdrive survival embodied in many of our leaders. This makes sense, given that many of us arrive in movements because of our experiences of harm and oppression. We have to remember that we are fighting for a new way, and in order to do that we have to start by practicing something new: in our bodies and with our comrades.

Extractive and exploitive systems can also become embodied and shape our personal relationships, including how we receive and give care. Even when we consciously want to be offering ourselves to our loved ones, contractions in the body due to trauma and oppression can cut off our capacity for mutual connection in a way that ultimately perpetuates individualism and maintains existing structures of power. In organizers, providers, and practitioners, one way this shows up is in a deep contraction or shrinking around scarcity, feeling like there isn't enough time, space, or energy. The healing industrial complex confines our healing relationships to brief blocks of time, including the standard fifty-minute therapy session, which often does not allow for a more organic and expansive process to unfold, and the ten-minute doctor appointment to talk about sexual health. Overall, this feeling of scarcity can lead to hoarding resources and a lack of generosity. I have seen this translate into overstating frameworks around emotional labor to include *any* time emotional support is being offered. Can we make space for mutual aid and collective care that isn't cynically categorized as a kind of extractive labor? This requires an embodied understanding of interdependence. When I am watching my cats clean each other, I know that they aren't thinking of it as labor. They understand in an embodied—not intellectual—way. Caring for each other is essential to their survival, so they extend that care freely, knowing they will receive what they need in return, even if not in that moment. The radical Jewish philosopher Rabbi Abraham Joshua Heschel makes the important distinction between "laboring" and "toiling." In this framework, "toiling" implies some kind of struggle or even suffering, while "labor" is simply that which makes our relationships with our bodies, each other, and the land possible. This distinction is important: we have to be able to care and show up for each other without keeping an extractive bank log of debt. We must see the longer arc of mutuality as we widen into a framework of collective care.

Unfortunately, practices of "self-care" are prone to lead people into a state of dissociation. Self-care can become performative and prescriptive. Rather than practice building presence and capacity to be with what is alive in our bodies and communities, we seek distractions and coping mechanisms. This is not to say that we don't need breaks or time away from the relentless onslaught of information and violence. But isolating oneself to dissociate is different from creating space for oneself to rest, feel, and heal as part of a broader community. That said, either can be done in a more choiceful or centered way. In 2023, as the ethnic cleansing and genocide in Gaza escalated, many organizers were going all out: staying up all night, going to actions every day, and struggling to meet basic needs like sleeping and eating. We knew this wouldn't be sustainable and that even if we wholeheartedly tried to override our bodies' needs, they would eventually catch up to us. We had all heard the saying "It's a marathon, not a sprint," and we needed to remember that, but the suggestion still sits within an individualistic framework and doesn't account for the acute moments when sprinting is required. What we began to practice was rooted more in collectivity. When we believe and feel ourselves as a part of a collective body, then we know that if we have to slow down or take a break, someone else will be there to make the signs, block the bridge, call Congress members, or otherwise organize for an end to war and all forms of violence. Just like dolphins and whales take turns shutting off different parts of their brain so they can rest while still protecting against predators, we can allow different parts of our collective body to rest while the other parts stay vigilant in protecting our people.

In *Self as Other: Reflections on Self-Care*, CrimethInc. asks, "Who is working so you can rest?" This complicated question is posed as an important challenge to self-care, but in another way it could be legitimate to ask this in a positive framework of collective responsibility. It perhaps presents rest as a luxury rather than as a necessity and shames people for their needs, but it might also be seen as a deeply important inquiry, particularly for those of us with wealth inherited at the expense of oppressed people's labor. It complicates an extractive care narrative in which certain people are afforded the opportunity to rest and receive care while other people are expected to provide that care. Conventional notions of self-care ignore the reality that for many people, caring for themselves requires caring for another. Many of us cannot suspend commitments to family, community, or movement and take ourselves out for self-care. Black and Brown people in particular are expected to make white people feel comfortable as we are still living in the embodiment of white supremacy and, in many ways, the embodiment of slavery. In the care model of the healing industrial complex, only certain people have access to healing, and this is largely centered around gender, race, and class. Projects like the Nap Ministry are working to change this through the commitment to Black rest as resistance. Self-care and mutual aid are truly inseparable, as the branch of our nervous system related to social engagement is what keeps us calm and regulated.

In Jewish tradition we practice rest each week on Shabbat, sundown Friday to sundown Saturday. There are a range of practices from nonobservance to saying the blessings before Shabbat dinner to being fully shomer Shabbat. "Shomer Shabbat" generally refers to following a range of halakha (Jewish law), such as refraining from writing, handling money, operating vehicles, cooking, gardening, or using anything with electricity from dusk on Friday until three stars appear in the night sky on Saturday. My Shabbat practice growing up was to have a special dinner every week: a time to feast, rest, recline, and get deep into conversation. We often joked about how often my mom used the phrase "the way you are in the world." Like, "of course you helped your friend move this week, because that's the way you are in the world"; or, "Of course you found beauty amidst your struggles, because that's the way you are in the world." I see this now as an invitation to embodiment of the world to come, Olam Ha-ba. As an adult, I have rekindled a connection to my Shabbat practice, which now includes turning my phone off to quiet external demands and practice self-responsiveness. Shabbat is a time for me to listen to my body and follow its longings. On Saturday mornings I bathe, either in the tub or in the Eno River near my house, giving myself a mikvah, a ritual cleansing to release and begin again. Sometimes I go dancing, sometimes I stay in bed all day, sometimes I adventure with a friend. For me, it is about leading with ease and pleasure in a world that otherwise asks us to override our embodied desires. Shabbat is a practice of *olam ha-ba*, the world to come—a world where we all get to rest in the abundance of the earth and each other. Rabbi Abraham Joshua Heschel describes this in *The Sabbath:*

> To set apart one day a week for freedom, a day on which we would not use the instruments which have been so easily turned into weapons of destruction, a day for being with ourselves, a day of detachment from the vulgar, of independence of external obligations, a day on which we stop worshipping the idols of technical civilization, a day on which we use no money, a day of armistice in the economic struggle with our fellow [people] and the forces of nature—is there any institution that holds out a greater hope for [people's] progress than the Sabbath?[16]

One of the blessings said on Shabbat reminds us that resting on that day is for *all of us*. In practice, most families need help—whether it's attending to the sheep that happened to give birth on Shabbat or heating up the food they prepared the day before. This is where the idea of the Shabbas goy comes in. The Shabbos goy refers to the non-Jew who works for us so we can rest. In many places, this is a beautiful example of diasporic interdependence, so when the goy needs rest, we reciprocate. In other times, this dynamic has been exploited in a one-directional manner rooted in classism, where Jews pay people to serve them during Shabbat. So how do we live into Olam Ha-ba, the world to come? How do we cultivate a world in which rest is available to all of us, not a scarce resource only afforded to the rich? How do we build a culture that transforms self-care into collective care?

The Myth of Self-Reliance

Self-reliance can be an incredible survival strategy, particularly in cases of developmental trauma or other scenarios where we are left without the resources or care we need to survive. However, when left unexamined, self-reliance can become habitual and impede our ability to build community. As the youngest of three, I grew up with a lot of independence; both of my parents worked full-time, and at that point their parenting was more hands-off. When my sisters and I grew out of sharing a room, my parents proposed that one of us move to the room in the basement. My older sisters were too spooked, but I jumped at the opportunity—at the young age of seven—to live in the basement entirely separate from the rest of my family. Throughout the years, I continued to foster my independence. I dropped out of high school and got my diploma through the public independent study program, and I traveled internationally for six months on my own at age eighteen. I made my own way. While I am deeply grateful for these opportunities, I also recognize how I was continually shaped to be able to fulfill all my own needs, to make things happen on my own. Today, as an adult, I still catch myself falling into this tendency—never fully leaning on anyone else, building relationships in which I bury my own needs to make room for others, assuming that in order for anything to get done, I have to do it on my own. This myth of being self-reliant has prevented me from having the kind of symbiotic relationships I long for. Class has also shaped this for me; as my family's wealth has grown in our lifetimes, we increasingly relied more on paid services and less on our community. From child care to rides to the airport, we learned to rely on our pockets and not on each other. Many children raised in the dominant culture in the United States are rewarded for being self-reliant—taught to meet their own needs and desires or to export or repress them. This is a twisted mentality in which people's bodies are repressed and then shamed for having needs related to the impacts of this repression.

The repression of individualism occurs not only within our borders but also internationally, as US imperialism and globalization strip away other nations' self-determination and subsequently punish and control them. Border imperialism and capitalism make us increasingly depend on institutions and systems of production while simultaneously isolating us from each other and interrupting systems of collective care. We have come to rely on the systems that repress us rather than being able to care for each other. Somatically, whether internally or internationally, this can show up as a narrowing of the eyes, unable to take in more of the possibilities around us; or a caving in of the shoulders, closing off our vulnerability to protect against disappointment rather than taking the risk to ask for what we need.

Concepts of care are also embedded in the heteropatriarchal exploitation of women and femmes' bodies. Women (whether or not they identify as such) are expected to take care of the children, without receiving wages or compensation, while men work for wages to take care of their wives and children who are thus entirely dependent on them. However, it is not even the husbands that they are depending on, it is their bosses—it is capitalism. In this narrative, queer and trans lives are pushed to the margins making financial sustainability particularly difficult for people outside of the heteropatriarchal nuclear family norm.

Women's roles expanding out of the home and into the workplace has only increased the level of responsibility. Capitalism's success depends on mothers and wives (of any gender) doing all of the reproductive and emotional labor, both at home and—thanks to second-wave feminism—in the workplace. This includes certain types of feminized labor, such as secretarial work, nursing, feeding, and teaching. Women are facing sexism and sexual harassment in the workplace, unequal pay, and inadequate maternal leave. The embodiment of the second-wave-feminist-empowered woman can do it all: take care of the kids, work a 9–5 job, and still be home in time to cook dinner for her husband. Women continue to be trapped at the intersections of capitalism and sexism, making possibilities for healing and care extremely limited.

Outside of the care that is expected and assumed from women and other caregivers, when people more heavily rely on each other it is frowned on or labeled as needy or codependent. One example is the US cultural myth that becoming an adult means leaving your family and being able to entirely sustain yourself and only yourself until you reproduce, get a white picket fence, and start the cycle all over again. In cases where people are still living with their families, taking care of elders, nieces, et cetera, there is often judgment largely based on racism and classism. Similarly, living in queer collective homes for all of my adult life, I have received judgment around not being independent, even though straight couples are not questioned for their choices to live as a family. Anything that strays from the nuclear family will meet significant barriers. This is because the state depends on the self-reliant, heterosexist, individualistic nuclear family.

Embodying Mutual Aid through Joint Struggle

> The history of disabled queer and trans people has continually been one of creative problem-solving within a society that refuses to center our needs. If we can build an intersectional climate

> justice movement—one that incorporates disability justice, that centers disabled people of color and queer and gender noncon-forming folks with disabilities—our species might have a chance to survive.
>
> —Patty Berne and Vanessa Raditz

The dominant culture of the state is one of disconnection and misuse of power. These fractures can show up in how we treat our bodies as disparate systems as well as how we conceive of our movements as separate. Many physicians trained in the US medical system lack understanding of the role of the nervous system in regulating our organs and the rest of our body. Porges writes, "The neural regulation of the old subdiaphragmatic vagus could be involved in several physical health symptoms that are frequently comorbid with trauma, such as irritable bowel syndrome, fibromyalgia, obesity, and other gut issues."[17] These conditions disproportionately impact trauma survivors and people with chronic mental health struggles. They are often addressed by doctors who reduce the physical symptoms to being psychosomatic and send the patient to therapy. Although many conditions are connected to our thoughts and emotions and can be healed this way, mainstream medicine often misses the point: these are real nervous system conditions impacting multiple organs and systems in the body. To make up for this bias in the medical industrial complex, sick and disabled people have found ways of making our own medicine and taking care of each other through what some might call mutual aid.

The concepts and practices of mutual aid are a radical counter to individualism and the dependence on institutions, nonprofit agencies, and corporations for getting our needs met. Dean Spade, author, professor, and part of a Seattle-based group called the Big Door Brigade, writes, "Mutual aid is a term to describe people giving each other needed material support, trying to resist the control dynamics, hierarchies and system-affirming, oppressive arrangements of charity and social services. Mutual aid projects are a form of political participation in which people take responsibility for caring for one another and changing political conditions, not just through symbolic acts or putting pressure on their representatives in government, but by actually building new social relations that are more survivable."[18]

Mutual aid is one of many ways we can build interdependence and take the state out of our care practices. Rather than depending on oppressive systems, mutual aid depends on building intersectional movements and interdependent relationships over time. Mia Mingus, a prominent disability justice activist, talks about a form of mutual aid in sick and disabled communities as "access intimacy." This sort of framework takes away the savior complex and allow for a more symbiotic and embodied form of support. While at times building these systems of support is not a choice but rather a necessity, there is a lot of power and possibility in integrating mutual aid into our lives. Black and Brown, disabled, and queer and trans communities have had to develop alternatives to policing and ways to respond to crisis that don't create further harm. It was these communities, particularly Black women, who identified the need for sophisticated and accessible systems of care to address community violence and meet people's basic needs without engaging the state. It is out of practical necessity, not lofty ideals, that mutual aid and transformative justice have sprung. The Underground Railroad, which provided food and shelter to people escaping enslavement; the Black Panthers and their community safety work, education, and food distribution in Oakland and across the United States; Black cooperative economics in the segregated South, where relying on the state for safety was not an option; the Janes providing safe abortion access in the 1960s; informal loan clubs in Mexico (tanda), and Africa (asue or susu); and community-based medical professionals in Gaza operating with limited to nonexistent infrastructure are all examples. Some of these are understood as forms of mutual aid, others are called something else, but all of these communities have built practices and systems for showing up for each other's safety and well-being. The practices of mutual aid invite us to follow the lead of frontline communities toward creative interventions in seeking justice and liberation.

In connection with mutual aid, different movements have grown and supported each other as they fought to expand rights and transform culture. Black and Palestinian solidarity around state violence, the interweaving of queer and feminist theory, and the connections made between immigrants and climate justice, none of these would be the same without the others. Another movement, one that relates directly to the politics of the body, is disability justice, which profoundly challenges individualism and the hyper-focus on productivity in capitalism. For example, the concept of "pods" developed by Mia Mingus and the Bay Area Transformative Justice Collective originated as an expansion of how we think about community as rooted in abolitionism and disability justice. A pod is a network of people we can turn to in the event of violent, harmful, and/or abusive experiences to support safety, accountability, transformation, healing, and collective resilience. The term "pod" and the practices that go along with it then came to be used by people across many walks of life during the COVID-19 pandemic as a way of navigating contagion, consent, and communication. Because of the interconnections between these movements, many of us had access to community practices of care that accounted for the variations of vulnerability and risk in different populations. At its core, disability justice complicates the ways we think about bodies and what makes a body worthy of belonging—it invites us into a decolonized framework around the embodiment of care. As was illuminated through the economic devastation of the pandemic, capitalism ties our worthiness and belonging to our productivity. Disability justice subverts capitalism by honoring differently abled bodies and deconstructing the notion that these bodies don't belong and need to be fixed, cured, or made better in some way. Mingus talks about "stretching," meaning that there are times when we must reach beyond our boundaries to support someone in meeting their needs. She says that, particularly in sick and disabled communities, we have to learn to stretch for each other: interdependency is not optional. She notes that systems of oppression are built on ableism: "Ableism set the stage for queer and trans people to be institutionalized as mentally disabled; for communities of color to be understood as less capable, smart and intelligent, therefore 'naturally' fit for slave labor; for women's bodies to be used to produce children, when, where and how men needed them; for people with disabilities to be seen as 'disposable' in a capitalist and exploitive culture because we are not seen as 'productive'; for immigrants to be thought of as a 'disease' that we must 'cure' because it is 'weakening' our country."[19] If we want to dismantle oppression, we must recognize the interdependence of our bodies and our movements. This is a powerful contrast to even some of the ways that alternative cultures or countercultures talk about boundaries and having to take care of ourselves before caring for others. While I agree that we cannot show up well for other people when we aren't taking care of ourselves, I think these kind of sentiments create a false binary and reinforce individualized ideas of self-care. Instead, we can call on the legacies of intersectionality and joint struggle to remember that the more we weave our webs of connection in our own bodies as well as our movements, the more powerful we are in the face of state violence. As German pastor Martin Niemöller spoke about in regard to his own early complicity in Nazism and his eventual change of heart:

> First they came for the socialists, and I did not speak out—because I was not a socialist.
> Then they came for the trade unionists, and I did not speak out—because I was not a trade unionist.
> Then they came for the Jews, and I did not speak out—because I was not a Jew.
> Then they came for me—and there was no one left to speak for me.

Politicized Healing

Along with being heavily shaped by systems of trauma and oppression, our bodies have the tools, skills, and magic to heal and transform these patterns in ourselves and our relationships. Embodied healing offers a pathway for unraveling contractions, unlearning individualism, and returning to what our bodies know best: embodied mutual connection.

Healing justice—the theory and practice popularized by Cara Page and the Kindred Southern Healing Justice Collective—is rooted in histories of Black and Indigenous feminist healing traditions and builds on practices that keep communities surviving and thriving in the face of violence. Kindred defines healing justice as a political strategy "to intervene and respond on generational trauma and systemic oppression, and build community/survivor led responses rooted in southern traditions of resiliency to sustain our emotional/physical/spiritual/psychic and environmental well being."[20] Holding historical, social, and political context is critical to healing. When we can see the ways we are shaped by our relationships and environments, we can build new pathways that will remain open, not only inside a therapy office but also when we move out into the world. Given that oppression is traumatizing, to challenge oppression we must also heal our trauma. The split between healing and political organizing actually perpetuates oppression. Many of us have experienced fractures within organizing: calling each other out and fighting over already scarce resources. Often these splits take place around issues of safety and belonging and reopen old wounds that haven't fully healed. As mentioned, one way this shows up in movements is in a constant sense of urgency. Most likely what we are fighting for is urgent, like stopping the construction of a new jail or campaigns against the colonization of

Palestine. However, the email being sent today rather than tomorrow is probably not as urgent as we make it out to be. This sense of needing to rush harms our nervous systems and our bodily well-being, and it also tends to lead to mistakes or even harm. Witnessing people who are fighting for liberation turn on each other and perpetuate oppressive behavior is heartbreaking, but also understandable given that we live inside of these systems and thus are bound to reenact them. But we do have some agency, and somatics can be a useful tool and practice. We can build in more choices so that rather than reacting from urgency, a place of trauma, and fight or flight, we can recenter in our safety, dignity, and belonging. We can feel our connections and refocus on the bigger picture of what we are fighting for. Even when I am working with a client one on one, I am investing not only in their own healing but in their movement role and their commitment to justice. When we are able to recenter on our personal and political commitments, we can make better choices that result in deeper connection with ourselves and our communities. In order to do this, we have to reintegrate what for many movements has always been true: healing is part of liberation.

Rather than being separate or re-traumatizing, organizing can be a source of healing in and of itself. Engaging in political organizing can often create a deeper sense of community and hope for a better future. So many of our traumas are around being neglected or harmed, so regenerating nurturing connection in political community can help heal that trauma. Many people come to movement spaces seeking healing. People who have been marginalized by society can find home in a political space that doesn't just tolerate their existence but celebrates it. The unfortunate side of this is when people seeking healing end up being re-traumatized, as folks act out their unresolved trauma on each other. In the U.S. movement for Palestine I have experienced this full range: from turning against each other (in ways that reify the exploitation of power and weaken our movements) to profound healing in action. Over the years, during calls to action regarding settler violence in the West Bank, the repression of BDS activism, and the war on Gaza, we have gathered as comrades, friends, and loved ones to move our grief and rage into action. The most powerful campaigns I have participated in were not symbolic or performative—they were direct and raw with emotion. We cannot let these emotions be relegated to therapy rooms. We must take them into the streets where we weep, yell, and demand better conditions for everyone. The movement for Palestine has taught me to feel more deeply than ever, to stay connected to something bigger than life itself, and to never lose hope—because every life is sacred.

Embodied practices in a politicized framework offer a new way of being in our bodies and with each other. I believe that when we engage with these practices consistently, and over time, we begin to create the kind of culture that can hold our full selves and more lovingly and effectively fight for liberation. When trauma is collective, the healing must be collective. When trauma is politicized, the healing must be politicized.

In creating liberatory spaces, we can start to get a sense of what liberation feels like in our bodies and use that as a compass for what we are striving toward. I find this to be a powerful demonstration of how we can use our bodies as tools for generating visions of justice. The field of healing justice is already being reduced to a one-on-one, self-care practice: people seeking out healing justice practitioners. The idea that you cannot participate in political movements *and* take care of yourself but instead have to remove yourself for self-care is deeply problematic and rooted in patriarchy, ableism, and racism. While taking yourself out may be what is needed at times, we need to create organizing cultures in which our healing is valued as part of our organizing. I have watched so many people burn out and leave the movement or stay in beyond their capacity and effectivity. We want to be able to choose to stay in movements for liberation while also attending to what needs healing. In this way, we are de-individualizing healing, and self-care becomes collective care. We do what we need to do to survive the day-to-day while also fighting for a radically different future in which we are liberated from the systems that oppress us, traumatize us, poison us, and otherwise inflict harm on our bodies. We need healing justice to be a part of our commitment to transforming from a culture of consumption, extraction, and destruction to one of regeneration, healing, and connection.

Embodied Practices

"Caring for myself is not self-indulgence, it is self-preservation and that is an act of political warfare."

—Audre Lorde

You are invited to engage with these practices when the time is right for you and at your own pace. With everything, practice consent, self-responsiveness, accessibility, and mutual care. These practices are intended as applied learning and transformation–before entering, read through the content of the preceding chapter to better land the social, political, and/or ecological relevance of these practices. Also, you will need to refer to the author's note at the beginning–A Guide to Embodied Practice and Lineage–for a more comprehensive orientation and key to symbols.

- **Healing through Touch:** ♁ ☉ ☉ ☉ ☆ ☆ There are many different forms of bodywork that support the release of trauma and nervous system regulation. Somatic bodywork is heavily informed by practices like craniosacral therapy, Rolfing, and polarity therapy. If you don't have access to a practitioner or would prefer to practice alone, you can explore your different armoring bands using attentive touch around the eyes, jaw, throat, chest, diaphragm, abdomen, pelvis, thighs, lower legs, and feet (see Embodied Practices in chapter 2). Notice what areas are more contracted or expanded, where there is more sensation or numbness, or other ways of sensing and feeling in your body.*

- **The Machine/Image Theater:** ♁ ♁ ♁ ☉ ☉ ☉ ☆ ☆ This practice invites creative and embodied ways of knowing to deconstruct systems of oppression. In a group, determine who will be the spectators and who will be the actors. Invite the actors to create a static sculpture with their bodies, representing the medical industrial complex. This could represent different dynamics, roles, scenarios, and/or how your body feels inside that system. Now have the actors to move in relationship with each other, sculpting a moving, dynamic image. Then invite the actors to slowly shift their bodies out of that shape and into the shape of healing justice. Try not to use shortcuts—really get curious about what it takes to shift from one shape to the other. Once you have arrived at the new image, turn to the spectators for reflections and feedback. Do this for a couple of rounds, slowly shifting from the medical industrial complex to healing justice. Debrief together about what you learned from your embodied sensations and movements about just transitions. You can also choose other themes and systems to work with, like shifting from the shapes of self-care to collective care.

- **Centering:** ☖ ☉ ☆ We center to make more room for our feelings and sensations, just as they are, and to align our bodies and actions with what we care about. We can center in anything: rage, joy, grief, pleasure, et cetera. We do not center to settle our systems or become more complacent in our conditions. This is also why we practice centering with our eyes open: to build the capacity to simultaneously be present with ourselves and our social and ecological surroundings. To practice, tune in to decide if you want to be seated, standing, or lying down, and settle into whatever position you choose.

  1. Begin to bring your attention deeper into your body and sensations. You can do this through movement, breath, and attention. Notice temperatures, pressure, contraction, movement, numbness, et cetera. Let your focus move from thinking to feeling and other sensing. Before centering on purpose, just notice where you are without trying to change or override it. Remember, we center to be present, open, connected, and on purpose.

  2. Now bring your attention to your center of gravity. You can place a hand there if you like. For some people this is just below the belly button. We center in multiple dimensions, so center can be thought of as length, width, and depth. Or we can look to our bodies as we do the shaking of the lulav (date palm frond) on Sukkot, moving in the cardinal directions: length being above and below, width being east and west, depth being north and south, and center being center! Take your time moving through each of these dimensions, with movement, breath, attention, and touch. Feel free to get creative and add in your own ways of connecting to each dimension. Track your physical experience as well as the spiritual connection with each dimension as follows.

  3. Length represents our relationship to dignity. Let gravity be heavy as you drop your weight down toward the earth and lengthen toward the sky at the same time. Allow more space between the vertebrae of your spine. Center in your length.

  4. Width is our capacity for mutual connection and boundaries. Again, from center, fill into your width or from side to side. Feel

your sensations and fill out from shoulder to shoulder, hip to hip. Feel your left and right sides and everything in between. Find your right-sized width, where you can take up the space you need and also make room for others. Center in your width.

5. Depth is our relationship to time, space, and ancestry. Feel yourself from back to front. Feel all along your back body, including the backs of your thighs, your butt cheeks, and your upper and lower back, all the way through the back of your skull. Then find the aliveness inside your body: your breath, digestion, and heartbeat. Now fill into your front side; maybe feel the clothes on the front of your body, the muscles in your face, chest, and belly. Feel for our descendants and what is ahead, the known and unknown futures. Center in your depth.

6. Finally we will come directly into our centers and feel for what we care about and what we are committed to. Centering in length, width, and depth, say your commitment to yourself. If you are unsure about what that is, or if it is changing, from a centered place, ask yourself: "What matters to me?" "Who or what do I love?" "What do I long for?" Let your commitment fill you. Let it inform your nervous system. We are practicing embodying our commitments so we can act from them.

7. Mood check: If you are alone, check in to feel for your mood and take a note of it. If you are with others, go around and have folks say one or two words about their mood in the moment. We do this to recognize and broaden our range of emotions, to be revealing with each other, to learn how to shift our mood when we need to, and to align with what we care about.

- **Collective Centering:** ♙ ♙ ⏱ ⏱ ☆ Practice centering (as above), with two or more people. Take turns leading the different dimensions: one person does length, another does width, another does depth, and another does center. Use your own embodied experience as a reference point as you lead. For example, you might say: "As I feel into my length and dignity, I can feel my feet sinking into the floor." At the end for your mood check, share two different parts of what surfaced in the following format: "There is a part of me that feels _____. There is another part of me that feels _____."

- **Mutual Connection:** This practice helps us listen and speak from center, from our whole body up and, not just from our brains or saying what we think we should say. It taps into a deeper knowledge and wider listening. Before beginning the practice, partners should decide whether they want to practice with touch or instead with energy. If a partner chooses touch, ask if palm on their heart or upper chest is okay or whether they prefer touch on the shoulder. If you choose touch, try it out before you begin. Then decide on two questions. The first question (referred to as "Question 1" below) could be, for example: "What do you care about?" Or "What are you fighting for? Or "What is transforming in you?" The second question ("Question 2" below) could build on the first one. I like to have the second one simply be "Why?" Even though you know the questions in advance, instead of thinking of the answer, allow yourself to go through the steps below to listen from a deeper place of knowing.

  1. Partner A and Partner B sit or stand facing each other about arm's distance apart.
  2. Both partners sit or stand with one leg in front of the other for a secure base.
  3. Both partners take a moment to center together by grounding their feet, deepening their breath, and doing whatever else helps you become present and connected.
  4. Partner A extends their arm (or energy)
  - Their arm extends toward the other person's heart (or shoulder). With consent, you can make contact.
  - Partner A's arm is extended, and their elbow is relaxed and pointed toward the floor.
  - Partner A's full palm is on Partner B's sternum, with fingers facing toward the outside of their body.
  - If Partner A's palm is on Partner B's shoulder, it is cupped on the outer edge (not top) of the shoulder.
  - Partner A checks in with Partner B: is pressure and contact okay?
  - Partner B answers or otherwise helps any adjustments to touch.
  - With time and practice this becomes smoother and more natural.

5. With your centers facing each other, partner A asks Question 1.

6. Partner B responds using their embodied cues to speak differently than they might otherwise respond just using their thoughts. This often requires slowing down.

7. Partner A listens from their center without verbal comment, letting their body and presence show listening and understanding.

8. When Partner B finishes, partner A releases their hand (or energy), and both partners switch their foot stance as well.

9. Partner A extends their other arm (or energy) on the same side as the new foot in front. Their arm extends toward the other person's heart (or shoulder). With consent, you can make contact. Partner A's arm is extended, and their elbow is relaxed.

10. With your centers facing each other, partner A asks Question 2.

11. Partner B responds using their embodied cues.

12. Partner A listens from center without comment.

13. When Partner B finishes, partner A releases their hand (or energy), and each partner switches their foot position.

14. Repeat steps 3–11 with Partner B asking the question and Partner A responding.

15. Share with each other how was it to listen and respond from the body. Were you surprised about your answer?

Access note: You do not have to make contact during this practice. Extending your energy can be as powerful as touch. You can choose to extend energy with your arm raised and no contact—or remaining center to center, with arms at your sides. Another variation is to practice with each person touching their own heart or chest for each round as asker and answerer. This is also a great adaptation if you do this practice on a video call.

CHAPTER 6

Mycelia: Collective Care

The connection between mycelia and plants is the oldest-known rela-
tionship that has evolved to bring most of the plant life we see today
into existence. Mycelia comprise a fungal network that engages in the
exchange of energy between plants and fungi. This connection is referred
to as mycorrhiza. Fungi help plants absorb water and provide nutrients
through their mycelia while the plants give fungi food in the form of carbo-
hydrates. Trees' relationship with mycorrhiza is critical, with the fungi
consuming sugars from trees photosynthesized from sunlight, and trees
receiving mineral nutrients from the mycorrhiza.

It is easy to romanticize these plant-fungal relations as perfectly
symbiotic and altruistic, but upon deeper probing one finds that there is
a lot of push and pull, choice, discernment, strategy, and boundaries in
these connections.

Mycelia are a model of mutual aid and community defense. They
link into a network to support neighbors with nourishment and informa-
tion while also defending against harmful plants and insects that would
otherwise colonize their communities. Older trees with more resources
and connection in this network can sense distress and distribute resources
to trees in distress through the mycelia.

This web of connection demonstrates the principle that all of life
depends on each other. Even organisms that seem to be separate are often
connected. These complex connections are threatened by the clearcutting
and destruction of forests to make way for mono-cropping and develop-
ment that destroys the mycorrhiza and makes the land more vulnerable
to deterioration, disease, and invasion. Once a nonnative invasive species
takes over, the mycelia are impacted in a way that makes them less

hospitable to native plants. The destruction of flora, fauna, and fungal communities endangers native life, makes all of us less food-secure, and overall diminishes everyone's quality of life.

This chapter reminds us of the interconnection of our struggles to ensure that nobody's trauma can be weaponized against other communities.

When we see ourselves as part of a collective body—a whole and unified organism made up of many units—we subvert the cultures of isolation and individualism that are fostered in capitalism and colonization. Collective care moves us toward decolonization by turning to each other and the land for mutual support rather than relying on capitalist forms of consumption and extraction. Collective care suggests considering our bodies to be a part of a broader body, a body that includes not only humans but also other animal, plant, and fungal bodies that make up our ecosystems. It means caring for ourselves *within* our community. Models of care in mainstream culture in the United States are reduced to individualistic acts of self-care. Additionally, we are told that we must care for others at the expense of ourselves, which breeds a culture of saviors ineffective at scalable and sustainable change making. In this chapter, I invoke mycelium as a model for how we humans might also link into a network to support neighbors with nourishment and information while also defending against others that harm our communities.

Individualism has been engrained in our bodies and movements in ways that limit possibilities for mutual care and connection. Individual leaders are placed on pedestals and made into famous icons. People build their activist résumés by posting pictures of themselves at protests on social media, while base-building organizations are struggling to get the numbers they need for a mass movement. Even in certain single-issue organizations, people are under the illusion that they can fight for one people's liberation at the expense of another. What we know now, particularly while living through the ongoing novel coronavirus pandemic, is that the health and safety of all of us is bound together. If we want true freedom, we can leave nobody behind.

Collective care invites us all into deeper practice around building the kinds of cultures we want to live in and not just taking each other down. For many of us, the trauma we experience in our lives is part of a collective experience, and it is important that the approach to healing matches the site of harm. Thus, healing collective trauma requires collective care and collective action. This is what we mean by joint struggle—the practice of moving from the intersections of harm and oppression toward futures that ensure safety and dignity for all of us. For Jews, we might hold the collective trauma of the Nazi genocide, being continually displaced from our homes, targeted as scapegoats, and living under Christian hegemony and/or other forms of antisemitism. Joint struggle means joining in fights against Islamophobia and other forms of racism as well as understanding the impacts of racism in our own communities. Joint struggle means joining with Jews of color, Mizrahi and Sephardic liberation, and pushing back against Ashkenormativity, the centering of white European Jewish culture.[1] Joint struggle means exposing the ways white nationalism targets both Jews and people of color. And it means joining with Palestinians in the fight for the decolonization of their land. We cannot truly win any of these freedoms in our bodies and cultures without fighting for all of them.

In order to stay centered in our collective struggles for liberation, we will explore different tools for self-regulation in the face of trauma activation and reactivation. In this chapter, we will also explore co-regulation and our need for social engagement as part of healing trauma, settling our nervous systems, and returning to interdependence as an antidote to the isolation of oppressive systems. After antelopes escape their predators, and "shake off" the trauma, one of the first things they do is run back to their herd.[2] Individual or even interpersonal processes are not sufficient for collective healing. Like the antelope, we depend on our broader communities. We need the tools of political education *and* healing to create cultures of collective care that strip away the underpinnings of the oppressive systems we otherwise rely on. Let's now turn to examine the role of embodied transformation in shifting historical and collective patterns toward interdependent relationships with each other and the land.

Isolation as Trauma, Interdependence as Survival

Isolation is more harmful for humans than attaching, even in disorganizing ways. Our systems simply can't take shape without others; so, even if the attachment is not secure, our bodies understand that connection is always safer than isolation. As much as painful attachments are hard to bear, the primacy of connecting—a biological imperative for our nervous systems means we will keep seeking as best we can to stay in contact with what is offered and eventually find more nourishing attachments.[3]

Interpersonal neurobiology is a scientific, interdisciplinary study of how we influence and impact each other's nervous systems. This emerging field has given way to discoveries about the nervous system, including the polyvagal theory and other neuroscience to back up what we all know on a deep level: we are interconnected and depend on each other for our survival. Scientists have shown that when we are in the presence of warm and responsive relationships, our orbitofrontal cortex becomes interwoven with our amygdala in the right hemisphere. As this wiring gets stronger through practice and repetition, there is increased myelination—a process in which a sheath is formed around the nerve, creating a faster pathway—and our window of tolerance for intense emotions, which we can experience while remaining connected to ourselves and each other, gets wider.[4] The implications of this on our personal and political lives are massive. Through practice we can move from stuck, combative, or defensive places towards more generative, connected, and authentic experiences of collaboration.

Neuroscientist Marco Iacoboni writes about neural mechanisms of mirroring. The distinction between our nervous systems is perhaps fictitious; this would explain why we can empathize with each other in embodied ways. Beyond describing the concept of connecting self with other, he writes that "our neurobiology puts us 'within each other.'"[5] This idea of being "within each other" points to a politics beyond intersectionality, one of inseparability. How might our movements be different if we embodied these principles?

In white settler cultures like those of the United States and Israel, because of the destruction of land-based community, the dehumanizing competition inherent in capitalism, and the confines of heteronormative family structures, we have created a hyper-individualistic culture in which it becomes antithetical to cultivate and sustain interdependent connections. Many of the practices that have gained traction in the United States, such as yoga and meditation, have been misinterpreted and contorted into individualized and capitalistic models of "self-care." By taking these practices out of context, we are not only being disrespectful and culturally appropriative, we are also missing out on the co-regulatory process in which people's bodies support each other in an effective collective practice.

We are all steeped in the cultures and environments we live in, so in order to heal individually, we must heal collectively. Feeling alone in an experience of suffering is a central factor in having potential trauma (experiencing the activation of a survival response) becoming embedded trauma (the survival response getting stuck in activation without resolution). Moving from a sense of isolation toward a sense of connection, co-regulation, and alliance is almost always a critical part for opening a healing process. When we feel safe and held, we become more open to and aware of our sensations, feelings, and thoughts.

Interdependence Is Not Codependence

> If one tree fruits, they all fruit—there are no soloists. . . . Not one tree in a grove, but the whole grove; not one grove in the forest, but every grove.

> —Robin Wall Kimmerer

Unlike the white settler culture in the United States, Indigenous cultures recognize the inseparability of self and other. Potawatomi author and botanist Robin Wall Kimmerer illustrates this inseparability through every part of her book *Braiding Sweetgrass*, saying in countless ways what she says here: "The boundaries of self and the living world are not very distinct at all."[6] She tells the story of the pecan as an example. A pecan tree builds mutual and symbiotic relationships with its community and depends on the support of other organisms that share its ecosystem. Kimmerer describes how mast-fruiting trees (trees and shrubs with fruits, seeds, and nuts eaten by wildlife) all bear fruit at the same time as an entire grove, never individually, which scientists have never been quite able to explain. The pecan, a mast-fruiting tree, demonstrates a complex and interwoven system of interdependence. Kimmerer says that the pecan trees are not only connected with each other but also with other species and that, by feeding squirrels and humans, the trees are also guaranteeing their own survival. Pecans remind us that when one of us thrives, all of us thrive.

In navigating the realm of relationships and attachment, there are many different perspectives on codependence and independence. The idea that self-regulation and autonomy are signs of health comes from a patriarchal, white Christian supremacist, individualist culture. From a physiological perspective, we can also think of this as a left hemisphere–centric culture (as detailed in chapter 4). Left hemisphere–centric views tell us that it isn't safe to trust or rely on other people, meaning we are likely going to prioritize strategies for self-reliance. But when we engage our whole brain, we can prioritize relationships supported by the capacity for connection in our right hemisphere, still backed by the discernment of our left hemisphere.

Co-regulation is the process by which one person's settled nervous system is able to sync with another and allow both people to feel grounded and connected. The polyvagal theory and other work in interpersonal neurobiology outline the ways our systems are wired to seek connection and regulation with each other. With this incredible capacity for attunement, we can also experience co-dysregulation, in which someone else's activated state impacts our neuroception and sense of safety. Whether for safety or for threat, our bodies being binary and separate from each other is a part of the myth of individualism.

Individualism is a force of oppression rooted alongside racism, sexism, and classism. When critiquing systems of oppression, individualism often gets left out from our analysis and even condoned in our communities and movements. There are so many forces in dominant culture—including our relationships to land and food—that shape us to strive for individualism. Some of these forces can leave us with no choice but to be self-reliant, particularly those of us who have survived a lot of intimate loss. But when we systematically overvalue independence without enough attention toward forming secure bonds with ourselves, each other, and the land, we contribute to a culture of individualism. Individualism breeds authoritarianism and fascism by justifying the idea that one person (or corporation) can govern everyone and that we should trust that one entity rather than trusting each other.

This extreme form of independence is a fundamental contradiction to our biology. When our evolutionary ancestors were born, they could go out on our own without any caretakers, as most modern reptiles and fish do today. But humans are mammals that evolved to require caretakers, especially in our first several years of life. Evolutionary biologists understand this as the reason why some mammals developed the ability to read facial expressions along with other embodied cues to track for safety through the social engagement system (a newly named branch of the nervous system discussed in the chapter 4).

Despite this brilliant evolution, white supremacist capitalist patriarchy and right-wing authoritarianism have bred a culture of individualism, in which interdependence is misconstrued as co-dependence. This culture values self-reliance, independence, and autonomy, and it pathologizes interdependence—which shows up in the ways we talk about codependency. "Codependency" was originally used to describe people who are heavily impacted by their relationship(s) with people who are chemically dependent. This came out of research that revealed similarities between alcoholics and people in close relationships with alcoholics. In 1979 the word "codependency" emerged to refer to "people whose lives had become unmanageable as a result of living in a committed relationship with an alcoholic."[7] As time went on, the meaning expanded to include "a person who has let another person's behavior affect him or her, and who is obsessed with controlling that person's behavior." While both versions describe a valid and specific condition, the second definition is what has led to the overuse of the word. As we know from the polyvagal theory, our nervous systems are interwoven, and we are all constantly impacted by the behavior of those around us. There is nothing wrong with that. On the contrary, it is an important part of building sustained connections. Obsession and control we might then understand as adaptations for insecure attachments. It is important to destigmatize codependency but also to not overuse the term to describe what is actually just the reality that we are always impacting each other. Being able to offer care and rely on others for care and support is a natural part of social engagement and secure attachments.

In this framework, it is indeed important to learn to come back into our own bodies and build self-reliance. However, our relationships to interdependence are often based on the families and cultures we come from. Many families depend on each other to show up in big and beautiful ways. Dominant cultural narratives rooted in classism, ableism, homophobia, and racism are projected onto those who live beyond the hetero-nuclear family structure and timeline. Within individualistic culture, the families that form outside of the confines of the state are blocked from accessing resources, othered, and/or labeled as codependent.

Throughout time and place we see examples of societies that are set up with interdependence at their core, where it is not an option to go off on your own either because it is physically dangerous or culturally taboo. We now know it can be fatal for infants not to receive enough connection through touch in the earliest phase of their lives. We have deep evolutionary drives toward connection, belonging, and community. As we have (d)evolved, there is less and less of a sense of needing each other for our survival, and with that has come a culture of disposability. This is not to say that we should always stay in relationships or feel like we have to—it is important to continue cultivating cultures of consent, to have agency around with whom and how we are in connection with people. But so much is lost as we become less dependent on each other and more dependent on giant corporations and state institutions.

Between 2017 and 2019, California's primary energy company, Pacific Gas and Electric (PG&E) received multiple rounds of bankruptcy bailouts from the state government to cover their liability for the major wildfires. PG&E's lack of maintenance resulted in the most devastating fires in the history of California, with destruction of land and life. Many of the people fighting these massive fires were prisoners of the state being paid eight cents per hour, while wealthy people hired private firefighters to protect their mansions and second homes. The government backing of PG&E failed to serve communities' needs, and power to thousands of homes was shut off as a precautionary measure. In several cases, this led to chronically ill and disabled people being in critical condition as they were unable to power their medical equipment. Campaigns such as No PGE Bailout were formed to respond to this dependence and reinvestment in faulty systems, and people demanded public dominion over the electricity grid infrastructure. As we look into a future and continued climate chaos, it is ever more crucial to be discerning about what systems we are investing in to meet our basic needs. There have been incredible efforts of mutual aid during these times of crisis including groups formed to pass out N95 masks in houseless communities and offer herbal lung support, earthquake preparedness education, and mutual aid listservs for disabled and chronically ill folks through power outages. During the 2017 Tubbs fire, thousands of undocumented people lost their homes due to PG&E's negligence and then couldn't receive federal emergency support and/or weren't able to get the fair reimbursement from insurance, if any at all. After these devastating fires, organizations in Sonoma County came together to start the UndocuFund, which provided direct assistance to undocumented people by distributing $6 million to people impacted by the fires. This kind of emergency response efforts in combination with sustained organizing around climate justice and environmental racism are critical to ensure that people on the front lines of systemic injustice are included in our systems of collective care.

In all these cases and more, we can see that dependence on community to delegate responsibilities is often threatened or taken over by the state. This does not mean we are independent, it just means we depend on other things besides each other. These systems leave so many people behind as it becomes a privilege to afford basic resources such as clean water and electricity. Responding to these horrendous conditions can often lead to a sense of urgency, particularly in times of climate emergency. In these moments, if we aren't attuned to our collective needs, we can end up putting our weight behind reforming the systems at the root of our struggles that leave many of us behind. Instead, we must re-attune to our communities' creative solutions and power.

But there are many layers of nuance to an antiauthoritarian politics of interdependence. While many of us in social movements proclaim "We Take Care of Us" as a response to policing, failed health-care systems, and the COVID-19 pandemic, we must be careful not to let the state off the hook for providing basic needs. With private GoFundMe fund-raisers becoming one of people's primary ways to afford health care, along with precarity nationwide in progressive democratic representation, we are in a time where we risk losing fundamental human rights to health care, housing, education, food, and justice for all. So while we don't want to give up our power to a state that does not take care of us, we also must fight to get our people in positions of power to ensure these basic rights and freedoms. With that, we can continue to build organizations to hold accountable the people who take on these roles, ensuring that they enact legislation in our interests, and supporting them when they come under fire. Through this multiplicity of strategies and tactics, we can set the terrain on which we can struggle and live into our true liberation.

In my lifetime I have been far too extreme on both ends of the spectrum, either falling into liberal reformist politics or disregarding the state entirely, leaving gaps in my analysis regarding the importance of social services and democratic representation. In the course of writing this book, I grappled with how my relationship to the state is susceptible to individualism and shaped by my race, class, gender, sexuality, and religion. In both the 2014 and 2023 US-backed military attacks on Gaza, I would call my members of Congress, sometimes daily, identifying myself as a Jewish person in support of Palestinian freedom and hopelessly beg my representatives to call for a ceasefire. Often I would receive formulaic email responses, assuring me that they were going to fight for the security of the state of Israel (making it obvious that they hadn't even read my comments). At times I gave up on this tactic and opted for more direct action, and other times I wondered if we might have been able to achieve a ceasefire sooner had we won more progressive representation in the previous election. Whatever our theoretical stances are, people's lives are on the line when it comes to matters of the state, so, rather than subscribing to dogmatic politics, I choose to grapple with the complexities of what it means to be alive in this world and find ways to fight for liberation. However creative, subversive, or radical the strategy may be, I always reground myself in the material conditions required for true liberation.

Our explorations of embodied trauma responses help to explain part of what happens when people respond to personal and/or political crisis in narrow, one-dimensional, or dogmatic ways. In times of crisis, our nervous systems are in an activated state that literally cuts off access to creative thinking centers. By building tools for resilience and co-regulation in our bodies, we can slow down, listen to people on the front lines of these crises, and open up our bodies to a vast realm of possibility. Ultimately, we need solutions that are transgressive and scalable, *and* we need governance that represents and cares for us. As we fight to preserve basic freedoms through progressive electoral campaigns, we can use embodied practices to nurture alternative communities of care and governance.

There is a somatic principle that says we are always practicing something and always embodying something. So when we talk about "getting more embodied," this misses the point that we are already embodied, it just may not be how we want to be embodied. In the same vein, we always depend on something—we are never entirely independent. So, in building models of collective care, we can strive for more agency and self-determination around what it is that we depend on and how we can embody that.

We can also learn about the pitfalls of hyper-individualism through dystopian sci-fi by Octavia E. Butler, N.K. Jemisin, and Ursula K. Le Guin. In these dystopian futures, hyper-individualism takes over, and everyone has their own unit and is out for themselves. The only relationships between units are violent or exploitative or both. Utopian sci-fi stories, on the other hand, often illustrate complex webs of relationship, survival, and co-creation. How can we move these stories from fictional fantasy into a grounded reality of interdependence?

If we want to survive these apocalyptic times, we must build cultures of interdependence. We cannot let forces of individualism pathologize our basic human needs for connection. Whether through narratives around codependence, institutionalized racism, dependence on failed systems, or the devaluing of queer family, we must resist individualism and recenter visions of collective care.

Mutual Connection in Healing and Community

Interdependence is a series of small repetitive motions.

—adrienne maree brown

Collective care lives in the ways we build our lives and communities together as well as how we create and experience healing spaces in them. Since I was quite young, I have had the opportunity to be in collective healing spaces. From going to temple on the High Holidays, to my first exposure to somatics, embodied dance, and movement practices, I have experienced the power of healing in a collective body. Having struggled with depression most of my life, I have been in and out of therapy. At times this has been lifesaving, but it has mostly felt limiting and confusing. Why was I sharing so much vulnerability with this person in an entirely unidirectional way? There is no right or wrong way to heal, but I have always felt that there is a certain kind of healing that can only happen in connection with community. There is now a plethora of community-based research showing how people around the world have survived and stayed resilient in the face of extremely painful conditions. Whether people are grieving the loss of a loved one or facing state violence, their resilience most often involves collective grieving, movement, ceremony, or celebration.

Pumla Gobodo-Madikizela's doctoral work was founded in the restorative justice process named the Truth and Reconciliation Commission during and after South African apartheid. Her research in Black South African communities that had experienced state violence, including political assassinations, found that collective movement, drumming, and song increased collective resilience and decreased intra-community violence.[8] Anecdotally, I have found the same to be true in our movement's response to the violence of Israeli apartheid, particularly in the 2023–24 genocide in Gaza. Our hearts were breaking, and the grief and rage were too big to hold alone. We came together to feel and to not let the numbness required to endure state violence keep us from building power together. We gathered for weekly protests, sat-in at the US Capitol, interrupted business as usual, and sang freedom songs from the Black liberation movement and contemporary protest songs written by anti-Zionist Jews. In every way we knew how, we demanded that the humanity of Palestinians be dignified through calls for a ceasefire, an end to the occupation, and the Palestinian right to return. While there were strategic goals for these protests, rarely did we scratch the surface of impacting material conditions for people in Palestine. But still we gathered, and we organized—to feel our power in numbers and remind the world that while a small imperialist owning class controls the state's resources, the masses want collective liberation.

Creating spaces for mutual connection as healing, whether through protest or through music and dance, is one of the most powerful somatic practices. In many somatic practices, we keep our eyes open to let our environments in, whereas in other traditions you might close your eyes so you can connect with yourself. There is a place for that too, bringing all your focus internally, as is done in certain meditations. At the same time, it is important to build in the muscle of being deeply connected with ourselves while simultaneously staying connected with each other and our environments. When I am in a difficult or exciting conversation, anything with a lot of charge or energy, if I come back and scan my body, I will find that my thighs and perineum are clenched. For me, that has felt like cutting off my energy, access, and connection with the lower half of my body. This gets in the way of my ability to fully connect with other people in a moment of high intensity, regardless of whether it's intense excitement or struggle. Through my own somatic practice, I have learned to work with these contractions so that, firstly, I am aware when it is happening. Secondly, I have built new pathways in my body to be able to unclench or just decrease the intensity of the contraction so that I am able to access other—perhaps less traveled—pathways. When we restore access to more of ourselves, we are better able to experience mutual connection.

Our capacity for mutual connection also depends on a solid embodiment of boundaries as detailed in chapter 4. In communities I have been a part of, I have seen people, myself included, repeatedly cross our own boundaries, leading to inevitable breakdowns. Due to overpromising based on ideals and therefore overstepping boundaries, I have witnessed the collapse of numerous political projects, queer collective houses, and land projects. It can feel like an uphill battle to build interdependent communities in a system that continues to require your dependence on it. In *Relational Bodies* (2019), Zoë Poullette proposed that there are three critical components to building resilient communities: proximity, participation, and play. We need to be able to be physically close enough to feel for each other, to participate in shared experiences, and create opportunities to be playful with each other. I believe that to create and sustain cultures and communities of interdependence it is critical to build these muscles. We need to deepen this pathway to mutual connection where we can be in touch with our own sensations, needs, and desires, while also being present with another.

Transformation through Collective Accountability

Transformative justice, a specific practice for addressing harm through accountability, has been developed by Black women, queer, and trans people. At its root, transformative justice is about taking the state out of the body—turning to community-based practices for healing and justice rather than policing or other forms of the state. Many of our ancestors practiced forms of care that can help us approach and understand transformative justice. In my own Jewish tradition, I find ancestral connection to transformative justice through the principles of *teshuvah, tefillah,* and *tzedakah.* The common translations of these Hebrew words from Hebrew—"repentance, prayer, and charity"—have led English-speaking Jewish communities to misunderstand what these foundational principles truly mean. Growing up, these principles of teshuvah, tefillah, and tzedakah were very present in my home. We went to temple to pray, we chanted prayers asking for repentance on the High Holidays, and we made donations to Jewish nonprofits and charities. As an adult, I've come to understand teshuvah, tefillah, and tzedakah as a return to our embodied self and connections, the redistribution of wealth, and the restoration of justice. What follows is a case for teshuvah, tefillah, and tzedakah as transformative justice practices.

"Teshuvah" is often translated as "repentance," but the root of "teshuvah" is "returning"—returning to the good within you. This approach shows a way toward healing and forgiveness that, unlike in Christianity, is not founded in shame or guilt. How do we return? We return through our bodies. One of the great medieval philosophers of Jewish law, Rambam (Maimonides), talks about how teshuvah is only complete when we return to the same situation in which something went awry and choose to behave or act differently. This is the foundation of somatic practice—to be able to face the pressures in our lives with an embodied awareness of our conditioned reaction, and to engage the embodied practice of centering, returning to the center from which we can then move with more aligned choices. Our missteps occur when we have fallen off center, when we are taken away from our bodies through the internalization of trauma and oppression, or simply through the humanness of being flawed and imperfect. We do things that are out of alignment with our values all the time. Our lives are full of contradictions. The question is not "How do we avoid making mistakes?" but rather "How do we come back to ourselves and our connections, make amends, and move forward together?" So in this first step of Jewish transformative justice, we return to ourselves—we transform in our own bodies and in our relationships.

"Tefillah" is commonly translated as "prayer," but the literal translation is "to attach oneself." We can understand tefillah as reaching toward something bigger than ourselves, to cultivate divine connection or simply to cultivate secure attachment with oneself. Through the lens of transformative justice, this is the step where you bring your learning and returning to yourself into relationship with your community, with the land, and with whatever other divine power or connection you feel.

"Tzedakah" is often translated as "charity," giving the sense that a gift is given out of the goodness of your heart and that the recipient did not ask for anything or maybe even "deserve" it—a philosophy that lines up closely with philanthropy. However, "tzedakah" can also be translated as "righteousness" or "justice," meaning that the giver is motivated by duty, because as humans on this planet we are indebted to each other and the earth. We owe our lives to each other, and tzedakah invites us into mutual aid and collective care.

The principle of tzedakah has been shaped by Zionist investment in the state of Israel. At the majority of synagogues and Jewish day schools, and even in many Jewish homes, you may find a blue metal tin, kind of like a piggy bank, where people put donations. I remember the one in my house growing up, faded and rusty, with a map of historic Palestine and a Jewish star, which read: "Jewish National Fund." While my family made donations to many different communities and movements, the idea with this "Tzedakah box" was to consolidate Jewish money toward support for the development of the state of Israel. The Jewish National Fund (discussed in chapter 1) is an institution instrumental in occupying and confiscating Palestinian land for the exclusive use of Jewish people. The JNF is also responsible for the "plant a tree in Israel" program, for which donations are frequently made in the name of young people when they have their bar or bat mitzvah, a Jewish coming-of-age ritual. I find it abhorrent and even sacrilegious that these ancient Jewish principles of transformative justice have been misused and through disembodied ethnonationalism, toward the establishment and maintenance of a colonial state.

Reclaiming embodied Jewish traditions such as teshuvah, tefillah, and tzedakah helps us come back to movements grounded in self-determination and justice, both in the United States and in Palestine. These principles of returning, connection, and justice not only guide us in collective reparation and other movements but also are a part of how we repair intimate relationships. Mutual connections, particularly those sustained over time, require being able to navigate conflict and repair after hurt or harm. In these moments of conflict we have the opportunity to practice embodied and accountable ways of making amends. In cases where mutual repair isn't an option, we can still move through these processes in our own bodies, without actually involving the other person or people.

As we embark on an exploration of accountability, we must lay a foundation that recognizes all of our inherent worth rather than treating people as disposable. This also invites us into our own sense of belonging in a way that makes it more likely for us to be committed and successful in an accountability process. Another piece of foundation that needs to be built is honoring people's self-determination and understanding what they are seeking through these processes rather than projecting what we think "success" looks like. Finally, we must find the right pace, which often means slowing down, as urgency can lead to rigidity in our bodies and our mutual processes.

Accountability is an invitation to stay in relationship, and we must hold it with the utmost respect. Approaching accountability through transformative justice practices can be daunting and is often unsuccessful, as we are trying to practice something that contradicts every system of oppression we have been steeped in all our lives. While there are sometimes big, multiyear processes of healing and transformation and holding accountable people who have done harm, there are also smaller ways we can practice transformative justice. There are all the little moments and interventions we can make to deescalate, practice harm reduction, and honor people's inherent worth in our day-to-day lives.

Conversations around accountability are often complicated by different layers of social, political, and individual context. I believe that in order to maintain integrity we must engage with each of these layers. This often means moving through a trauma healing process, having difficult conversations about harm in our communities, and taking action to intervene in cycles of violence.

There are many different ways people talk about the principles of transformative justice, and these often overlap. Abolition activists like Dean Spade and Tourmaline talk about the importance of prevention, intervention, reparations, and transformation. Generation Five, the aforementioned organization developed to end child sexual abuse and find alternatives to mandatory reporting within methods of addressing harm talks about four components: (1) safety, healing, and individual agency for survivors; (2) accountability and a transformation for people who harm; (3) community action, healing, and/or group accountability; and (4) transformation of the social conditions that perpetuate violence. Generation Five explains: "Transformative justice seeks to provide people who experience violence with immediate safety, long-term healing and reparations; to demand that people who have done harm take accountability for their harmful actions, while holding the possibility for their transformation and humanity; and to mobilize communities to shift the oppressive social and systemic conditions that create the context for violence."[9]

Making amends through apology can be difficult for a variety of reasons: it can mean admitting you hurt someone, and it can mean holding that even if you wronged someone, you are not wrong. We tend to think in binary ways, that one person is right and one person is wrong and therefore that if we apologize we are saying that we are the wrong ones. Most of the time, it is more complicated than that. Forgiving ourselves is not to be used as a way of dodging responsibility. Rather, it is an essential part of any transformative accountability process. The prison industrial complex teaches us to criminalize, shame, and deem deviant bodies not worthy of love and belonging in community. Instead of reproducing these systems in our relationships, we have the choice to do the hard but worthwhile work of transformative justice and centered accountability. While guilt becomes embodied in feeling one *did* something wrong and thus can seek repair, shame is embodied as one *being* fundamentally wrong, and this can get stuck in the body.[10] Making amends is an important part of processes of transformation illustrated in the models listed above as well as many twelve-step programs aimed at supporting people who are working to change behaviors and heal from addiction. Through self-forgiveness we can liberate the energy that has been held captive by our trauma and internalized oppression. Collective accountability and forgiveness can be powerful practices to heal shame and rebuild love and belonging.

Such transformative processes do not end with "I'm sorry." We must commit to doing the work of changing behavior so that we don't continue to harm others and are able to have access to different choices in the future. To me, this kind of commitment is the most powerful apology, and it is also one that requires practice toward embodiment. Mia Mingus of the Bay Area Transformative Justice Collective writes:

> Accountability is not just a buzz word, it is a critical skill for dismantling oppressive, punitive systems and creating transformative spaces for us to learn to show up for ourselves and each other. Being accountable to others and ourselves is something we must learn how to do well, just like anything else. These are hard skills that require the discipline of practice, commitment and faith, knowing that we will make mistakes and fall short many times—most times. This is especially true in a society steeped in punishment, privilege and criminalization; that actively avoids accountability and does not encourage the kind of culture, relationships or skills needed to support true accountability.[11]

Somatic theory and neuroscience both teach us that certain pathways in our skull-encased brains and "body brains" (described in chapter 4) get grooved through repetition, so making any significant change means rewiring our bodies to be able to take new actions under the same conditions.

We all have different tendencies when it comes to accountability. In generative somatics we talk about over-, under-, and centered accountability. Both over- and under-accountability are often rooted in a sense of being bad; the shame we feel about ourselves overpowers and inhibits centered accountability. If we are over-accountable, we tend toward taking on more responsibility than is ours to hold. This can show up on the intimate level of survivors of violence feeling that the experience was their fault (victim blaming). It can also show up on a systemic level in which individuals feel immobilizing shame for their position of privilege, which does not result in taking action to dismantle such systems but rather maintains them. Under-accountability manifests as immediate defensiveness and not engaging in the process of repairing relationships. Often we contain both tendencies, or one leads to the other. Over-accountability can lead to resentment, and then we may burn out, ghost, or otherwise disappear from that process or relationship (under-accountability). Centered account-ability has room for complexity in that people can each be accountable to what is our responsibility and also discern what is not our responsibility without cutting off connection. While we all contain all of these tendencies, different bodies are often conditioned to be over- or under-accountable. Leah Lakshmi Piepzna-Samarasinha in *Care Work* writes about how disa-bled femmes of color are expected to consistently be available to receive any and all feedback, leading to the sense that everything is their fault and that they need to immediately take responsibility. Within our different social contexts, we can use our bodies and connections as teachers to find our own centers in accountability.

While we can apply these principles of accountability in our rela-tionships, we must be cautious not to individualize processes that are meant to be held collectively. For example, the concept of reparations is at times taken out of context and misused in people's personal campaigns to remedy interpersonal harm. The origin of reparations as defined by the National Coalition of Blacks for Reparations in America (N'COBRA) is "a process of repairing, healing and restoring a people injured because of their group identity and in violation of their fundamental human rights by governments or corporations. Those groups that have been injured have the right to obtain from the government or corporation responsible for the injuries that which they need to repair and heal themselves." N'COBRA is a mass-based coalition organized for the sole purpose of obtaining reparations for African descendants in the United States.[12] Today calls for reparations range from Black descendants of people enslaved under chattel slavery to the Land Back movement of Indigenous communities across Turtle Island, and from poor and working-class people calling for wealth redistribution to Palestinian civil society calling for BDS and right to return. It is clear that nothing will ever make up for what was taken; but collective reparations, including elimination of discriminatory laws and the redistribution of land and wealth, begin to chip away at the extractive, oppressive systems that made vigilante, interpersonal, and state violence possible in the first place. Being able to speak out against these oppressive systems is a form of collective accountability. Lewis Raven Wallace and Micah Bazant echo this sentiment in their zine *Miklat Miklat*: "Our challenges to scapegoating, isolation and retribution in our selves or our communities will be more effective when they go hand in hand with political struggles against the creation of scapegoats, against the root causes of oppression and marginalization and violence.... The healing of transformative justice is not just individual but [also] collective; it is intertwined with the empowerment of groups of people to change the conditions they/we live in."[13] Accountability has to happen on this broader scale. There needs to be reconciliation both for histories of settler colonialism as well as the current realities of settler life on unceded, stolen land as part of an ongoing process of genocide and colonization.

The systems that allow impunity for people in power while punishing marginalized communities need to be transformed. We must transform them into community-based models of care and accountability that support people in their struggles and in getting their needs met in ways that also consider the collective. We must transform the systems that genetically modify food and poison our soil into systems of food sovereignty, food security, and food justice for all. We must transform the systems that that exploit and extract resources from people and land into systems that value and respect the native plants, animals, waters, and indigenous peoples from the United States to Palestine. Resistance to transformative accountability keeps us in cycles of violence, repeating history, extinguishing species, and stalling progress toward justice. Transformation is necessary for humans', animals' and the earth's ability to survive and thrive.

The punitive dynamics of policing and prisons has seeped into our communities; thus deep transformation is also required to practice better ways of holding each other accountable. While there have been incredible attempts in my somatic practice, political homes, and communities—we still have a long way to go as a culture in embodying transformative justice. In our movements for justice, I have seen a leader with decades of abusive behavior toward other organizers refuse any kind of mediated process and continue to wield destructive power in numerous prominent political projects. Some years ago I personally had an experience around harm and the failings of community that challenged the very thesis of this book. I asked myself every day: how can I generate a sense of safety in my body without relying on police or other state apparatuses? My abusive ex was stalking and threatening me. Even with access to all the tools and resources, without the support of her community I was unable to engage in a transformative accountability process or even just find reassurance that I could be safe in my day-to-day life. After several failed attempts at reaching out to her friends during incidents of emotional and/or physical abuse, I decided to write a letter to her community, asking for more collaboration to ensure that my ex—their friend—had the support she needed to stop harming me, other members of our community, and herself. I consulted with friends working on transformative justice, survivor-centered account-ability processes, and abolitionist systems of care to figure out the best way forward, one that was both values-aligned and effective. I wrote:

> I believe we all have a shared commitment to keeping each other safe without engaging the state. I feel incredibly unsafe as [my ex] has been threatening and abusive for a year and a half and I need support to further intervene. She has been in a mental health crisis and using substances again. Her unpredictability is destabilizing.... I care about her safety and ours, and I believe a transformative approach is possible if we can all come together. The goals of this meeting are to: 1) develop shared understandings of the situation 2) assess risk 3) share resources, tools, and strategies 4) coordinate a plan of action 5) make space for different people's needs and bound-aries 6) cultivate a supportive network to ensure collective safety.

This letter never even made it into her friends' hands. Her community of self-proclaimed radical anarchists did not want to "infringe on her auton-omy" and thus stood by, offering no interventions to keep us safe without engaging the state. At this point, she had figured out where I lived and had come to my house late at night, throwing beer cans at my door and slashing my tires. The fear and hyper-vigilance in my body escalated—I couldn't sleep, had a hard time eating, and could barely leave the house without having a panic attack around the possibility of running into her. Without a community to hold this process, I was at a loss. I called the local domestic violence hotline to see if they had any ideas. They told me to call the police and file a restraining order. However, even if I wanted to pursue this action (which I did not), on hearing the details of my situation they said I did not qualify because in the state of North Carolina you have to be "opposite sex" and/or live together to file a domestic violence restraining order. The layers of homophobia, gendered violence, and failings of the state were far from lost on me. I reached out one last time to some of her closest friends, and that is when they told me I should just call the cops and that they wouldn't judge me for it, given how volatile the situation had become. While I appreciated their acknowledgment of how I was backed into a corner, I was shocked and disappointed that this community would turn to the state before they would risk their own vulnerability to engage in a transformative justice process. I decided to turn my attention toward creating physical barriers at my home, implementing a phone tree in case rapid response was required, and most of all to practice finding strength and safety in my body. I wish this story had a happy ending for all of us, but it does not. Her aggression toward me decreased, but we still live in the same community. I just drove past her the other day—years have gone by—and she made sure to lean out a window and flip me off with both hands. She is still carrying her own unhealed attachment trauma and unprocessed rage, and her community remains fractured by insufficient practices of collective care. But perfection isn't the goal, and our ideas around success and failure are often shaped by the state, so I still claim this as a story of transformation and healing. I like to think that some part of her was touched by the attempts to extend care through accountability. Regardless, I found my own power through it all. However small and scared she made me feel, my power was never hers to begin with, and it definitely wasn't the state's. I have rebuilt my sense of safety through years of embodied practice and remain committed to cultivating communities that are accountable to our politics from the interpersonal to the systemic. Culture-making takes time, generations even. This is our work: in the face of a state that has left us all carrying an undue burden of trauma and oppression, we keep practicing and holding each other with love and rigor, despite messiness and contradictions, as we find our way to embodied collective safety.

In the world of transformative justice we can find a lot of mistakes, attempts, failures, and some successes, all of which give great fodder for learning and growth. In the context of my somatic practice I have had clients react to being activated by our work by suddenly ending our sessions. In these cases, because of the healing container, I have been able to address why they shut down or turned away from the painful work, to uncover what was evoked and ultimately foster a reparative process. Politicized healing and somatics create safer, relational ways to be inside of an experience of activation after causing or experiencing hurt—to come back to ourselves, each other, and our shared commitments.

There are also organizations that have engaged in incredibly transformative accountability processes. One led by Mariame Kaba at Black Youth Project 100 ended with the survivor of sexual assault participating in a healing circle with the person who caused this harm, as they shared their apology, their growth, and their commitment to repair.[14] Kaba, a leader in the transformative justice movement, went on to write *Fumbling towards Repair* with Shira Hassan, a book that offers "reflection questions, skill assessments, facilitation tips, helpful definitions, activities, and hard-learned lessons intended to support people who have taken on the coordination and facilitation of formal community accountability processes to address interpersonal harm & violence."[15] As this movement grows, we have more and more tools to use and resources to practice.—I first learned about the possibilities of transformative justice at a reproductive justice conference in 2014 in Oakland, where Mimi Kim, cofounder of INCITE Women of Color Against Violence, spoke about a recently compiled tool kit through her work with Creative Interventions. At that point, the tool kit was a giant stack of paper that I excitedly gathered and carried around, devouring every word with hope. This stack of paper is now a published book, *The Creative Interventions Toolkit,* referred to as a fundamental text in the field. With every step we take toward transformation and justice, we are practicing something new, something that makes a culture of embodied safety, dignity, and belonging possible for all.

In our times shaped by prisons and policing, we are only a couple of generations into practicing transformative justice. So, what does it mean to be committed to a politics and practice that we are individually and collectively still fumbling our way through?[16] It means that we have to ground the intellectual ideals of transformative justice in the realities of our current conditions, and this requires practice.

Building Embodied Movements of Care

> Decolonization presents expansive and universal visions of self-determination over our own bodies, lives, cultures, land, and labor.
> —Harsha Walia

Embodying collective care in movement building challenges individualism, policing, militarized borders, and nationalism. There is a shift from the idea that the smallest unit is me to the idea that the smallest unit is we—and that *we* cannot be divided. The forces of the state shape relationships into extractive exchanges in which everything has a price, including basic human needs for care and connection. Taking the state out of our movements and systems of care means embodying reciprocity, interdependence, and generosity for all peoples and lands.

As we embody mutual connection and accountability in our relationships, we get a taste of what these things could look like on a systemic level. Robin Wall Kimmerer (the Indigenous author referenced earlier) takes a broad and long view—one that shifts the emphasis on the state taking care of us to our connecting with the ancestors and descendants of all species. She writes, "For all of us, becoming indigenous to a place means living as if your children's future mattered, to take care of the land as if our lives, both material and spiritual, depended on it."[17] Kimmerer emphasizes the importance of relearning and remembering our mutually beneficial relationships with each other and the earth rather than just critiquing the negative impacts of human life. If we are only focused on our collective traumas, how can we envision the social and ecological future we want? Somatics is a way of not only imagining a more just future but also actually experiencing it in our bodies, in the present moment. Building critiques and understanding the ways trauma and oppression pass through our bodies and through generations is important, but this is made much more powerful when we remember that resilience to gets passed on through our cells, our bodies, and our ancestors. Our capacity to experience joy, pleasure, and connection is critical for building movements that care.

Taking care of our connections and being accountable in our communities builds stronger movements for justice. Given that oppression includes the aggregate of individual and collective instances of trauma, and our movements are designed to fight oppression, we must also take care to resolve past traumas and prevent ongoing harm. By doing this healing work, not only is our energy freed up to fight for collective liberation, we also become less susceptible to the state's weaponization of our trauma. When we recognize the impacts of oppression in our bodies and in our movements, we can more clearly identify the ways they compromise our ability to fight back and make change. When we see that our healing does not stop at an intellectual understanding of oppression, we can actually loosen the grip of the state.

Transformation means moving toward more fully inhabiting our bodies as agents of change and healing and thus is absolutely essential to our movements for justice. In order to move from a society based on consumption, exploitation, and individualism to one that values shared resources, creativity, and collectivity, we must undergo a complete transformation. In reading the work of James Baldwin, you can feel the embodied nature of his politicized writing with descriptions of emotion and illustrations of relationships like this: "Love takes off masks that we fear we cannot live without and know we cannot live within."[18] In footage from a documentary on Malcom X, you see him leading a contingent of people to march to a hospital to demand medical attention and the release of their comrade from prison—the level of embodied and collective coordination as they all move together is palpable. If we look at these images, listen to the recordings, and read deeply into their words, we can perceive with all of our senses that here was someone leading collective action with a relaxed body and focused mind. There are many other examples throughout history of how collective embodied resistance built powerful movements. In 1957, facing extreme backlash, nine Black students walked with dignity into the previously segregated Little Rock Central High School, each step bringing them (and generations to come) closer to an equitable future in education. In 1960 four young Black students sat in nonviolent protest at the Greensboro Woolworth's lunch counter and were joined by over sixty more students who occupied every seat until Woolworth's agreed to desegregate the establishment and serve everyone equally. Their embodied perseverance inspired similar direct actions across the country.

In my lifetime, one of the most formative organizing experiences that illuminated both the importance of cross-movement solidarity and the impacts of a politicized somatics was the 2014 Block the Boat action led by the Arab Resource and Organizing Center (AROC).[19] This was a boycott, divestment, and sanctions action aimed at stopping ZIM—Israel's largest cargo shipping company, a transporter of weapons—from unloading at the Port of Oakland. Along with turning out thousands of people to a rally and picket line, a big part of our work was to coordinate with the International Longshore and Warehouse Union (ILWU) Local 10 to organize their workers to refuse to unload the ship. Because of their longstanding political history, including resisting the South African apartheid regime, as well as the call from the Palestinian General Federation of Trade Unions to unions worldwide to act in solidarity, the ILWU respected AROC's picket and joined in the protest. Clarence Thomas, a third-generation member of the union and community activist, spoke out at the rally, invoking an old IWW slogan: "I want everyone to know an injury to one is an injury to all."[20] This action inspired direct action at ports around the world, blocking ZIM ships in 2014, 2021, and again in 2023. Israeli ZIM ships have now gone years without docking at these ports due to this successful organizing. The main organizers of the first Block the Boat action were not only deeply embedded in an intersectional anti-Zionist politic of joint struggle but also all had a history of practicing somatics. In a Generative Somatics newsletter, Chris Lymbertos (deputy director of GS at the time) and Lara Kiswani (executive director of AROC) spoke to the significance of their embodied practice in being able to stay in this sustained coordinated action. "We needed to be alert and grounded at all times, and constantly had to make tough decisions with little time to reflect. Our somatics training supported us to take care of ourselves in that context. Our participation in SOEL (School of Embodied Leadership)--a GS course that builds endurance, agility, core strength, and power—was critical in preparing us to sustain through the long and intense days, and to remain present, clear, precise, and strategic in each decision."[21] These leaders showed us the way toward liberation, not only through their politics but also through their bodies. I will never forget the feeling of biking away from the Port of Oakland that day: the warm August breeze, my comrades at my sides, and music blasting in the background—there was a contagious embodiment of hope, possibility, and connection through collective action.

Embodied Practices

A good scar allows healing, it even covers over, but the covering always exposes the injury, reminding us of how it shapes the body. Our bodies have been shaped by their injuries; scars are traces of those injuries that persist in the healing or stitching of the present. This kind of good scar reminds us that recovering from injustice cannot be about covering over the injuries, which are the effects of injustice; signs of an unjust contact between our bodies and others. So "just emotions" might be ones that work with and on rather than over the wounds that surface as traces of past injuries in the present.

—Sara Ahmed

You are invited to engage with these practices when the time is right for you and at your own pace. With everything, practice consent, self-responsiveness, accessibility, and mutual care. These practices are intended as applied learning and transformation—before entering,

read through the content of the preceding chapter to better land the
social, political, and/or ecological relevance of these practices. Also,
you will need to refer to the author's note at the beginning—A Guide
to Embodied Practice and Lineage—for a more comprehensive orien-
tation and key to symbols.

- **Pleasure Bowl:** Pleasure is a critical part of embodiment, particularly in practicing somatic opening. Focus your attention on a pleasurable sensation. This could be the sun on your skin, the smell of spring, the expansiveness of your breath, the taste of a delicious treat, the sound of your favorite song, a sensual touch, or anything else that brings you joy or pleasure. Keep your attention there and notice when it drifts towards less pleasurable thoughts or sensations. Practice training your attention towards joy and pleasure—as it wanders, use sensation to bring you back and notice how it opens you. This can look like laughter, yawning, tears, or orgasm, as well as more subtle ways of somatic opening. You don't have to ignore what is hard or pulling you away, just keep turning up the dial of attention on pleasure and connection.

- **Teshuvah, Tefillah, and Tzedakah:** Writing can be a practice of embodiment as you let your hands move to externalize your process. Take some time to journal about the following questions. If you start to drift into theoretical frameworks and jargon, recenter, breathe, and return to your body. Ask yourself: What would it look like to apply the principles of transformative justice to your political organizing? For example, what do teshuvah, tefillah, and tzedakah (making amends, offering prayers, and giving righteously), mean for Jewish anti-Zionism? For the Palestinian right to return? You can reference the section in this chapter titled "Transformation through Collective Accountability."

- **Somatic Alliance:** We can experience collective care somatically by positioning our bodies in ways that support each other. This allows our bodies to learn what types of support we respond to, which in turn could help us communicate that need.
  1. Partner A: Name a longing, commitment, or something you are extending toward (e.g., "I want long term partnership," "I need rest," "I am committed to transforming intergenerational harm").

2. Partner B: Make a statement that allies you with your partner (e.g., "You deserve deep love," "You are allowed to rest," "Healing is possible").

3. Partner A: Orchestrate your partner's body, movements, or words to support your longing or commitment (e.g., have them stand at your feet while you lie down to rest, or sit back-to-back).

4. Experiment, and try different things until it feels right. Contact or no contact. Close proximity or more distant. In front, behind, or to your side.

5. Once you have found the right positions and language, have Partner B repeat back the same phrases as Partner A practices integrating and allowing more and more of their partner's presence in.

6. Switch roles and repeat steps 1–5.

7. Share with each other: what about that position had you feeling supported?

- **Body Scan:** Next time you are having a conversation with a friend or group of people, check in and scan your body: Are you in touch with sensations in your body? Are you able to simultaneously feel yourself while also perceiving and connecting with the bodies around you?

- **Body Scan for Care:** Next time you are being cared for or taking care of someone, scan your body: What sensations do you notice in your body when someone is extending care to you? When you are extending care, how do you feel and perceive others' reception of your care?

- **Learn from animals:** Watch how they clean and care for each other's bodies.

- **Centered Accountability:** 𝍫 𝍫 ◔ ◔ ◔ ☆ ☆ ☆ This practice is akin to the "Pressure" practice at the end of chapter 1 and is intended to support reflection around your accountability responses and practice how to find a centered way to be accountable.

1. Each person thinks about an example related to accountability.

2. Each person chooses a phrase to represent that accountability example. It could be "I need you to be accountable" or "You messed up" or "Can we talk about what happened in the

meeting?" Similar to the "Pressure" practice, find an example at a level of intensity of 3 or 4 on a scale of 1–10,.

3. Once you know the content you are working with, set up.

4. Position yourself at a right angle, perpendicular to each other. Person A (practicing accountability first) looks forward. Person B (representing the example) faces Person A's profile (either side).

5. Both people take a moment to center. (The centering practice is detailed in chapter 5.)

6. Round 1:

- When Person A is ready, they will nod their head.
- Person B will speak the phrase Person A shared.
- Pause, and notice what happens in your body.

7. Optional Rounds 2 and 3:

- Repeat step 6 and try taking on over-accountability—you can let yourself exaggerate what that feels like.
- Next try under-accountability.

8. Debrief, switch roles, and repeat. When you are switching, and at the end, be sure to shake off your roles. In the debriefing, note which responses felt familiar and which felt new. Where do you need more practice?

9. With these reflections, try one last round and practice centered accountability.

Access note: This can be done seated or standing, and you can extend your energy without lifting your arms.

- **Resilience:** ♀ ⏱ ☆ Our capacity to be with what is challenging is intimately tied to our capacity to be with what is working. Resilience refers to our ability to process, reintegrate, and bounce back. We engage with this practice as distinct from the common abstraction of resilience used to excuse or permit harm or oppression. We practice resilience to reestablish safety, hope, and connection, so we can cultivate a positive imagination of our collective futures. To do this practice, recall something that brings you resilience. For many people this is often some form of nature, creativity, and/or spirituality.

  1. Once you have an example of resilience in your imagination, close your eyes.

2. What sensations do you notice? What do you smell, taste, hear, feel, or see?

3. Experiment with turning your resilience up and down. Turn it up 50 percent: allow the image to be more vivid and vibrant, the smell to be stronger, the taste to be fuller, the sound to be louder, the touch to be more felt. Now experiment with turning it down, to 50 percent less sensation than where you first started. Take your time to explore sensation, images, emotion, and aliveness.

4. Now find the sweet spot, and hang out there. Take a somatic snapshot so you can return.

5. Debrief: Where did you land on the spectrum? Was your sweet spot higher or lower on the spectrum of intensity? How can you return to this place of resilience with intention?

- **Collective Resilience:** ⚥ ⏱ ⏱ ☆ In a group of two or more people, gather in a circle and share your resilience practice. What do you do to connect to resilience? Where do you go? Tell the details and sensations of the dance floor, the community dinner, the beach, or wherever it is for you. Notice what you feel in your body as you share, as well as what you see and experience in the others' as you listen. If you are in ongoing relationship, take note of each other's resilience practices so you can remind each other when you need it.

Closing

> Our bodies are not merely blank slates upon which the powers-that-be write their lessons. We cannot ignore the body itself: the sensory, mostly non-verbal experience of our hearts and lungs, muscles and tendons, telling us and the world who we are.
>
> —Eli Clare

As we have made our way in, around, and through this book, we land here at the end, ideally with a more fleshed-out sense of embodied safety, dignity, and belonging. We have traversed the realms of collective trauma, individualism, nationalism, Zionism, antisemitism, and border imperialism. We have delved into politicized healing and somatic interventions that open us to more permeable and vulnerable boundaries, interdependent nervous systems, intersectional movements, and collective care. The invitation here, as we close, is to let the words you read and the practices you engaged sink deeper, beyond your fascia and into your bones. I hope we continue together to build deeper understandings of these areas of inquiry, to build embodied ways of intervening in systemic injustice, to remember our inherent interdependence, and to show up for each other powerfully.

Engaging with *Taking the State out of the Body* has worked me in a profound way. The more I tried to shape it, the more it shaped me. I continued to be called into closer relationship with the contradictions and complexities of a queer anti-Zionist Jewish identity, perspective, and project. In my intimate community, there were many difficult conversations as we moved beyond collective survival responses to make room for more liberatory futures. I have been a part of incredible communities and projects supporting Palestinian and Arab organizers and leaders, confronting the dangers of the misuse of antisemitism, and challenging Jewishness exceptionalism. This has entailed resistance to Zionism, deconstruction of Ashkenazi assimilation into whiteness, the addressing of breakdowns in organizations, mitigation of Zionist backlash, and the continued search for embodied and creative ways to organize toward the dismantling of colonialism and imperialism in the United States and Palestine. My deepest intention in writing this book was to reach a wide range of people to help build a collective analysis and practice that embodies joint struggle in both our personal and political lives. By moving from intellectual and individual understandings of trauma to embodying collective commitments to dismantle systemic oppression, our bodies can become sites of resistance and sources of resilience in social and ecological movements for justice.

May we continue to unfold, peel back layers, and spiral deeper. May we know that healing and transformation are possible in fractal and scalable ways, whether micro or macro: from shifting relational boundaries to winning fights against militarized borders, from de-platforming the cops in our heads to closing down jails, from decolonizing occupied lands to taking the state out of our bodies. By the time this is published, there will be countless new ways of thinking about the body and our relationships to safety outside of the state. With the constantly shifting political tides, we must remain adaptive in our bodies to respond swiftly, precisely, and in ways that leave nobody behind. Forces of the state, such as fascism, imperialism, capitalism, colonialism, and Zionism, attempt to strip away our embodied relationships to place. Through collective movements that include politicized embodied healing, we can generate a sense of safety and belonging that upends nationalism and militarized borders and policing by restoring the power that lives in our bodies and our communities.

Notes

INTRODUCTION

1   "Homonationalism" is a term popularized by Jasbir Puar that refers to the co-optation and assimilation of queerness into nationalist ideology.

2   Ejeris Dixon, "Fascism Is Rising, but It Does Not Have to Be Our Future," Truthout, May 21, 2023, https://truthout.org/articles/fascism-is-rising-but-it-does-not-have-to-be-our-future.

3   I learned this while training with Generative Somatics (https://www.generativesomatics.org), an organization dedicated to politicized embodied healing and social transformation.

CHAPTER 1 Calendula: Resisting Ethnonationalism

1   Mark Rifkin, *The Erotics of Sovereignty: Queer Native Writing in the Era of Self-Determination* (Minneapolis: University of Minnesota Press, 2012), 38.

2   Harsha Walia, "Indigenous Sovereigntists Speak," rabble.ca, February 7, 2013. https://rabble.ca/indigenous/indigenous-sovereigntists-speak.

3   "Erica Violet Lee Speaks @ The Peoples Climate Week—Idle No More," Idlenomore.ca., accessed March 8, 2020, https://idlenomore.ca/erica-violet-lee-speaks-the-peoples-climate-week-idle-no-more.

4   Theodor Herzl and Marvin Lowenthal, *Diaries of Theodor Herzl* (Gloucester: Smith, 1978), 6.

5   Zanaib Ramahi, "Kashmir and Palestine Share the Struggle for Self-Determination Against Colonial Occupation, *Mondoweiss*, August 8, 2019, https://mondoweiss.net/2019/08/palestine-determination-occupation.

6   Sara Kershnar, co-founder of IJAN, informed much of my understandings around what joint struggle really means and looks like. IJAN, "A Case of Joint Struggle across Borders—the Case of Palestine," July 24, 2012, http://www.ijan.org/uncategorized/a-case-of-joint-struggle-across-borders-the-case-of-palestine/

7   "Bassem Tamimi Injured and Arrested with 3 Others at Boycott Israel Protest," International Solidarity Movement, October 24, 2012, https://palsolidarity.org/2012/10/bassem-tamimi-injured-and-arrested-with-3-others-at-boycott-israel-protest.

8   IJAN, "Who We Are," IJAN, March 5, 2014, https://www.ijan.org/who-we-are.

9   Steven Salaita, *Inter/Nationalism: Decolonizing Native America and Palestine* (Minneapolis: University of Minnesota Press, 2016), 145.

10   Edward W. Said and Jean Mohr, *After the Last Sky: Palestinian Lives*, 1986, http://ci.nii.ac.jp/ncid/BA24068807.

11   "Refugees," Holocaust Encyclopedia, accessed November 19, 2019, https://encyclopedia.ushmm.org/content/en/article/refugees.

12   Zena Al Tahhan, "More Than a Century On: The Balfour Declaration Explained," *Al Jazeera*, November 2, 2018, https://www.aljazeera.com/features/2018/11/2/more-than-a-century-on-the-balfour-declaration-explained.

13   Ilan Pappé, *The Ethnic Cleansing of Palestine* (Oxford: Oneworld, 2006).

14   Intl Jewish Anti-Zionist Network, "Never Again for Anyone," February 23, 2024, https://vimeo.com/117251606.

15   Ze'ev Jabotinsky, "The Iron Wall," 1923, https://en.jabotinsky.org/media/9747/the-iron-wall.pdf.

16   Jabotinsky, "Iron Wall."

17   "More than 350 Survivors and Descendants of Survivors and Victims of the Nazi Genocide Condemn Israel's Assault on Gaza," IJAN, accessed March 25, 2024, http://www.ijan.org/projects-campaigns/nafa/survivors-and-descendants-letter.

18   A lot of the political analysis around Zionism in this chapter came from years of organizing with the International Jewish Anti-Zionist Network, doing political education, campaign work, and direct action.

19   Jabotinsky, "Iron Wall."

20   Jabotinsky, "Iron Wall."

21   Jabotinsky, "Iron Wall."

22   *Israel's Worldwide Role in Repression* (International Jewish Anti-Zionist Network, 2012), http://www.ijan.org/wp-content/uploads/2016/03/IWoRR.pdf.

23   Salaita, *Inter/Nationalism*, 101.

24   Adolf Hitler, 1922 speech. "Adolf Hitler," n.d., https://history.hanover.edu/courses/excerpts/111hit1.html.

25   "CUFI Reaches 10 Million Members," Christians United for Israel, December 22, 2020, https://cufi.org/press-releases/cufi-reaches-10-million-members.

26   Christian Zionism holds the belief that Jesus will not return to Earth until all Jews have returned to the "Land of Canaan," interpreted as historical Palestine. In the theology of Christian Zionism, Jesus will not unleash his judgment and usher in the End Days until these conditions of Zionism have been met. Many Christians support the existence of Israel as a Jewish state and the immigration of Jews to Palestine because they wish to hasten the second coming of the Messiah and with it their own salvation. For more on Christian Zionism and the Messianic narrative: Judy Maltz, "Inside the Evangelical Money Flowing into the West Bank," *Haaretz*, December 9, 2018; Matthew Avery Sutton, "Jerusalem: Trump's Gift to Evangelicals," *Seattle Times*, December 16, 2017.

27   Quoted in Mimi Kirk, "Countering Christian Zionism in the Age of Trump," MERIP, August 8, 2019, https://merip.org/2019/08/countering-christian-zionism-in-the-age-of-trump. Steve Niva, "Countering Christian Zionism in the Age of Trump," MERIP, August 23, 2019, https://merip.org/2019/08/countering-christian-zionism-in-the-age-of-trump.

28   Noah Kulwin, "After Squirrel Hill," *Jewish Currents*, September 23, 2021, https://jewishcurrents.org/after-squirrel-hill.

29   Eric K. Ward, "Skin in the Game," Political Research Associates, June 29, 2017, https://politicalresearch.org/2017/06/29/skin-in-the-game-how-antisemitism-animates-white-nationalism.

30 For more on pinkwashing, see Astraea Lesbian Foundation For Justice, "Aswat–Palestinian Feminist Queer Movement for Sexual and Gender Freedoms–Astraea Lesbian Foundation for Justice." February 7, 2019, https://www.astraeafoundation.org/stories/aswat-palestinian-gay-women. Maya Mikdashi, "Gay Rights as Human Rights: Pinkwashing Homonationalism," Jadaliyya, December 16, 2011, https://www.jadaliyya.com/Details/24855.

31 Jasbir K. Puar, *Terrorist Assemblages: Homonationalism in Queer Times* (Durham, NC: Duke University Press, 2007).

32 Noah Graerci, *Doykeit* 1 (2012): 18 (zine compiled by Solomon Brager).

33 "Beyond Propaganda: Pinkwashing as Colonial Violence," *alQaws*, October 18, 2020, https://www.alqaws.org/articles/Beyond-Propaganda-Pinkwashing-as-Colonial-Violence?category_id=0.

34 Yuval Bagno, "Israel Sees Record Number of Anti-LGBTQ+ Incidents in 2022—Report," *Jerusalem Post*, March 19, 2023, https://www.jpost.com/israel-news/article-734812.

35 For more on greenwashing, see "'Making the Desert Bloom': A Myth Examined," *Journal of Palestine Studies* 8, no. 2 (Winter 1979), https://www.palestine-studies.org/en/node/38553.

36 "Documentary Film: *Enduring Roots: Over a Century of Resistance to the Jewish National Fund*," International Jewish Anti-Zionist Network, accessed March 8, 2024, http://www.ijan.org/projects-campaigns/stopthejnf/enduringroots.

37 Mariam Barghouti, "On October 7, Gaza Broke out of Prison," *Al Jazeera*, October 15, 2023, https://www.aljazeera.com/opinions/2023/10/14/on-october-7-gaza-broke-out-of-prison.

38 Samuel Farber, "Lessons from the Bund," *Jacobin*, January 3, 2017, https://jacobin.com/2017/01/jewish-bund-poland-workers-zionism-holocaust-stalin-israel.

39 Quoted in Miriam Weinstein, *Yiddish: A Nation of Words*, reprint ed. (New York: Ballantine Books, 2002), 127.

40 Solomon Brager, *Doykeit*1 (2012): 2, (zine compiled by Solomon Brager)

41 Originating from Algonquian- and Iroquoian-speaking peoples in what is now the northeastern United States, "Turtle Island" is a name for North America. ("America" was first used on European maps in reference to Italian "explorer and navigator" Amerigo Vespucci.

42 Puar, *Terrorist Assemblages*, 171.

43 "Palestinian Civil Society Call for BDS," Palestinian BDS National Committee, July 9, 2005, https://bdsmovement.net/call.

44 LANDBACK, https://landback.org.

45 "Reparations," Movement for Black Lives, accessed March 25, 2024, https://m4bl.org/policy-platforms/reparations.

46 "Queer Indigenous Studies: Critical Interventions in Theory, Politics, and Literature," *Choice/Choice Reviews* 49, no. 05 (January 1, 2012): 34, https://doi.org/10.5860/choice.49-2748.

CHAPTER 2 **Redwoods: Collective Trauma**

1   Ngọc Loan Trần, "Calling IN: A Less Disposable Way of Holding Each Other Accountable," *BGD*, December 18, 2013, https://www.bgdblog.org/2013/12/calling-less-disposable-way-holding-accountable.

2   This idea is rooted in understandings of cycles of harm as defined by Generation Five as well as Sarah Schulman, *Conflict Is Not Abuse: Overstating Harm,*

Community Responsibility, and the Duty of Repair (Vancouver: Arsenal Pulp Press, 2021).

3   Saliem Shehadeh, "Struggling for Justice at San Francisco State University," *Mondoweiss*, July 13, 2017, https://mondoweiss.net/2017/07/struggling-francisco-university.

4   Benedict Anderson, *Imagined Communities : Reflections on the Origin and Spread of Nationalism*, rev. ed. (London: Verso, 2016).

5   For more on Marissa Alexander's case see "Marissa Alexander TED Talk," Survived & Punished, June 1, 2019, https://survivedandpunished.org/2019/06/01/marissa-alexander-ted-talk. For more on the Tamir Rice case see "The Killing of Tamir Rice: Cleveland Police Criticized for Shooting 12-Year-Old Holding Toy Gun," *Democracy Now!*, December 18, 2014, https://www.democracynow.org/2014/12/5/the_killing_of_tamir_rice_cleveland.

6   Erin McKenna and Scott L. Pratt, *American Philosophy: From Wounded Knee to the Present* (London: Bloomsbury, 2015).

7   Roxane Dunbar-Ortiz, *An Indigenous Peoples' History of the United States* (Boston: Beacon Press, 2014).

8   Edmund S. Morgan, *American Slavery, American Freedom: The Ordeal of Colonial Virginia* (New York: W.W. Norton, 2003), 102.

9   Joy DeGruy, *Post Traumatic Slave Syndrome: America's Legacy of Enduring Injury and Healing* (New York: HarperCollins, 2017).

10 The Shuumi Land Tax is a voluntary annual financial contribution that non-Indigenous people living on traditional Chochenyo and Karkin Ohlone territory make to support the critical work of the Sogorea Te' Land Trust. The tax directly supports Sogorea Te's work to acquire and preserve land, establish a cemetery to reinter stolen Ohlone ancestral remains, and build urban gardens, community centers, and sacred arbors so current and future generations of Indigenous people can thrive in the Bay Area.

11 Resmaa Menakem, *My Grandmother's Hands: Racialized Trauma and the Pathway to Mending Our Hearts and Bodies* (Las Vegas: Central Recovery Press, 2017), 63.

12 Qwo-Li Driskill, Chris Finley, Brian Joseph Gilley, and Scott Lauria Morgensen, eds., *Queer Indigenous Studies: Critical Interventions in Theory, Politics, and Literature* (Tucson: University of Arizona Press, 2011), 34.

13 These stories are cited from years of family discussion. Quotes are from Erik Lundegaard, "Remembering the St. Louis," *Super Lawyers*, July 8, 2010, https://www.superlawyers.com/articles/california/remembering-the-st-louis.

14 International Jewish Anti-Zionist Network, *Israel's Worldwide Role in Repression* (2012), http://www.ijan.org/wp-content/uploads/2016/03/IWoRR.pdf.

15 For statistics on refugees from the Holocaust moving to Palestine see "Refugees," *Holocaust Encyclopedia*, https://encyclopedia.ushmm.org/content/en/article/refugees; Jenny Brodsky, Assaf Sharon, Yaron King, Shmuel Be'er, and Yitschak Shnoor, *Holocaust Survivors in Israel: Population Estimates, Demographic, Health and Social Characteristics, and Needs* (Jerusalem: Ryers-JDC-Brookdale Institute, 2010), http://www.claimscon.org/wp-content/uploads/2014/02/553-10-Holocaust-Survivors-REP-ENG.pdf.

16 "The Nakba Did Not Start or End in 1948," *Al Jazeera*, May 23, 2017, https://www.aljazeera.com/features/2017/5/23/the-nakba-did-not-start-or-end-in-1948.

17 Menakem, *My Grandmother's Hands*, 41.

18 Rachel Yehuda, Adam Morris, Ellen Labinsky, Shelly Zemelman, and James Schmeidler, "Ten-Year Follow-up Study of Cortisol Levels in Aging Holocaust Survivors with and without PTSD," *Journal of Traumatic Stress* 20, no. 5 (2007): 757–61; Rachel Yehuda, James Schmeidler, Larry J. Siever, Karen Binder-Brynes, and Abbie Elkin, "Individual Differences in Posttraumatic Stress Disorder Symptom Profiles in Holocaust Survivors in Concentration Camps or in Hiding," *Journal of Traumatic Stress* 10, no. 3 (1997): 453–63; Rachel Yehuda, Sarah L. Halligan, and Linda M. Bierer, "Cortisol Levels in Adult Offspring of Holocaust Survivors: Relation to PTSD Symptom Severity in the Parent and Child," *Psychoneuroendocrinology* 27, nos. 1–2 (2002): 171–80.

19 Jonathan Ofir, "Concentration Camps—at the US Border and in Gaza," *Mondoweiss*, June 24, 2019, https://mondoweiss.net/2019/06/concentration-camps-border.

20 Ben Lorber, "Taking Aim at Multiracial Democracy: Antisemitism, White Nationalism, and Anti-immigrant Racism in the Era of Trump," Political Research Associates, October 22, 2019, https://politicalresearch.org/2019/10/22/taking-aim-multiracial-democracy.

21 Eli Clare, Dean Spade, and Aurora Levins Morales, *Exile and Pride: Disability, Queerness, and Liberation* (Durham: Duke University Press Books, 2015), 143.

22 Gail Weiss, "Pride and Prejudice: Ambiguous Racial, Religious, and Ethnic Identities of Jewish Bodies," in *Living Alterities Phenomenology, Embodiment, and Race*, ed. Emily Lee (Albany: State University of New York Press, 2014)

23 Bell Hooks, "Love is an Action Never Simply a Feeling" (RISD Zine Library, 1999)

24 This model was developed through Generation Five and generative somatics.

CHAPTER 3 **Fascia: Borders and Walls**

1 "Fasces," Etymonline, accessed March 18, 2024, https://www.etymonline.com/word/fasces.

2 "CBP Releases March 2023 Monthly Operational Update," US Customs and Border Protection, accessed April 15, 2023, https://www.cbp.gov/newsroom/national-media-release/cbp-releases-march-2023-monthly-operational-update; "What's behind the Influx of Migrants Crossing the US Southern Border?," *PBS NewsHour*, September 21, 2023, https://www.pbs.org/newshour/politics/whats-behind-the-influx-of-migrants-crossing-the-u-s-southern-border.

3 Harsha Walia and Andrea Smith, *Undoing Border Imperialism* (Oakland: AK Press, 2013,

4 Quoted in Walia and Smith, *Undoing Border Imperialism*.

5 Clare, Spade, and Levins Morales, *Exile and Pride*

6 Walia and Smith, *Undoing Border Imperialism*, 9.

7 "Sioux Indians Want Land, Not Millions," *Washington Post*, October 14, 2001.

8 Harriet Sherwood, "Israel PM: Illegal African Immigrants Threaten Identity of Jewish State," *Guardian*, May 20, 2012.

9 Philip Rucker, "'How Do You Stop These People?': Trump's Anti-immigrant Rhetoric Looms over El Paso Massacre," *Washington Post*, August 4, 2019.

10 Will Parrish, "The U.S. Border Patrol and an Israeli Military Contractor Are Putting a Native American Reservation under 'Persistent Surveillance,'" *The Intercept*, August 25, 2019, https://theintercept.com/2019/08/25/border-patrol-israel-elbit-surveillance.

11 Reece Jones, *Border Walls: Security and the War on Terror in the United States, India, and Israel* (London: Zed Books, 2012).

12   Frank Furedi, "The Only Thing We Have to Fear Is the 'Culture of Fear' Itself," *Spiked*, April 4, 2007, https://www.spiked-online.com/2007/04/04/the-only-thing-we-have-to-fear-is-the-culture-of-fear-itself.

13   Menakem, *My Grandmother's Hands*, 27.

14   Mohammed al-Hajjar, "War on Gaza: Israeli 'Massacre' Kills over 100 Palestinians Seeking Food in Gaza City," *Middle East Eye*, February 29, 2024, https://www.middleeasteye.net/news/war-gaza-israeli-massacre-kills-dozens-looking-food-gaza-city.

15   Sara Ahmed, *The Cultural Politics of Emotion*, new ed. (Edinburgh: Edinburgh University Press, 2014), 212.

16   Malcom X Grassroots Movement, *Operation Ghetto Storm*, April 2013, https://www.prisonpolicy.org/scans/Operation-Ghetto-Storm.pdf.

17   Ahmed, *Cultural Politics of Emotion*, 70, 75.

18   Jeremy Scahill, Ryan Grim, and Daniel Boguslaw, "The Story behind the *New York Times* October 7 Exposé," *The Intercept*, February 29, 2024, https://theintercept.com/2024/02/28/new-york-times-anat-schwartz-october-7; David Corn, "The Iraq Invasion 20 Years Later: It Was Indeed a Big Lie That Launched the Catastrophic War," *Mother Jones* (blog). https://www.motherjones.com/politics/2023/03/the-iraq-invasion-20-years-later-it-was-indeed-a-big-lie-that-launched-the-catastrophic-war.

19   Ahmed, *Cultural Politics of Emotion*, 75.

20   Ahmed, *Cultural Politics of Emotion*, 3.

21   Puar, *Terrorist Assemblages*, 47.

22   Walia and Smith, *Undoing Border Imperialism,* 54.

23   Greg Afinogenov, "The Jewish Case for Open Borders," *Jewish Currents*, July 15, 2019, https://jewishcurrents.org/the-jewish-case-for-open-borders.

24   Eric A. Stanley and Nat Smith, eds., *Captive Genders: Trans Embodiment and the Prison Industrial Complex* (Oakland: AK Press, 2011).

25   "Marissa Alexander TED Talk."

26   Les Fehmi and Jim Robbins, *The Open-Focus Brain: Harnessing the Power of Attention to Heal Mind and Body* (Boulder, CO: Shambhala Publications, 2008).

27   Bonnie Badenoch, *The Heart of Trauma: Healing the Embodied Brain in the Context of Relationships* (New York: W.W. Norton, 2017), 80.

28   Badenoch, *Heart of Trauma*, 75.

29   Trần, "Calling IN."

CHAPTER 4 Vagus Nerve: Membranes and Boundaries

1   Silvia Federici, *Caliban and the Witch: Women, the Body and Primitive Accumulation* (London: Penguin Modern Classics, 2021).

2   This chapter draws on the work of prominent feminist, anti-imperialist activists and writers such as Harsha Walia and Gloria Anzaldúa.

3   Stephen W. Porges, *The Pocket Guide to the Polyvagal Theory: The Transformative Power of Feeling Safe* (New York: W.W. Norton, 2017), 44.

4   Badenoch, *Heart of Trauma*, 5.

5   Badenoch, *Heart of Trauma*, 7.

6   Sara H. Konrath, Edward H. O'Brien, and Courtney Hsing, "Changes in Dispositional Empathy in American College Students over Time: A Meta-analysis," *Personality and Social Psychology Review* 15, no. 2 (2011): 180–98.

7   Badenoch, *Heart of Trauma*, 20.

8   Elliot Kukla, "Terms for Gender Diversity in Classical Jewish Texts," TransTorah,

2006, http://www.transtorah.org/PDFs/Classical_Jewish_Terms_for_Gender_Diversity.pdf.

9 Relationship anarchy is a form of nonmonogamy in which one has a nonhierarchical assortment of romantic, sexual, and/or intimate connections.

10 Jessica Fern, *Polysecure: Attachment, Trauma and Consensual Nonmonogamy* (Portland, OR: Thorntree Press, 2020), 173.

11 Somatics & Trauma Training, 2018, Generative Somatics.

12 adrienne maree brown, *Emergent Strategy: Shaping Change, Changing Worlds* (Chico, CA: AK Press, 2017).

13 Pragya Agarwal, *Sway: Unravelling Unconscious Bias* (London: Bloomsbury Publishing, 2020).

14 Bruce H. Lipton, *The Biology of Belief: Unleashing the Power of Consciousness, Matter & Miracles* (Carlsbad, CA: Hay House Incorporated, 2008).

15 Porges, *Pocket Guide to the Polyvagal Theory*, 123.

16 Susan Sangha, Andi Scheibenstock, and Len Lukowiak, "Reconsolidation of a Long-Term Memory in Lymnaea Requires New Protein and RNA Synthesis and the Soma of Right Pedal Dorsal 1," *Journal of Neuroscience* 23, no. 22 (September 3, 2003): 8034–40.

17 Badenoch, *Heart of Trauma*, 176.

18 "Introduction to the Inherent Treatment Plan: Craniosacral Biodynamics with Franklyn Sills," 2019, http://www.craniosacral-biodynamics.org/introduction-to-inherenttreatmentplan.html.

19 Bruce K. Alexander, "The Globalization of Addiction," *Addiction Research* 8, no. 6 (2000): 501–26, https://doi.org/10.3109/16066350008998987.

20 Porges, *Pocket Guide to the Polyvagal Theory*, 15.

21 Porges, *Pocket Guide to the Polyvagal Theory*, 20.

22 Porges, *Pocket Guide to the Polyvagal Theory*, 20.

CHAPTER 5 Oak: Individualistic Embodiment and the Colonization of Healing

1 Nita M. Renfrew, "Traditional American Indian Bodywork: The Origin of Osteopathy, Polarity, and Craniosacral Therapy," *Journal of Contemporary Shamanism* 8, no. 1 (2015), researchgate.net.

2 "Somatics Living Lineage" generative somatics and the Strozzi Institute, June 2022, https://www.stacihaines.com/lineage.

3 "Lineage of Embodiment Panel: How to Honor the Lineage of Embodiment," Embodiment Institute, accessed March 22, 2024, https://prentishemphill.podia.com/how-to-honor-the-lineage-of-embodiment; "Embodied Ancestral Skills," wildbody, accessed March 11, 2024, https://wildbody.ca/ancestral-skills; Cara Page and Erica Woodland, *Healing Justice Lineages: Dreaming at the Crossroads of Liberation Collective Care and Safety* (Berkeley: North Atlantic Books, 2023).

4 Susan Raffo, "Building Collective Liberation: Wondering about a Protocol for Healers," February 21, 2020, https://www.susanraffo.com/blog/building-collective-liberation-wondering-about-a-protocol-for-healers.

5 Wilhelm Reich, *The Mass Psychology of Fascism* (Farrar, Straus and Giroux, 1933), 19.

6 Reich, *Mass Psychology of Fascism*, 163.

7 I learned about Reich's influence on contemporary somatics through Richard Strozzi Heckler and Zoë Poulette.

8   Frantz Fanon, *The Wretched of the Earth* (London: Penguin Classics, 2001)

9   Renfrew, "Traditional American Indian Bodywork."

10   Ruti Wagaki, RCST, "Decolonizing Our Origin Story: A Pathway Toward Healing," *Cranial Wave*, 2022, https://www.craniosacraltherapy.org/assets/docs/Cranial_Wave/2022.23_Decolonizing_Our_Origin_Story.pdf.

11   Lewis Mehl-Madrona, Josie Conte, and Barbara Mainguy, "Indigenous Roots of Osteopathy," *AlterNative: An International Journal of Indigenous Peoples* 19, no. 4 (2023), doi.org/10.1177/11771801231197417.

12   The somatic bodywork I am referencing is a modality that Generative Somatics cultivated that pulls from craniosacral and polarity therapy as well as decades of hands-on experience working with somatic clients.

13   Evan L. Ardiel and Catharine H. Rankin, "The Importance of Touch in Development," *Paediatrics and Child Health* 15, no. 3 (2010): 153–56.

14   Barbara Pease and Allan Pease, *The Definitive Book of Body Language: The Hidden Meaning Behind People's Gestures and Expressions* (New York: Bantam, 2008).

15   Leah Lakshmi Piepzna-Samarasinha, *Care Work: Dreaming Disability Justice* (Vancouver: Arsenal Pulp Press, 2018).

16   Abraham Joshua Heschel, *The Sabbath* (London: Macmillan, 1951), 28.

17   Porges, *Pocket Guide to the Polyvagal Theory*, 159.

18   Dean Spade, "Mutual Aid Toolbox," https://www.deanspade.net.

19   Mia Mingus, "Moving toward the Ugly: A Politic beyond Desirability," Femmes of Color Symposium keynote speech, Oakland, August 21, 2022.

20   Kindred Southern Healing Justice Collective, "What Is Healing Justice?," accessed May 7, 2024, https://kindredsouthernhjcollective.org/what-is-healing-justice.

CHAPTER 6 Mycelia: Collective Care

1   "Ashkenormativity" refers to a form of Eurocentrism in Jewish culture that privileges Ashkenazi Jews over Jews of Sephardi, Mizrahi, and other non-Ashkenazi backgrounds. Ashkenormativity is embedded in white supremacy and assumes Ashkenazi culture is the default Jewish culture.

2   Zoë Poullette (friend and somatic practitioner) in discussion with the author, December 2018.

3   Badenoch, *Heart of Trauma*, 172.

4   "Window of tolerance" is a term coined by Dan Siegel and further developed by Pat Ogden.

5   Marco Iacoboni, *Mirroring People: The New Science of How We Connect with Others* (New York: Farrar, Straus and Giroux, 2009), 57.

6   Quoted in Scott F. Parker, "Stories of Self (Vol. 7): Reciprocity with Robin Wall Kimmerer," March 15, 2017, https://www.thebeliever.net/logger/stories-of-self-vol-7-reciprocity-with-robin-wall-kimmerer.

7   Melody Beattie, *Codependent No More: How to Stop Controlling Others and Start Caring for Yourself* (Center City, MN: Hazelden, 1986), 34.

8   Pumla Gobodo-Madikizela, *A Human Being Died That Night : A South African Story of Forgiveness* (Boston: Houghton Mifflin, 2003).

9   generationFive, *Ending Child Sexual Abuse: A Transformative Justice Handbook* (June 2017), https://generativesomatics.org/wp-content/uploads/2019/10/Transformative-Justice-Handbook.pdf.

10 Nathan Shara (Generative Somatics teacher) in training with the author, June 2018.

11 Mia Mingus, "Bay Area Transformative Justice Collective," May 30, 2019,https://leavingevidence.wordpress.com/2019/12/18/how-to-give-a-good-apology-part-1-the-four-parts-of-accountability/

12 "What Is N'COBRA?," National Coalition of Blacks for Reparations in America, accessed February 11, 2024, https://ncobra.org/aboutus.

13 Micah Bazant and Lewis Raven Wallace, "Miklat Miklat," https://www.micahbazant.com/miklat-miklat.

14 "Summary Statement Re: Community Accountability Process (March 2017)," *Transforming Harm*, March 8, 2017, https://transformharm.tumblr.com/post/158171267676/summary-statement-re-community-accountability.

15 Mariame Kaba and Shira Hassan, *Fumbling Towards Repair: A Workbook for Community Accountability Facilitators* (Chicago: Project Nia, 2019).

16 Kaba and Hassan, *Fumbling Towards Repair*.

17 Robin Kimmerer, *Braiding Sweetgrass: Indigenous Wisdom, Scientific Knowledge and the Teachings of Plants* (Minneapolis: Milkweed Editions, 2013), 9.

18 James Baldwin, *The Fire Next Time* (New York: Dial Press,1963).

19 About IJAN and AROC collaboration: Daikha Dridi, "The Women behind the Block the Boat Movement," *CounterPunch*, October 24, 2014, https://www.counterpunch.org/2014/10/24/the-women-behind-the-block-the-boat-movement; Block the Boat movement: "Block the Boat #BDS," accessed September 20, 2015, https://blocktheboat.org/about-block-the-boat.

20 Julia Wong, "Oakland Activists 'Block the Boat' for Three Days Running," *In These Times*, August 20, 2014, https://inthesetimes.com/article/oakland-activists-block-the-boat-for-three-days.

21 Chris Lymbertos and Lara Kiswani, "Block the Boat and Somatics," *Generative Somatics Newsletter*, December 5, 2015.

About the Author

Eliana builds transgressive relationships with bodies, land, and lineage through their work as a somatic practitioner, politicized facilitator, anti-Zionist organizer, full-spectrum doula, queer pleasure instigator, and land steward. Their practice centers queer and trans organizers in developing embodied leadership as well as Jewish organizers in healing intergenerational trauma for the sake of collective liberation. They were born and raised by the dramatic landscapes and freaks of the San Francisco Bay Area, and are now rooted in the southern movement history and red clay of Durham, North Carolina. At their core, Eliana loves their people, plants, rivers, and the dance floor.

ABOUT PM PRESS

PM Press is an independent, radical publisher of critically
necessary books for our tumultuous times. Our aim is to
deliver bold political ideas and vital stories to all walks
of life and arm the dreamers to demand the impossible.
Founded in 2007 by a small group of people with decades
of publishing, media, and organizing experience, we have
sold millions of copies of our books, most often one at a time, face to face. We're
old enough to know what we're doing and young enough to know what's at
stake. Join us to create a better world.

PM Press
PO Box 23912
Oakland, CA 94623
www.pmpress.org

PM Press in Europe
europe@pmpress.org
www.pmpress.org.uk

FRIENDS OF PM PRESS

These are indisputably momentous times—the financial system is melting down globally and the Empire is stumbling. Now more than ever there is a vital need for radical ideas.

In the many years since its founding—and on a mere shoestring—PM Press has risen to the formidable challenge of publishing and distributing knowledge and entertainment for the struggles ahead. With hundreds of releases to date, we have published an impressive and stimulating array of literature, art, music, politics, and culture. Using every available medium, we've succeeded in connecting those hungry for ideas and information to those putting them into practice.

Friends of PM allows you to directly help impact, amplify, and revitalize the discourse and actions of radical writers, filmmakers, and artists. It provides us with a stable foundation from which we can build upon our early successes and provides a much-needed subsidy for the materials that can't necessarily pay their own way. You can help make that happen—and receive every new title automatically delivered to your door once a month—by joining as a Friend of PM Press. And, we'll throw in a free T-shirt when you sign up.

Here are your options:

- **$30 a month** Get all books and pamphlets plus a 50% discount on all webstore purchases

- **$40 a month** Get all PM Press releases (including CDs and DVDs) plus a 50% discount on all webstore purchases

- **$100 a month** Superstar—Everything plus PM merchandise, free downloads, and a 50% discount on all webstore purchases

For those who can't afford $30 or more a month, we have **Sustainer Rates** at $15, $10, and $5. Sustainers get a free PM Press T-shirt and a 50% discount on all purchases from our website.

Your Visa or Mastercard will be billed once a month, until you tell us to stop. Or until our efforts succeed in bringing the revolution around. Or the financial meltdown of Capital makes plastic redundant. Whichever comes first.

A People's Guide to Abolition and Disability Justice

Katie Tastrom

ISBN: 979-8-88744-040-8 (paperback)
       979-8-88744-054-5 (hardcover)
$19.95 / $29.95   256 pages

Disability justice and prison abolition are two increasingly popular theories that overlap but whose intersection has rarely been explored in depth.

A People's Guide to Abolition and Disability Justice explains the history and theories behind abolition and disability justice in a way that is easy to understand for those new to these concepts yet also gives insights that will be useful to seasoned activists. The book uses extensive research and professional and lived experience to illuminate the way the State uses disability and its power to disable to incarcerate multiply marginalized disabled people, especially those who are queer, trans, Black, or Indigenous.

Because disabled people are much more likely than nondisabled people to be locked up in prisons, jails, and other sites of incarceration, abolitionists, and others critical of carceral systems must incorporate a disability justice perspective into our work. *A People's Guide to Abolition and Disability Justice* gives personal and policy examples of how and why disabled people are disproportionately caught up in the carceral net, and how we can use this information to work toward prison and police abolition more effectively. This book includes practical tools and strategies that will be useful for anyone who cares about disability justice or abolition and explains why we can't have one without the other.

"An essential movement tool. Tastrom convincingly shows that police and prison abolition and disability justice are core strategies for liberation and that we can't win one without the other."
—Alex Vitale, professor of sociology and coordinator of the Policing and Social Justice Project at Brooklyn College and the CUNY Graduate Center, and author of *City of Disorder and The End of Policing*

"A People's Guide to Abolition and Disability Justice is a clear, accessible, and invaluable tool for not only dissecting the depths of disability and criminalization but also illustrating how the fights for disability justice and prison abolition are inextricably linked."
—Victoria Law, author of *Resistance Behind Bars: The Struggles of Incarcerated Women* and *"Prisons Make Us Safer" & 20 Other Myths about Mass Incarceration*

P Is for Palestine: A Palestine Alphabet Book

Golbarg Bashi, illustrated by Golrokh Nafisi

ISBN: 979-8-88744-076-7 (paperback)
979-8-88744-084-2 (hardcover)
$16.95 / $29.95   72 pages

Embark on an alphabetic odyssey through culture and heritage.

Imagine a world where every letter of the alphabet unlocks the colorful tapestry of a rich and ancient culture. This enchanting book does just that, guiding young readers on a journey through language, history, and traditions with each turn of the page.

Can we sing the ABC anywhere? With a woolly bear or on thin air? Set off on an alphabetic adventure to Palestine, a land that tells a story with every letter. From the A that stands for Arabic, a beautiful language sung by millions, to the Z for za'atar, a flavor that's as bold as the history it accompanies, *P Is for Palestine* is more than just an ordinary ABC.

It's also an odyssey through heritage, a cultural immersion that connects young minds to the world beyond their own. It's where the traditional T for thob dresses meets the modern, where the ancient Q for Quds (Jerusalem) sits at the heart of spirituality, and where the resilience symbolized by I for intifada teaches the value of standing up for what is right.

With engaging illustrations and sweet rhymes, this book is a celebration of identity, a bridge spanning generations, and an invitation to friendship. Whether you're a child, a parent, or simply a lover of wisdom and wonder, let this journey inspire you with every letter you explore.

"The book should be outright banned from American bookstores."
—Fox News

"The first ABC picture book about Palestine is definitely an important book for people of Palestinian heritage who want to share it with their children."
—Alex Supko, librarian at Baltimore County Public Library, writer at Intellectual Freedom of the American Library Association

"Cheerful little book, in which a curly-haired young girl guides us through her homeland. . . . A genuine celebration of the historical diversity of Palestine, the book does a stellar job of reminding Westerners, many of whom believe Christianity is a Western religion, that it is Palestine that is the birthplace of Christianity."
—Nada Elia, Palestinian author and journalist

Surviving the Future: Abolitionist Queer Strategies

Edited by Scott Branson, Raven Hudson, and Bry Reed with a Foreword by Mimi Thi Nguyen

ISBN: 978-1-62963-971-0

$22.95   328 pages

Surviving the Future is a collection of the most current ideas in radical queer movement work and revolutionary queer theory. Beset by a new pandemic, fanning the flames of global uprising, these queers cast off progressive narratives of liberal hope while building mutual networks of rebellion and care. These essays propose a militant strategy of queer survival in an ever-precarious future. Starting from a position of abolition—of prisons, police, the State, identity, and racist cisheteronormative society—this collection refuses the bribes of inclusion in a system built on our expendability. Though the mainstream media saturates us with the boring norms of queer representation (with a recent focus on trans visibility), the writers in this book ditch false hope to imagine collective visions of liberation that tell different stories, build alternate worlds, and refuse the legacies of racial capitalism, anti-Blackness, and settler colonialism. The work curated in this book spans Black queer life in the time of COVID-19 and uprising, assimilation and pinkwashing settler colonial projects, subversive and deviant forms of representation, building anarchist trans/queer infrastructures, and more. Contributors include Che Gossett, Yasmin Nair, Mattilda Bernstein Sycamore, Adrian Shanker, Kitty Stryker, Toshio Meronek, and more.

"Surviving the Future *is a testament that otherwise worlds are not only possible, our people are making them right now—and they are queering how we get there through organizing and intellectual work. Now is the perfect time to interrogate how we are with each other and the land we inhabit. This collection gives us ample room to do just that in a moment of mass uprisings led by everyday people demanding safety without policing, prisons and other forms of punishment.*
—Charlene A. Carruthers, author of *Unapologetic: A Black, Queer, and Feminist Mandate for Radical Movements*

"Surviving the Future *is not an anthology that simply includes queer and trans minorities in mix of existing abolitionist thought. Rather, it is a transformative collection of queer/trans methods for living an abolitionist life. Anyone who dreams of dismantling the prison-industrial complex, policing, borders and the surveillance state should read this book. Frankly, everybody who doesn't share that dream should read it, too, and maybe they'll start dreaming differently.*"
—Susan Stryker, author of *Transgender History: The Roots of Today's Revolution*

Working It: Sex Workers on the Work of Sex

Edited by Matilda Bickers, peech breshears, and Janis Luna

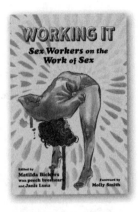

ISBN: 978-1-62963-991-8
$17.95   240 pages

Fiercely intelligent, fantastically transgressive,
Working It is an intimate portrait of the lives of sex
workers. A polyphonic story of triumph, survival,
and solidarity, this collection showcases the vastly
different experiences and interests of those who have traded sex, among them a
brothel worker in Australia, First Nation survivors of the Canadian child welfare
system, and an Afro Latina single parent raising a radicalized child. Packed with
first-person essays, interviews, poetry, drawings, mixed media collage, and
photographs, *Working It* honors the complexity of lived experience. Sometimes
heartbreaking, sometimes hardboiled, these dazzling pieces will go straight to
the heart.

"*If you ever want to know what is really up, talk to a sex worker.* Working It *is chock-
full of harsh realities, hopeful activism, hot takes, sharp writing, electric intellects,
dark humor—all from the culture heroes making their dollars at the intersection of
all our country's worst problems. This is true outlaw writing, and the stories inside
are of crucial importance for us all.*"
—Michelle Tea, author of over a dozen books, including *Rent Girl*, *Valencia*, and
Against Memoir

"*Under neoliberal late capitalism—where wage growth fails to meet the ever-growing
cost of living, and the already-frayed social safety net is ever-receding—laborers in
many sectors of the economy struggle to provide for themselves, their families, and
their communities. Sex workers are among these laborers, and* Working It *offers
what the editors rightly refer to as a 'kaleidoscope' of thought-provoking historical
commentaries, academic examinations, personal narratives, and interviews.
Interspersed with beautiful poems and creative images, the pieces in this collection,
written by contributors representing a wide range of identities and experiences, offer
readers an expansive view of sex work, while also highlighting sex workers' broader
struggles, triumphs, and collective efforts. Variously confronting issues including but
not limited to racism, classism, sexism, police brutality, consent, and respectability
politics,* Working It *indicates the challenges—but also the hope and radical
imagination—of workers striving to meet their own needs and support each other in
a broader sociocultural, political, and economic climate that is often hostile to their
interests.*"
—Samantha Majic, author of *Sex Work Politics: From Protest to Service Provision*,
coeditor of *Negotiating Sex Work: Unintended Consequences of Policy and Activism*,
and coauthor of *Youth Who Trade Sex in the US: Agency, Intersectionality, and
Vulnerability*

Where Are the Elephants?

Leon Rosselson

ISBN: 978-1-62963-973-4
$16.95   184 pages

Fierce and funny, this memoir in essay and song is full of wonderful tales of art and protest. Leon Rosselson's *Where Are the Elephants?* is a rare behind the scenes look at the life and times of one of England's foremost folksingers. This clear-eyed portrait of an activist who never gave up and whose talent, wit, and verve brought the world into finer focus provides a model for a whole new generation of radicals. Fans will love revisiting the lyrics from his hits—and behind the scenes glimpses of the stories and events that inspired his songs, but Rosselson's story of growing from a red diaper baby into a modern troubadour up against the barricades is a tale for the ages.

"In many ways, Leon Rosselson is the embodiment of the original ideals of punk rock. His hair isn't spiky, but his music is, using fearless wit and political integrity to highlight the hypocrisies of those in power. Alone among the great British songwriters of the past sixty years, Leon has sought to make art that stays true to Karl Marx's demand that we should concern ourselves with the ruthless criticism of all that exists."
—Billy Bragg

"Rosselson remains fearless. He provides something that the world is in dire need of currently—dissent that seeks dialogue versus greater division and disconnection."
—Ian Brennan, Grammy-winning music producer and author, *Silenced by Sound* and *Muse-Sick: a music manifesto in fifty-nine notes*

"His songs are teeming with colorful characters, wonderfully descriptive passages and witty observations."
—*Washington Post*

"Proof that the art of songwriting is not dead. Occasionally, acid flows from his pen but always the end-product is thoughtful, witty and provocative."
—Sheffield Telegraph

"His songs are fierce, funny, cynical, outraged, blasphemous, challenging and anarchic. And the tunes are good too."
—*Guardian*

"Some of the most literate and well-made topical songs now being written"
—*New York Times*

It Did Happen Here: An Antifascist People's History

Edited by Moe Bowstern, Mic Crenshaw, Alec Dunn, Celina Flores, Julie Perini, and Erin Yanke

ISBN: 978-1-62963-351-0
$21.95   304 pages

Portland, Oregon, 1988: the brutal murder of Ethiopian immigrant Mulugeta Seraw by racist skinheads shocked the city. In response disparate groups quickly came together to organize against white nationalist violence and right-wing organizing throughout the Rose City and the Pacific Northwest.

It Did Happen Here compiles interviews with dozens of people who worked together during the waning decades of the twentieth century to reveal an inspiring collaboration between groups of immigrants, civil rights activists, militant youth, and queer organizers. This oral history focuses on participants in three core groups: the Portland chapters of Anti-Racist Action and Skinheads Against Racial Prejudice, and the Coalition for Human Dignity.

Using a diversity of tactics—from out-and-out brawls on the streets and at punk shows, to behind-the-scenes intelligence gathering—brave antiracists unified on their home ground over and over, directly attacking right-wing fascists and exposing white nationalist organizations and neo-nazi skinheads. Embattled by police and unsupported by the city, these citizen activists eventually drove the boneheads out of the music scene and off the streets of Portland. This book shares their stories about what worked, what didn't, and ideas on how to continue the fight.

"By the time I moved my queer little family to Portland at the turn of the millennium, the city had a reputation as a homo-friendly bastion of progressive politics, so we were somewhat taken aback when my daughter's racially diverse sports team was met with a burning cross at a suburban game. So much progress had been made yet, at times, it felt like the past hadn't gone anywhere. If only we'd had It Did Happen Here. *This documentary project tells the forgotten history of Portland's roots as a haven for white supremacists and recounts the ways anti-racists formed coalitions across subcultures to protect the vulnerable and fight the good fight against nazi boneheads and the bigoted right. Through the voices of lived experience,* It Did Happen Here *illuminates community dynamics and lays out ideas and inspiration for long-term and nonpolice solutions to poverty and hatred."*
—Ariel Gore, author of *We Were Witches*

The George Floyd Uprising

Edited by Vortex Group

ISBN: 978-1-62963-966-6
$22.95   288 pages

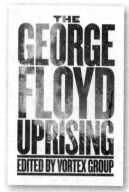

In the summer of 2020, America experienced one of the biggest uprisings in half a century. Waves of enraged citizens took to the streets in Minneapolis to decry the murder of George Floyd at the hands of the police. Battles broke out night after night, with a pandemic-weary populace fighting the police and eventually burning down the Third Precinct. The revolt soon spread to cities large and small across the country, where protesters set police cars on fire, looted luxury shopping districts, and forced the president into hiding in a bunker beneath the White House. As the initial crest receded, localized rebellions continued to erupt throughout the summer and into the fall in Atlanta, Chicago, Kenosha, Louisville, Philadelphia, and elsewhere.

Written during the riots, *The George Floyd Uprising* is a compendium of the most radical writing to come out of that long, hot summer. These incendiary dispatches—from those on the front lines of the struggle—examines the revolt and the obstacles it confronted. It paints a picture of abolition in practice, discusses how the presence of weapons in the uprising and the threat of armed struggle play out in an American context, and shows how the state responds to and pacifies rebellions. *The George Floyd Uprising* poses new social, tactical, and strategic plans for those actively seeking to expand and intensify revolts of the future. This practical, inspiring collection is essential reading for all those hard at work toppling the state and creating a new revolutionary tradition.

"Exemplary reflections from today's frontline warriors that will disconcert liberals but inspire young people who want to live the struggle in the revolutionary tradition of Robert F. Williams, the Watts 65 rebels, and Deacons for Defense and Justice."
—Mike Davis, author of *Planet of Slums* and *Old Gods, New Enigmas*

"This anthology resists police and vigilante murders. It is not an easy read. We will not all agree on its analyses or advocacy. Yet, its integrity, clarity, vulnerability, love and rage are clear. As a librarian who archives liberators and liberation movements, I recognize essential reading as a reflection of ourselves and our fears. With resolution, this text resonates with narratives of mini-Atticas. The 1971 prison rebellion and murderous repression by government and officialdom reveal the crises that spark radical movements and increasing calls for self-defense. This volume offers our cracked mirrors as an opportunity to scrutinize missteps and possibilities, and hopefully choose wisely even in our sacrifices."
—Joy James, author of *Resisting State Violence: Radicalism, Gender, and Race in U.S. Culture*

Beyond the Periphery of the Skin: Rethinking, Remaking, and Reclaiming the Body in Contemporary Capitalism

Silvia Federici

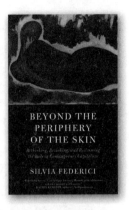

ISBN: 978-1-62963-706-8
$15.95   176 pages

More than ever, "the body" is today at the center of radical and institutional politics. Feminist, antiracist, trans, ecological movements—all look at the body in its manifold manifestations as a ground of confrontation with the state and a vehicle for transformative social practices. Concurrently, the body has become a signifier for the reproduction crisis the neoliberal turn in capitalist development has generated and for the international surge in institutional repression and public violence. In *Beyond the Periphery of the Skin*, lifelong activist and best-selling author Silvia Federici examines these complex processes, placing them in the context of the history of the capitalist transformation of the body into a work-machine, expanding on one of the main subjects of her first book, *Caliban and the Witch*.

Building on three groundbreaking lectures that she delivered in San Francisco in 2015, Federici surveys the new paradigms that today govern how the body is conceived in the collective radical imagination, as well as the new disciplinary regimes state and capital are deploying in response to mounting revolt against the daily attacks on our everyday reproduction. In this process she confronts some of the most important questions for contemporary radical political projects. What does "the body" mean, today, as a category of social/political action? What are the processes by which it is constituted? How do we dismantle the tools by which our bodies have been "enclosed" and collectively reclaim our capacity to govern them?

"Reading Federici empowers us to reconnect with what is at the core of human development, women's labor-intensive caregiving—a radical rethinking of how we live."
—Z Magazine

"Federici's attempt to draw together the work of feminists and activists from different parts of the world and place them in historical context is brave, thought-provoking, and timely. Federici's writing is lucid and her fury palpable."
—Red Pepper

"Real transformations occur when the social relations that make up everyday life change, when there is a revolution within and across the stratifications of the social body. . . . Silvia Federici offers the kind of revolutionary perspective that is capable of revealing the obstacles that stand in the way of such change."
—Feminist Review